RECOVERY

RECOVERY

THE SECOND EFFORT

BY

SIR ARTHUR SALTER, K.C.B.
Hon. D.C.L. (OXON)

LONDON
G. BELL AND SONS LTD
1933

First Edition, April 1932

Reprinted, April 1932, *May* 1932
June 1932 (*twice*)
September 1932

Revised and Cheaper Edition, February 1933
Reprinted, March 1933

Printed in Great Britain by the Camelot Press Limited
London and Southampton

TO

VISCOUNT CECIL OF CHELWOOD

CONTENTS

PAGE

PREFACE xiii
A general map of the world's present problems—The
inter-actions of policy in every sphere.

PREFACE TO SEVENTH EDITION . . . xvii

PART I
The Present Scene

CHAPTER I

RELAPSE AND RECOVERY: THE SECOND EFFORT   1
The first recovery after the war rapid but unstable—A
second effort of reconstruction now needed on sounder
lines—Dislocation not destruction the main effect of the
war—The problem difficult but essentially capable of
human solution.

CHAPTER II

THE PASSING OF AN ERA: THE COMPETITIVE
SYSTEM IN TRANSITION 7
No surplus world population except what is caused by
defects in the world's economic system—'Laissez-aller'—
how in the last century supply and demand were adjusted
automatically—The decline of free competition—The
need for deliberate planning—A new system possible
which will secure order without sacrificing enterprise.

CHAPTER III

IMPOVERISHMENT AMID PLENTY: THE WORLD
ECONOMIC DEPRESSION 22
The world's remarkable advance in the first decade after
the war—The beginning of the economic depression in
the autumn of 1929—Its causes—The trade cycle—
Rigid organisation—Capriciousness of modern demand
—Agricultural mechanisation and over-production—
Speculation—Defects in the system of credit—Maldistribution of gold—Reparation and war debts—Restrictions on immigration—No scarcity but unbalanced
production.

CONTENTS

CHAPTER IV

PAGE

CONFIDENCE AND COLLAPSE: THE WORLD
FINANCIAL CRISIS 42

The crash in June 1931—The political causes—The
Credit-Anstalt—The German short-term debts—The
Hoover Moratorium—The fall of the pound—The
effect of the financial crisis upon the economic depression
—The essence of the crisis—'a gap in the balance of payments unbridged by new credit'—Its underlying causes:
deadweight debts, reckless lending and high tariffs.

PART II
Economic and Financial Reforms

CHAPTER I

GOLD: TYRANT OR CONSTITUTIONAL MONARCH?
THE WORLD'S MONETARY SYSTEM . . 55

The reign of gold—How it has become tyrannical and
capricious—The purpose of money—How the gold
standard used to work—Why it has ceased to work satisfactorily—Rigid economic systems—Commercial Policies—'Sterilisation' of gold.

The reforms needed—Increase of gold prices and then
stability—Controlled and limited inflation by countries
with gold surplus—How to maintain stability in the
general level of prices—The rôle of Central Banks and
of Governments—Managed currencies, national and
international—Their dangers and their possibilities—
How countries now off the gold standard should direct
their policy.

CHAPTER II

GOOD LENDING AND BAD: THE WORLD'S CREDIT
SYSTEM 86

The function of lending—Different kinds of capital—
The differing situations and systems of Great Britain,
America, France and Germany—Loans to Governments—the reckless borrowing of 1925–1928—Instances
of resulting evils.

The remedies—The control and direction of foreign
public loans—The rôle of the League and the Bank of
International Settlements.

CHAPTER III

THE DEAD HAND: REPARATION AND WAR DEBTS   122

The special characteristic of a reparation obligation—The
solution that should have been adopted—The history of
reparation in summary—Mr Lloyd George and M. Poincaré—The Balfour Note—'Pleasure resort' Conferences
—Ruhr occupation—Dawes and Young Plans—War
Debts—their origin and character—The Debt settlements—The present position.
The solution: War Debts: Reparation—Lausanne.

CHAPTER IV

PRECEPT AND PRACTICE: COMMERCIAL POLICY AND
TARIFFS   171

The normal effect of tariffs—The relation of commercial
policies to the depression and the crisis—The World
Economic Conference of 1927—The League's work of
the following four years—The 'Tariff Truce' Conference
—The 'United States of Europe' movement—The diffi-
culties of Zollvereins—The 'most-favoured-nation' clause
—'Self sufficiency' or world trade—'Scientific tariffs'
—The goal of future policy.

CHAPTER V

THE GOOD AND EVILS OF CARTELS: INDUSTRIAL
ORGANISATION   196

Rationalisation—Unemployment—Large scale organisation—International Cartels—Their benefits—Their
dangers—How to secure the first and avoid the second.

CHAPTER VI

SAFEGUARDS OF THE PUBLIC INTEREST: COLLECTIVE
LEADERSHIP AND CONTROL   208

The self-adjusting quality of the competitive system has
been lost—The need for planned direction—State management: its limiting conditions—Mixed private and
public control—Leadership in finance and industry—
National Economic Councils and a World Economic
Council as adjuncts to the machine of Government.

CONTENTS

PART III
The Political Scene

CHAPTER I   PAGE

ARMAMENTS AND ALLIANCES: THE EUROPEAN SCENE   223
Political tension a cause of the financial crisis—The
political anxieties of the preceding years—The Hitler
Election—The 'Anschluss'—French Policy and psychology—German policy and outlook—The basis of Italian
policy—Other European countries—The tendency of
Europe to fall into two opposing groups.

CHAPTER II

VERSAILLES AND GENEVA: A DECADE OF TREATY-
MAKING 241
The Treaty of Versailles—Its merits and defects—President Wilson, his character, policy and success—Monsieur
Clemenceau—The League of Nations: evolution, failures
and successes—The Locarno agreements and their effect
on the League—Monsieur Briand—Herr Stresemann—
Sir Austen Chamberlain—The British guarantee—The
main characteristics of British foreign policy—The 'Freedom of the Seas'—American foreign policy—The Kellogg Pact—The weaknesses of the 'collective' system.

CHAPTER III

THE WAY TO SECURITY: COVENANT AND KELLOGG
PACT 271
Confidence in the 'collective' system the only alternative
to big armaments and military alliances—This impossible
without America—The limits to American action set by
deep-rooted traditions of policy—What she could do
without transgressing these limits—The lasting foundations of peace.

PART IV

A Programme of Action in Summary

CHAPTER I

PAGE

FIRST AID MEASURES: THE IMMEDIATE TASK   280

Events have outrun control—The waste of 'natural' adjustment—What could now be done—Postponement and reduction of reparation—Increase of gold prices—Internal national reforms in America and Great Britain—The action of the Banks—Pacification and Disarmament.

CHAPTER II

A NEW WORLD ORDER: OUR SYSTEM REFORMED
AND TRANSFORMED   290

Stable Currency—A reformed and regulated credit system—Stable and sane commercial policies—The integration of industrial organisation—The functions of Government and the five ways in which it can be made adequate for its task—Assured Peace—The new world system—Initiative and enterprise within a strong and flexible framework of law and custom.

EPILOGUE   302

'A world now apprehensive and defensive needs most the qualities it has for the moment abandoned: courage and magnanimity.'

INDEX   303

PREFACE

THIRTEEN years after the war we seem to be back in the chaos that immediately followed it. The road to real recovery is more tortuous and more arduous than we had thought; but it is not beyond finding and following.

This book is an attempt at a general map of the difficult country over which we have now to find our way, showing the obstructions by which it is encumbered, and, so far as possible, the practicable routes through it. Sectional maps, with a scientific wealth and precision of detail to which this cannot pretend, are plentiful. But they do not indicate the general direction of our goal; and, made by specialists, they often need specialists to read them. We shall try to see the regions, there described separately and in detail, as a whole and in their due relation to each other, with the routes clearer for the omission of all features of the landscape which lie off the path of the traveller.

And we must know our main direction or we can never choose our path in any particular region. A general conception of policy must dominate every specialised solution. Less than ever can we now isolate our problems. Man's activities in every sphere react upon one another more rapidly, more directly, and more intimately than in any previous age. A shortage or misuse of gold, the rash extension or the sudden arrest of credit, will change the fortunes of the remotest factory or farm. But money and credit, and the whole framework of finance within which economic activity proceeds, are themselves profoundly affected by whatever happens in other spheres of human effort and ambition; by social demands or legislation; by political aspirations and dangers. And to all these interactions both rapidity and wide range are added by what is the cardinal feature of our period: the improvement in the mechanism for the transmission of news.

We shall therefore take in turn the special problems of Money and Gold, Credit and Finance, Reparation and War Debts, Commercial Policies and Tariffs, Industrial Organisation, Governmental Regulation and Control, and Political Security; we shall try to see what has been achieved, and what defects have developed, in each of these spheres; what are their mutual relations and reactions; what part each plays in the troubles of this time; and, so far as may be, along what lines we may in each case seek some remedy or reform.

Any picture of our immediate distress will be partial and misleading if it is not comprehensive. The eye must range over both hemispheres, and over many varying fields of effort and ambition – social and political no less than economic and financial. Nor must it look at the surface only. We shall find neither explanation nor cure for the present depression and financial crisis if we look only at the causes which immediately precipitated them. We must look to older and more obscure weaknesses and defects, of which recent events have only been the symptoms and expression. For this reason, while unemployment is the most visible and the most distressing feature of the scene before us, we shall dwell little on it here. For it reflects only the sum total of economic disturbances arising from many causes, each of which needs separate consideration and a different remedy. The action designed directly to deal with the unemployed, as a measure of social justice and of social necessity, may sometimes relieve, sometimes aggravate, the evils from which unemployment comes; but it does not reach the real root of the trouble.

Nor can this analysis attempt to probe beneath our economic processes to the profound changes in desires and aspirations unknown to the purely 'economic man' which underlie them. The demand for increased socialisation comes less from a desire for greater material comfort than a preference for working in the service of the community rather than that of the profit-making shareholder; the nationalism which finds its expression partly in tariffs is not itself mainly of an economic origin; the insistence upon peasant proprietorship which has transformed the conditions of agriculture in a large part of Europe reflects primarily the peasant's desire to feel himself his own master. So far as these human aspirations find an expression in the economic structure, they will be within our scope; but the underlying psychology of the modern world is outside our theme.

Analysis again will not alone suffice. It is not a static world with which we are dealing, but one which changes rapidly before our eyes. The time element is essential. We shall need, therefore, as we enter each successive sphere, to follow the main march of events at least during the thirteen years which have elapsed since the Armistice.

A slight book which yet aims at being in this sense comprehensive, analytic, and narrative, must obviously have very definite limits. It can sketch only in the broadest outline. It must have its own perspective and angle of vision. That of the present one is determined by the special experience of the writer. He has been an official for a quarter of a century, and, for the latter half of that time, an international official. As such he has participated in, or has been in intimate contact with, most of the attempts to deal with the world's economic and financial problems by international action, whether through the Supreme Economic Council, the Reparation Commission, the 'pleasure-resort' Conferences from Spa to Genoa, or the League of Nations. Such an experience has its advantages and its limitations. The writer has not the academic qualifications of an economist and has had no direct experience in business enterprise; but he has been brought into close and continuous contact with those who have both, and he has had the task of helping to relate their specific contributions to those which official action can offer. The proposals which he makes are these which seem, in the light of his own particular experience, to be practical and useful, and he has attempted to weave them into a coherent policy. The limitations of work in a particular groove are obvious, the bias of personal and national outlook not wholly avoidable; these he has tried to correct—but they will doubtless need further discounting by his readers. Such as it is, this sketch of a possible foundation upon which others may build is presented for what it may be worth.

I wish to express my gratitude to Mr. J. B. Condliffe, Mr. E. Grove, Mr. H. V. Hodson, Mr. N. F. Hall, Sir Walter Layton, Professor G. L. Schwartz, Sir Arnold Wilson, and Professor Alfred Zimmern, for valuable advice as to particular chapters, to Mr. T. P. Conwell-Evans, who read through the whole of the text, and to the Editor of the " Round Table " who has allowed me to reprint some passages from an article I had contributed to that journal.

January 1932

PREFACE TO SEVENTH EDITION

A YEAR and a half has now elapsed since the World Depression entered into its second phase; since the Financial Crisis supervened in the summer of 1931 upon the Economic Slump which had begun in the autumn of 1929.

Recovery was begun in October 1931, in the early months of this second phase; its text was complete, apart from a few amendments in proof, by the end of the following January, and it was published in April. Events have moved quickly since then and, now that a new edition in a more popular form is being prepared, it may be convenient to attempt a brief conspectus of them, so far as they relate to the contents of the book.

Neither the experience of this last year, nor the discussions in the reviews, suggest any substantial change in diagnosis or remedy. Nor is the situation yet radically different. The main troubles remain; the attempts to deal with them have (with little exception) not reached a definite issue in either success or failure.

The main conception of the book, that we should re-form our system radically rather than contemplate its replacement by one which leaves no room for political liberty or private enterprise, has been criticised from two opposing points of view. A few – a very few – critics have urged that we should, and can, retrace our steps and recreate the conditions under which the individualist system will function automatically as in large measure it did in the last century. Others have, perhaps more plausibly, argued that our existing system does not possess the constructive energy for self-reform, and that it is doomed to a collapse which will clear the way for something fundamentally different. I still believe that a planned society is indispensable; that planning is compatible with the essence of freedom; and that our policy should be one of deliberate and drastic reform, not a mere drifting to disaster of which the final outcome is beyond human calculation. Even if I believed the chances to be against success, I think that this generation of those born to the rich heritage of western civilisation would be betraying their trust if they did not make the attempt, and did not draw from the prospect of possible collapse an inspiration to action rather than counsels of despair. But I believe that, in a depression which is psychological as well as material, the real constructive forces in the world have been underestimated and that they need only to be evoked to make our task practicable.

A picture of the world at this moment is in main outline the same as one drawn a year ago. The original depression is dominated by the financial crisis. The actual or feared inability to meet obligations, or to secure payment of what is owed by others, has led individuals, corporations and public authorities to restrict their purchases. Whatever be the method adopted the result has been to depress prices, reduce incomes, immobilise production, increase unemployment and to lower indefinitely the level at which secure solvency seems practicable. The process affects both internal and external trade. It has operated, however, with redoubled force upon external trade, where individual action has been supplemented by national measures. Most national policy during the period has been inspired by a desire to redress or assure the national balance of trade. Both

debtor and creditor countries have attempted to secure a
'positive' balance, that is to sell more than they buy,
or, more exactly, since they are better able to restrict
purchases than extend sales, to buy less than they sell.
Debtor countries have said, with obvious reason, that if
they are to meet their obligations in respect of past
loans they must export more than they import.   But
creditor countries in their turn have been impressed with
the demonstration, afforded in the English experience of
1931, of the strains to which financial centres are subject
and have desired the additional strength given by a
positive balance.   As all imports must obviously be equal
to all exports, the above goal of policy, collectively considered, is clearly incapable of attainment.   Whether
the conscious objective of policy is that of securing a
positive balance of trade, or perhaps more usually and
immediately, that of keeping a currency on the gold
standard or saving it from further depreciation, it
expresses itself in measures which restrict imports and
therefore other exports; the circle is rapidly completed
– and is continually contracting.

During almost all this period, therefore, world prices
have been falling; existing enterprises have been made
unprofitable, new enterprises discouraged; the burden of
indebtedness, public and private, has been increased;
bankruptcy and default have been wide-spread; unemployment has increased.   The impediments to trade, in
the form not only of increased tariffs, but of quotas,
prohibitions and, above all, exchange restrictions, have
multiplied.   Panic and hoarding have in some countries
added seriously to the financial and currency difficulties.
Worst of all, the general political condition, on which the
growth of confidence and the resumption of international
investment and trade depend, has become more grave.

A1*

The position in the East and the armaments crisis have resulted in a more serious threat to the new 'collective system' against war than at any previous period.[1]

Nevertheless, there are several respects in which the situation is somewhat better. The natural forces which in time bring a turn to the ordinary trade cycle have been operating. Excess stocks have been running down. The position of some food-producing countries has been improving, partly through some increase in prices, partly in some instances as a result of moderate currency depreciation. The economic position of Germany has distinctly improved. The painful process of liquidation and default, while entailing new difficulty in other directions, has been in some respects clearing the situation. A less pessimistic mood is visible, for example in the United States, where the panic and hoarding which threatened the dollar have given way to a more cheerful outlook, which is reflected in the rise of values in the stock markets. If there were no special features in this depression, and special obstacles to recovery such as are described in this book, we should probably by this time have taken a definite upward turn. But unhappily these obstacles for the most part remain. The whole situation remains still doubtful. The signs of a real revival in trade are scarcely yet visible. Natural forces alone are insufficient. Leadership and bold policy remain essential.

In some cases, indeed, such policy has not been wanting. Three examples of it, in particular, have shown that bold policy is possible.

First, the American monetary policy, designed to counteract deflation and arrest the fall in prices (p. 85) has been continued; and it is showing definite results of

[1] At the same time, however, a very notable advance in political doctrine has been made by Mr. Stimson's classic speech of August 8, 1932 (see p. 276).

benefit not only to America, but to the world as a whole. There were those who said hastily, as prices continued to fall and pessimism spread in the early summer, that this policy had failed. They had not realised that a monetary policy of this kind requires, even in the most favourable circumstances, some months before it can show its results and that, in this instance, the new money made available had to meet three immediate needs before it could begin to effect a positive improvement in prices. It had to counteract the effect, first of domestic hoarding, then that of the outflow of gold through the withdrawal of foreign balances; next the banks required to make themselves more liquid. Only when this phase was passed could the new monetary policy begin to help prices to rise. There can be no doubt that this policy stemmed powerful deflationary forces that would otherwise have made the whole position much more serious, and has been paving the way for what may now be a real improvement.

The immediate future of this policy is of great moment both to America and the world. There have been some indications, it may be hoped fallacious, of a tendency to retrace some of the steps taken, now that its first objects have been realised.

Next, the Lausanne Agreement has brought a real settlement of reparation, on a basis which will mean that no future payments will ever again either upset the financial position of Germany or disturb the exchanges of the world. This is the one instance in which one of the major obstacles to recovery described in the first edition has been removed by deliberate collective action. The passage in which I made proposals for a reparation settlement is the only one which I have thought it necessary to re-write (apart from the occasional amendment of a phrase or a sentence). The actual settlement arrived at is such as I contemplated in that it does not amount to complete cancellation, but that it provides a moratorium, a reduction of the payments to a mere fraction of what was required by the Young Plan, and special safeguards to prevent even such reduced payments being injurious. The moratorium is shorter; but the annual payments are substantially less; and the safeguards are different in character from those I suggested. On the whole, the solution is definitely better (because the burden is less) than I had thought practicable when writing six months before. It has seemed to me useless to reprint proposals now obsolete; so I have inserted instead a summary of the actual settlement. Formally, the agreement requires ratification which is made conditional upon a war debts settlement. But in practice, if Germany herself ratifies, the settlement may be regarded as definitely relieving her of more than she therein agrees to pay. The Lausanne Agreement is, in my view, an immense achievement, and the principal encouragement which this last year has given to the hope that effective international action to deal with the problems that confront the world will be possible.

Thirdly, there is the great Conversion operation in Great Britain, followed by the similar, though smaller and less drastic, operation in France. Nearly £2,000 millions of the British indebtedness has been put, by a single act, on a $3\frac{1}{2}$ per cent. basis. In France about half this amount has been converted to $4\frac{1}{2}$ per cent. In both cases the immediate result is a substantial relief to the Budget. But the chief significance is the lead given towards the general reduction of the rate for long-term loans. If this reduction can be achieved it will be of great benefit, both in encouraging new enterprise and in enabling a substantial part (though of course by no means all) of existing private indebtedness to be placed on a tolerable basis.

We have thus three important instances of wise leadership and deliberate action, one American, one European, one British, successfully directed towards stemming the mere drift of uncontrolled forces. Each of them encourages us to hope that man can yet be master of his fate and overcome the more numerous and formidable obstacles that still remain.

There is first the question of war debts. A description is given in the second part of the book of the relation which these debts bear to the depression and the prospects of recovery, and it is perhaps better for having been written for that purpose and not with a view to current negotiations. It is therefore printed without change. But as this Preface is written after the interchange of notes, and the payments and defaults, of December 1932, it may be well to add a few comments upon the task that confronts statesmen on both sides of the Atlantic in the forthcoming months.

It is obviously incumbent upon persons of good-will to do all they can to secure an environment for the negotiations, and a reception for whatever may be their result, which is free of all avoidable provocation and passion. This can only be done by a very conscious and definite effort on each side to understand the psychology and point of view of the other.

To war debtors I would suggest that they should try to realise imaginatively the attitude of the great mass of the population of America, whose opinion and desires are reflected in Congress. Let them picture, for example, the American farmer of the Middle West. His farm is mortgaged; the price of the wheat he sells has fallen to about one-third, so that the burden of his mortgage is tripled. He knows that there is an immense deficit in the national budget; that the number of unemployed is not only unprecedented in the past but scarcely equalled elsewhere. He realises that reduction of war debts does not mean that the bondholder gets less but that he must be paid by the American taxpayer instead of the European taxpayer. In these circumstances his reluctance to transfer the burden is intelligible.

It is intelligible, but it does not follow that it is right, in either his own or the general interest. The loss resulting from the fall in prices, restriction of business and the depression in general is of course on an incomparably greater scale than any war debt payments. Would, then, a drastic reduction in the debts be a decisive factor in recovery ?

The American reader will find the greater part of such answer as I can give in the book which follows. He will see there how the restrictions upon world trade have reduced the capacity to make payments from one country to another; how the fall in prices has increased the difficulty; how the strain has helped to dislocate the world's monetary system. But he may at this moment find his best approach to understanding the relation between inter-governmental debts and the depression, and the present psychology of the debtor countries, if he considers carefully what the European creditors of reparation did at Lausanne and why they did it. He need not admit any legal or moral connection between reparations and war debts; what matters is their economic and financial aspects and consequences and these are obviously identical. In both cases the obligations are unlike ordinary investments in having no earning asset behind them: in both, the real burden has been more than doubled by the fall in prices, and further increased by the fall in the volume of trade; in both, the liability to pay had thrown a heavy strain on the world's monetary system and the exchanges and remained as an impediment to recovery.

The European creditors of reparation made a settlement which first gave Germany a further complete respite of three years beyond the Hoover moratorium year; and then fixed the remaining obligation at a total capital sum, nominally of 3,000 million gold marks. This obligation was to be met by the issue of bonds under conditions which would prevent the annual burden upon Germany ever exceeding 180 million gold marks, and further safeguards were added to prevent any danger to Germany's credit. The Young Plan, only three years old, had fixed the annual payments about ten times as high; and when the respite and safeguards are allowed for, the nominal capital obligation of 3,000 million gold marks would perhaps be excessively assessed at 2,000 millions.

The object of this settlement is obvious. It was not to transfer the burden to America or put pressure on her. No responsible person believes that, whatever happens in the war debts negotiations, Germany's payments under the Young Plan will or can be revived. Nor was the settlement an act of sheer generosity. It was due to the conviction of the European creditors that the old payments could not be maintained and that their drastic reduction would help to restore confidence and prosperity. And subsequent experience has tended to confirm their opinion. Lausanne was at once followed by a tendency of commodity prices to improve and an increase in Stock Exchange values. But the effect upon the general world situation was of course dependent on other factors. The European reparation creditors could deal satisfactorily with rather less than half the mass of inter-governmental indebtedness, but not with the remainder. Nevertheless, apart from the precarious effect of Lausanne upon world conditions, it definitely improved Germany's credit and financial position, and it enabled her to meet her commercial obligations – to the advantage of American no less than European creditors. It did more than this. There has been more definite improvement in the German economic situation, and more definite indications of recovery, in the last few months than in any other country. There is every presumption that a similar settlement of the remainder of inter-governmental indebtedness would give a powerful impulse towards recovery, and would render every other problem – for of course there are others – easier of solution.

As to what should be the nature of any new settlement, Lausanne at least affords an interesting analogy. The basic financial considerations are much the same; and Lausanne suggests both the general order of magnitude within which any settlement must be conceived, and also the best method, that of the fixation of a capital sum to be liquidated by the appropriate bond issues.

It cannot be stated too directly that the full execution of the existing agreements, under any conditions of world trade which can be conceived as possible, is physically impracticable. Loan operations to meet current obligations – the method by which Germany paid from the time of the Dawes Plan to the Hoover Moratorium – would, even if practicable, only postpone and aggravate the difficulties. The debtor countries cannot anticipate, either in direct or triangular trade, any such surplus balance as to support the payments. There remains then only gold. The substantial payment made in December was made from the English gold reserve, thereby reducing the chances or at least postponing the date of any practicable return of sterling to gold, at whatever parity. Had the payment been made in any other way – e.g. by the sale of sterling – the result must have been to depreciate the pound and to drive down gold prices everywhere. But payment in gold, possible for the December payment, obviously affords no alternative. The total gold stocks of the Bank of England are only equal to about four years British payments. Payment in gold would obviously make the retention of gold as the basis of debtors' currencies impossible – and might thus even make it useless to the recipient; and in the meantime the process would obviously both prolong and aggravate indefinitely the whole world crisis.

A new settlement is therefore both urgent and essential. The only alternatives are modification by agreement or default (partial or complete) under *force majeure*. The only choice left to the debtors, in the absence of agreement, is as to the date and extent of default; and if default is to come, further postponement of it, or an attempt to pay on an impracticably high basis, would merely postpone and increase the general difficulties.

When the time is so short and the issues so complex the method of negotiation is clearly of great importance. No settlement of course can be concluded without the approval of Congress. It does not, however, I suggest, follow that the actual negotiations would best be made through a Commission composed wholly or in part by members of Congress. The Young Plan for reparation was approved by the Parliaments of the creditor countries and its modification also requires their approval. But that did not prevent the executives of the countries concerned taking their responsibility and agreeing upon a scheme, subject to ratification. It is unlikely that the Lausanne settlement could have been negotiated if the negotiators had been, not Prime Ministers, but Parliamentary committees. Similar urgency would suggest a similar procedure as regards the war debts, even though the precedents and customary methods may be somewhat different.

It is clear that there are great advantages in the payments actually made being embodied in agreement, and not determined unilaterally by debtors who are prevented by *force majeure* from observing the existing settlements. I hope indeed that even if an agreed settlement should prove impossible the debtors would not default completely but would tender what they consider practicable – though this would clearly be less if their situation and that of the world lost the advantage which settlement by agreement would bring. Serious, however, as may be the repercussions of default (whether partial or complete), it can scarcely be doubtful that, if agreement is impossible, default in 1933 is better in the interest of the whole world, than an attempt to maintain impossible payments, with the only result, not of avoiding but only postponing, the default, and of incalculably aggravating the whole world depression in the meantime. The Lausanne settlement of reparation was one of the great (and few) constructive acts of government in 1932. It was not an act of altruistic abnegation but of enlightened self-interest. The ensuing year will complete it, and reap its benefits – or will in large measure destroy them.

Then there is the whole sphere of commercial policy. Here the situation has become definitely worse. Tariffs have been increased, and supplemented by exchange restrictions, quotas and prohibitions.

For the most part the new impediments to trade that have been created during the last year have been due mainly to the financial causes already described, that is their object has been to improve a balance of trade in order to enable obligations to be met in foreign exchange and to protect a currency. The only way to deal with this situation is by monetary and financial policy.

There remain, however, the tariffs and tariff policy of the kind with which we were familiar before the financial crisis. And several of the measures taken or projected represent conceptions of permanent economic policy rather than attempts to deal with a financial emergency. The principal Conference at which tariffs have been discussed, that of Ottawa, does not increase the volume of world trade as a whole, and it introduces or endorses certain regrettable principles. It is an innovation in the history of tariff policies that a country should engage itself to others to impose tariffs which it does not want in the real or supposed interests of its own producers or to retain others it may find injurious. The power of bargaining is restricted by agreements to maintain certain duties for five years. An incidental and qualified, but still regrettable, recognition is given to the miscalled 'scientific' tariff (see page 183). Meantime the attempt to improve the position in the Danubian States (page 191) did not succeed in the spring and, though renewed in a different form at the Stresa Conference of the summer, is still far from any real solution. The most-favoured-nation clause (page 175) remains at the centre of the problem of the world's commercial policy; and the issue has been sharply raised by the proposed Convention between Belgium, Holland and Luxembourg for the progressive reduction of tariffs, either between themselves alone or with the inclusion of any other countries which are prepared to join. It will be a tragedy if this promising initiative is blocked. The most useful contributions which the World Economic Conference could make to the tariff situation would, in my view, be the reform of the most-favoured-nation clause (page 190), and agreement upon certain principles (the first of which would be the explicit condemnation of the 'scientific' tariff) which should guide countries in their commercial policy. But the indications are not at present favourable.

As regards monetary policy, the chief event has been the continuance of the American action already mentioned. The situation is in general still as it was described in the first edition. The main need is a 'world policy of controlled reflation,' to arrest and reverse the fall in prices, and, thereafter, a policy directed to a reasonable stability of the general price level, whether through currencies linked to gold or not. In one respect, writing now, I should modify what I wrote nine months ago. I then advocated an increase in the general level 'preferably till it reaches the level of 1929.' Since then prices have fallen a great deal, so that the disparity with 1929 is greatly increased; and in the interval many adjustments have been made to a lower level. I should now therefore say 'to a point intermediate between the present level and that of 1929.'

Reference has been made to monetary policy in America. Even if America, however, as may be hoped, continues her policy with a view to achieving positive reflation, her action alone is insufficient. Concerted international action is necessary. The most effective method would probably be that recently advocated in an article published by Mr. Maynard Keynes. The proposal he makes which, as he explains, is not only his own but is supported by a number of other competent persons who have discussed it, is that the Bank of International Settlements (or another organisation created for the purpose) should be authorised to issue a specified number of certificates which the different countries would agree to accept as the equivalent of gold to the defined amount. These would be distributed to the participants in proportions determined by a formula based on their economic weight in the world, and would be gradually withdrawn in the event of an index number of the chief articles of international trade recovering to an agreed level. This plan would achieve several objects at the same time; it would enable the price level to be raised to the required point and could be so used as to relieve the financial strain which has led to exchange restrictions and secure their removal.

In the sphere of loans and credit the defaults in 1932 upon some (not all) of the unguaranteed League loans are especially disturbing because they constitute a serious impediment to one form of possible reconstruction. It is essential that the real nature of these defaults, and of the responsibility of the League of Nations, should be clearly understood.

What kind of special safeguard did the investor reasonably understand that issue 'under League auspices' implied ? Not certainly a guarantee against all risks, or why should the loans have been issued so as to yield about 8 per cent. ? Nor, in the nature of the case, could the League safeguard either a small economic unit such as Bulgaria, or Hungary, or any investor in it, against the impact of an unprecedented world depression. What the League did in effect was to assume a moral responsibility for securing every reasonable safeguard against the risks due to *internal* causes. In the case of loans to small, unstable and poor countries, these are usually the serious ones. The scheme may be unsound, or if sound in conception it may not be properly carried out, or the Government may fail to assign the necessary revenues for

the service of the bonds. Against these dangers the
League did safeguard the investor. When the world
depression began the schemes had been found to be well
conceived and carried out. The refugees were established in Greece and in Bulgaria and were making good.
The finances in Austria and Hungary had been restored,
and the position both of the public finances and the
National Banks compared favourably with those of other
countries. They had been re-established as normal units
in the European system. Moreover the assigned
revenues have throughout, apart from the difficulty of
'transfer,' been found more than adequate. The difficulty
has been one of securing foreign exchange in return for
national currency; and this reflects the essential fact that
the defaults are due not to defects in the schemes, or their
execution, as to which the League could and did take
precautions, but to the impact upon small economic units
of world conditions which the League was unable to
control. This is not to suggest that the League has no
continuing responsibility as regards these loans. On the
contrary it is evident that advice which will help each of
the countries in question to regain its prosperity as fast
as world conditions make this possible is more than ever
necessary. The important point is that the defaults are
due essentially not to defects in the League's schemes or
subsequent action; but to the reaction of external world
conditions. These external conditions can only be
alleviated by world policy and the operation of natural
curative forces throughout the world. But within a
setting of generally satisfactory conditions the League's
ability to restore a particular country which has fallen
below the general standard has been rather demon-
strated than disproved.

The difficulty of the world credit position is that it

involves not a single but triple problem. It comprises three tasks which inter-act, and to some extent conflict; first, that of dealing with existing indebtedness, then that of encouraging the investor to invest again abroad, and lastly that of preventing such misdirection of capital as was witnessed in the years preceding the depression. The burden of indebtedness, private as well as public, is now crushing upon enterprise. It is heavier when the obligation is payable in currency other than that in which the debtor earns his income; since the prices of exported commodities have fallen more than internal prices, and external trade has diminished more than internal trade. The combination of lower prices with restriction of trade has made this burden intolerable. In some way it must be lightened. A considerable rise in the level of prices would at least give relief, without making future loans more difficult. This would be one of the great benefits of a policy of reflation. But it is perhaps unlikely that the price level will be raised sufficiently to afford a real solution. In that case the only solutions consist of various forms of scaling down or individual defaults. Both obviously discourage the investor from new loans. On balance I believe it would be worth while for the World Economic Conference to recommend a remission of a defined proportion of interest receivable for certain classes of loans and for a specified period, after which the loans could be re-examined in the light of what proves to be the level of prices. But the problem is a very intricate one and needs fuller treatment than can be given here. It must in any case be regarded as the complement, if not the alternative, to reflation. As regards the two other tasks of encouraging and safeguarding future foreign lending, there is perhaps no occasion to add to what appears in the original text. No other new development, except the Conversion operation, needs special mention. For the most part, the process of increasing strain and successive default has continued. The conditions for the resumption of foreign lending and investment are still as far from being realised. In the instance in which a new loan to a Government has been arranged, that of Austria, the guarantees of external Governments (page 119) have proved necessary.

This is necessarily only a brief and superficial review of the events of a crowded year. In conclusion, I think it is probable that we are entering upon a phase of partial recovery due to the elimination, mainly by natural forces, of those factors in the depression which are customary in the evolution of a normal trade cycle. The recovery will, however, be partial, unless we can, to a much greater extent than at present, deal by deliberate policy with the major obstacles which characterise this depression as distinct from those of the past. Where this policy has been forthcoming, as in the three great instances cited, it has been successful. Where it has not, the need has in every case become greater.

The World Economic Conference affords the next occasion for a great constructive effort. Side by side with it are the Disarmament Conference; and the special League Assembly for the Far Eastern crisis which will determine the political conditions on which its own success must largely depend. The need for far-sighted, collective, action was never so great as during the coming months. If the difficulties are greater, their very gravity has made it more possible to deal with them. If the dangers are imminent, they are happily also obvious. The past year has in some directions brought encouragement, in others made the need for action more urgent. It has, I think, in all important respects, brought confirmation as to the main outline of policy which is required.

The whole system under which our rich heritage of western civilisation has grown up is at stake. Its fate depends, not only upon deliberate and concerted governmental action, but also upon constructive reform by those who organise and direct policy through every main sphere of economic activity. The sands are running out; but it is still not – quite – too late.

A. S.

January 1st, 1933.

PART I

The Present Scene

CHAPTER I

RELAPSE AND RECOVERY

THE SECOND EFFORT

IT is the second effort, after the first has brought disappointment, that tests the quality of a man or of an age. In this decade we have to do what we thought we had done in the last; we must re-establish a system in which man can once more, without intolerable waste or interruption, utilise the resources of nature and of his own skill. We have to build again and to build better; and to do so while the pillars of the structure so recently restored seem all to be tumbling about our heads together.

At first our tasks confronted us in succession, or with a certain priority of importance. There were periods in which revolutions and internal anarchy broke out sporadically and were arrested; others when reparation dominated the scene and then left it; still others when disordered finances and currencies needed and obtained reform. There were periods when the Peace machinery was supplemented by new Treaties at Locarno or elsewhere, or tested successfully in Greece and Bulgaria; and others when Conferences, designed for the limitation of Naval armaments, concentrated the attention and the resources of Governments and of public good will. And the world was not then so close-locked in a common fate as to prevent compensatory movements and the interplay of counteracting forces. When belligerent Europe was still in chaos other continents were enjoying a scarcely precedented progress; and soon the surplus of their new prosperity flowed back in capital to help Europe herself in her recovery.

But we achieved respite rather than settlement. Now every problem confronts us at once and in its most acute form. And no country or continent is exempt. An economic depression deepened by a financial crisis has spread impoverishment over both hemispheres. Revolutions arrested once are now again threatened. Reparation, 'finally settled' two years ago, has for the time stopped altogether, and its resumption is difficult and doubtful; and with reparation are now inevitably involved war debts as well. Currencies stabilized so recently, and so widely, that nearly every country was linked to gold, are again fluctuating; and three-quarters of the world is now on a managed basis. The peace machinery of Covenant and Kellogg Pact is being put to its most severe test in Manchuria and Shanghai, so far with not wholly reassuring results. The great Disarmament Conference is convened for a period when the obstacles to success and the penalties of failure both seem greater. The despatches of our daily papers announce new strokes of fate in unending succession, like the messengers of Job, each heralding disaster. 'And while he yet spake, there came another.'

The wounds of the war were deeper than they seemed. Or rather, perhaps, they reduced the world's resistance to older weaknesses and hastened their fatal consequences. How much the least of the evils of the conflict was its material destruction ! In mere production the war period bore its own burden. It made almost as much as it consumed. The human effort needed to rebuild devastated areas, or restore the fixed plant destroyed or worn out, would have been but a small toll on the world's capacity. Happily, no belligerent can utilise the production of the future; the shot fired to-day must be made yesterday, and not to-morrow. In material resources the world was therefore not very substantially poorer in 1918 than in 1913. It had indeed mortgaged the future disastrously by debts, but debts do not enable future products to be used or wasted. They only affect the distribution of what may be made in later years, and – but this is much – disturb and dislocate the processes of future production.

Here is the clue to our present distresses. It is one not of destruction, or of failure in production or in resources, but of dislocation. If we had had a system which enabled us to utilize fully our capacity to produce without paralysing interruptions, it would have been but a year or two before the world had not only repaired its war losses, but advanced to a standard of prosperity never before attained and scarcely imagined.

The tasks of the first post-war decade were to rebuild the framework within which man could pursue his normal life of making, selling, consuming, to clear the channels of trade that had been blocked by the operations of war and to open others, and finally to restore a single and stable medium of exchange in place of the fluctuating and disorganised currencies with which war finance had littered the belligerent world.

And for a time it looked as if we had succeeded to an extent and with a rapidity beyond all reasonable expectation. The shortages of 1918 had disappeared by 1920. A few years later currencies had again been linked with gold through the greater part of the world, and with a few, and those relatively unimportant, exceptions the world had a single medium for the conclusion of its contracts and the conduct of its trade. By 1925 the world's production and consumption per head, that is, the average standard of living, were higher than in 1913. A year or two later this was true even of belligerent Europe, though not of every country of it. When the full decade was passed in 1929, while some countries had lost in relative position, the world as a whole was well above all earlier standards and seemed to be advancing at an unprecedented pace to levels of prosperity never before thought possible.

Then came the depression, in intensity and in range beyond all previous experience, with a duration and with subversive consequences which none can yet with confidence forecast. Perhaps we had repaired too hastily and too carelessly the war damage to our economic structure. Perhaps we had too hurriedly assumed that our goal must be to return to our pre-war system and to re-establish all its main features; and had failed to realise that developments in the economic methods and social desires of man, already in progress before the war but accelerated by it, required us, in some vital respects, to rebuild on new foundations. In any case these questions now present themselves imperiously to our attention.

Our task is thus to do again. We have to gird ourselves for that second effort which, for those who have once known hope and disappointment, is so much more painful than the first. In Russia it is said that the terrific effort of the five years' plan is mainly supported by those who are too young to have lived through, with the understanding of adult experience, the high aspirations and deep disappointments of the first experiment; the middle-aged find it harder to renew their enthusiasm and, except for those who have the stimulus of leadership, go no further than endurance and acceptance.

The main energy for our new reform may well have to come from those who did not themselves directly participate in the first reconstructive experiments; perhaps the new insight into world conditions must come mainly from those who are not handicapped by having the very structure of their minds interwoven with old methods and earlier assumptions. But those who have been attempting to re-establish the framework of the world's economic structure, those who in the widest sense during this decade of accumulating disaster have been public servants, whether in the exercise of official or unofficial functions, cannot escape the responsibility involved by the frustration of their efforts, and they can only discharge it by doing their best to review the past and to discover where have been the mistakes and, if it may be, how they can be retrieved.

The responsibility is the greater, and the hope – indeed the assurance – of ultimate success is also the greater because, difficult as it may be, the problem facing us is in its nature capable of human solution. If nature's resources were failing us; if scientific invention and technical skill were inadequate to give us more than we now have, we might have no alternative but to economise and to endure. There have been periods in which impoverishment was due to scarcity, to an inadequacy of natural resources or of man's power to utilise them; and the time may come in future centuries when the increased population of the world will press hard upon its available supplies, and when diminished standards and ultimate starvation will be an inescapable necessity for its surplus mouths.

Happily, however, any such fate is distant, if not

doubtful. We have no such hard limits to our progress. Never was Nature so prodigal in her gifts; never was man so well equipped in skill and scientific resources to utilise them. Ours is a problem of the impoverishment that comes with plenty. It comes from defects in human organisation and direction, from imperfect planning, from weakness in our financial and distributive systems – from essentially remediable evils and essentially removable causes. It is incredible that such causes should permanently prevent the world from utilising and enjoying the resources at its disposal. Under the pressure of sufficient necessity man is an adaptable creature; and he will in time, beyond question, find the solution. But individual man is short-lived, and he finds a poor consolation for his present distresses in the thought that his descendants will escape them. If we are to avoid a period of misery and disruption which may threaten the fabric of our present civilisation, we need a renewed effort of searching analysis and constructive reform in our western world, comparable in boldness and in determination to that which is now being witnessed in Russia, however different be the goal and the method.

CHAPTER II

THE PASSING OF AN ERA

THE COMPETITIVE SYSTEM IN TRANSITION

THE Malthusian bogey has in these latter days assumed a strange and novel form; much more difficult to understand than the familiar spectre of the past, but once understood, much more certainly capable of being exorcised. Fate used to assume the form of a geometrical increase of population in a world of exhaustible resources; and it was easy to understand that this doom might overtake man, as here and there it has done in certain areas and periods throughout history, even while nature had riches in reserve, because he had not the skill or resources of knowledge and invention to wring from her what she has to give him. In this last century however this fatal doom has not come nearer but receded into a remoter distance. In addition to the familiar decimations of war and pestilence, though they have not been wanting, we have seen a tendency in many countries for the growth of population to slacken, and sometimes to stop. The birth rate in England and in France, for example, foreshadows a population soon stationary, perhaps even at no distant date in decline. Besides the obscure variations in natural fertility there is the effect of deliberate limitation, already considerable in the most industrialised countries and incalculable in its future range and consequences. The population of the world increases indeed, but at no rate of geometrical progression.

At least the obsession of a mathematically dated doom has disappeared. And recent increases have been more than off-set by prospects of new natural resources. Large regions of the world are capable of supporting many times their present inhabitants. Even with known resources, and known methods of exploiting them, the world could certainly maintain several times its present population at much more than its present standards.

And yet, in one sense, there is already a surplus population. Unemployment is its proof, expression and measure. It is in part temporary, during the depression; in part local, in countries whose resources and trade are inadequate. But in both cases the surplus is only relative to the framework and functioning of the particular system under which one man now exchanges the product of his labour for that of another. There is no absolute surplus independent of the defects of that system. Even during the period of the world depression more people work and live in comfort than a quarter of a century ago; before this period as large a proportion of a much increased number worked and earned at higher rates. So, too, with the apparent local surpluses, in Japan or in Italy, which sometimes cause unemployment and impoverishment even in times of world prosperity. The surplus is only relative to the character and the working of the system – of currency and credit and custom and commercial policy – under which world trade is conducted.

Belgium, for example, is the most thickly populated country in the world. It cannot live on its own resources, if by that we mean that it must grow all its own food and import nothing in return for exports from the outside world and its own colonies. But that is only to say that international trade is essential to it. Except in so far as there are impediments to external trade, there is no natural and inevitable limit to a particular country's population till the whole of its territory becomes a single crowded urban district. Belgium might, as far as limits of natural necessity are concerned – I am not suggesting, of course, that such an extreme is either likely or desirable – be a continuous great factory agglomeration, a specialised industrial area in a world economy, as Liège or Sheffield is in a particular country. When we speak therefore of a surplus population, generally or locally, in a world whose resources are, as they now are, immensely in excess of present needs, it is only a *relative* surplus, dependent upon defects in our system and removable with the remedying of these defects. The apparent surplus, of which unemployment, part-time, or abnormally depressed standards of living, are the alternative expressions, constitute the specific evil of our age. But it is a functional, not an organic, disease.

Our Malthusian bogey then, in the shape in which he now afflicts us, is like a djinn of the Arabian Nights who has temporarily escaped from the jar in which he was harmlessly confined, and can be sent back there if only we can find the proper formula. Sometimes indeed we have hit upon it nearly enough to get him back for a moment, but never yet for long enough to seal the jar. The real formula still eludes us.

§ *The Laissez-Faire System*

We thought, most of us, in the Nineteenth century, that we had found this formula in the magic words 'laissez-faire.' Within a mere framework of law and institutions, established by the public authorities of each country, of law to repress fraud, of currency to afford a medium of exchange, of order and security, the individual would work for the public advantage by pursuing his private profit. As no one need buy what he did not want, nor give more for anything than he thought it worth, none could earn for himself without bringing benefit to others. The strongest of all the motives to arduous work which is common to mankind, the desire for personal gain and fortune, was harnessed to the chariot of the public good. The individual, thus specialised and eager, could discover more exactly, and provide more skilfully, what others wanted than any planning authority with a wider range and a less stimulating motive.

The triumphs of this system – for the theory was embodied in practice with, for a time, but few though increasing exceptions – have often been sung; the marvellous outburst of scientific invention, multiplying nature's gifts beyond all imagining; the soaring fabric of material civilisation, sheltering hundreds of millions in a comfort far beyond that of the primitive life of the solitary peasant, which has been the normal lot of most men throughout the ages; the breakfast table of typist and artisan enriched with the products of every quarter of the globe.

But the distinctive feature of the system, which we need to emphasise as it passes from us, was its self-regulating and automatic quality. Over the whole range of human effort and human need, demand and supply found their adjustments without anyone estimating the one or planning the other. The individual producer pushed and groped his way to a new or expanding market. He rarely troubled to guess the total demand for his product; for the share of the market which he could capture was more to him than the total market in which he had to find his place. His guide was no estimate of world demand and production, but the moving index of changing prices. If he and his competitors made more than the consumer, within whatever market they could reach, would buy, prices would fall; the less efficient and advantageously placed producers would lose and be squeezed out; supply would thus in time fall below demand; prices would rise; and a little later the prospect of higher profits would again attract more capital and enterprise to production. So supply and demand would circle round a central, though moving, point of equilibrium – tethered to it by an elastic but limited attachment. Those who planned enterprises in every sphere would not so much see, as feel, their way to their market – like a blind man feeling his way with the limitations of his disability but also with the peculiar sensitive precision which that disability gives to the sense of touch. No extended range of vision was needed or was possible. Production and distribution were adjusted by a process that was automatic, elastic and responsive. The mechanism registered the desires of the myriads of consumers, and secured satisfaction for them, without the intermediate offices of any central institutions or authorities who surveyed those desires as a whole.

If for a moment there was some central control – as in a corner of wheat for example – it was through some defect or abuse of the normal system. The distinctive feature and signal merit of that system was that under it the multitudinous economic desires and activities of the world were, so to speak, democratised. They governed themselves with the liberty, elasticity and variety, of freedom.

Nor was it only the adjustment of the supply and demand for goods that partook of this character. The same principle permeated the whole of the financial and credit system. The very basis of the currency systems, gold in most countries, silver in others, was regulated in the same automatic way. And what changing prices would do for commodities, changing rates of interest would do for capital. If the sum of purchasing power withheld in the form of saving from expenditure on articles immediately consumed was insufficient to provide the capital plant for expanding enterprise, saving would be encouraged by a higher rate of interest, a greater reward for 'abstention.' So too the willingness of the investor to accept the extra risks of more adventurous enterprise, or of less calculable political hazards, would be adjusted by the higher return such investment would afford him. Within each country, and as between one country and another, capital and consumption would thus find their own equilibrium.

By a process almost as automatic, as we shall see in later chapters when we enquire how it has broken down, the balance of payments and the balance of trade between different parts of the world were adjusted by the working of the monetary system – not indeed without skill and intelligence, but an intelligence directed to the limited object of maintaining the metallic value of national currencies and not to the changes in the course of trade which were ultimately and automatically secured as a result.

Money, finance and credit indeed, and those who are concerned in their operations, are no more, under the orthodox economic system, the rulers of that system than are the individual entrepreneurs. The rôle of finance is to be the handmaid and servant of economic activity. Where it has exceeded this rôle it has been through some defect of the system, and the results which have usually followed suggest that, if something of a ruler's direction is in future required to qualify the unrestricted liberty and automatism of the past, this is not to be found simply in the elevation of finance to the vacant throne.

To imagine that at the centre of the intricate web of man's economic activities stand a few constructive and controlling intelligences is to entertain a romantic illusion. There are no such Olympians. The intricate system of finance has been built and is operated by thousands of men, of keen but limited vision, each working within the limits of his own special sphere. For the most part the system has constructed itself from the separate work of specialists who built into the environment they found about them. Those who have made and worked this system have normally not understood it as a whole; those who have come nearest to understanding it, the academic economists, have not made it and do not direct it. The economic and financial structure under which we have grown up was indeed, at the moment of its greatest perfection, more like one of the marvellously intricate structures built by the instincts of beavers or ants than the deliberately designed and rational works of man. Instinct works with a subtlety, a precision, an exactness, an ease, a regularity, that reason cannot rival – and with a practical success, so long as the environment in which it works is unchanged. But now our environment – of social ambition and of industrial technique – has changed. Reason alone can now correct what instinct has created.

In the days of its greatest triumphs, and its scarcely challenged supremacy, no one realised how miraculous was the self-adjusting quality of this individualistic, competitive, free, unregulated, unplanned and unplanning system; and upon what a fortuitous combination of conditions, precarious and temporary, its success was dependent. Realisation has come gradually as some of these conditions have slowly disappeared, as some latent defects have developed; as it proved incapable of sudden adaptation to a novel environment of needs created by war and had to be temporarily replaced, in large measure, by deliberate control and planning; and as it is now challenged by another system with its own defects and dangers, but different ones, in Russia.

The clue to the maze of intricate problems through which we have to find our way is to be found in the fact that we are now in a stage intermediate between these two systems – the self-regulating, automatic system in which supply adjusted itself to demand under the stimulus of competitive gain, with the guidance of changing prices, and the system under which future needs are estimated, production is directed and controlled, and distribution is organised. The distinctive merits of the automatic system are the enormous stimulus it gives to productive capacity, and the greater elasticity of the response which the consumer secures to his desires and caprices. Its defects are the waste involved by irregularities of demand and consequent interruptions of production and sale. The planning system has the opposite defects and qualities. It provides a weaker normal stimulus to productive capacity (although that may for a period be supplemented by the desire to win a war or an enthusiasm in establishing a new plan), but it tends to utilise what resources and productive capacity are available more regularly and to distribute such supplies as there may be in a shortage with less injustice. We tend to find this planning system in operation, therefore, where resources and productive capacity are limited and the urgent need is to utilise them fully and to distribute what is produced so as to reduce intolerable privation to a minimum. It is also clear that, since the periodical oscillations of boom and depression are a feature of the automatic system, it will be during times of depression that this system will be subjected to the most serious questioning and challenge.

A large part of the theme of this book will be concerned with the fact that we have, in our present intermediate position between these two systems, lost many of the advantages of both and failed to obtain the full benefits of either. Without securing the advantages of deliberate planning, we have enough official control and private privilege and monopoly to impede the automatic adjustments, and to restrict the benefits of competition to the consumer. From this worst of both worlds we must certainly escape. We shall have occasion later to consider the peculiar difficulties and perils of planned direction and control. But we are dealing with a system which, in every great country except one, is still one of undirected competition, modified in detail but not replaced in principle. Not because this system, with all its faults, is inferior to its opposite alternative, but because it is the system under which we live, we must begin by reviewing briefly the way in which it has in practice been changed, and the main defects which it has revealed in the course of its development. Later chapters will exhibit these defects in greater detail and suggest how they can be removed.

§ *The Passing of Laissez-Faire*

In its ideal form the 'laissez-faire' system assumes a world consisting of 'economic men' pursuing their personal advantage, themselves the best judges of what that advantage is, offering their services to the community in return for what they see to be the best reward available, and the whole process taking place within a framework of law which secures that the reward is obtained only by the creation of new wealth and not by diverting wealth which already exists.

No apologist of the system, of course, considered that either it or the 'economic man' corresponded exactly to man and society as they are; but the inherent differences have in the course of time developed exceptions to its theoretical working of much greater importance than was at first realised.

In the first place man is a short-visioned creature, more likely in a transaction to look at immediate consequences than to see it in due perspective as a part of his life as a whole, with perhaps fifty years to run. Especially is this so when there is inequality of status in the bargaining parties, and one of them, without reserves, is acting under the pressure of immediate necessity. The first expression of this flaw in the theory was found in the abuses of the early days of the industrial revolution, child labour, unhygienic conditions, and so on. In Great Britain, and many other advanced industrial states, these were, in varying degrees, corrected by factory legislation. Then the inequality in bargaining status tended to keep wages near subsistence level and leave the increase in the value of labour's output to swell profits; and this was corrected in some cases by the growth of the trade union organisations.

A third exception to the working of the theory began to have serious reactions on the responsibilities of the State. An individual firm could obtain the services of a man during his working years for little more than the cost of his maintenance during those years; it could organise (as at the London docks) in such a way as to be able to draw on the reserves of labour, required by the fluctuations in the work, at the expense of the State and of human demoralisation in the intervals between employment. A workman seeking a job is in a poor position to demand not only his immediate needs, a current living wage, but provision for the cost of educating his family, for his periods of unemployment and ill-health, and for his old age. But all these needs have to be met, and little by little, in advanced countries, the community accepted the responsibility; free education, poor law maintenance, unemployment and health insurance, old age pensions were provided largely, in some cases wholly, from rates and taxes.

In all these respects a flaw in the original conception of the theory, or a failure in its correspondence with actual men and conditions, involved definite exceptions to the working of the system in such a way as to make private profit coincident with public advantage. The consequent measures of collective or public regulation, necessary as they were, entailed further exceptions. To enact factory legislation may be merely to enlarge and improve the framework within which competition takes place, and need not change the character or impair the working of that competition. But legislation is national, and over wide and increasing areas of industry the market is international; so that differences in national legislation distorted the normal operation of the competitive process and changed the channels of trade. Trade union organisation again has in practice not only corrected a disparity in bargaining status. Its wage agreements have not merely, as was both just and fair, increased the worker's share of the profits, but in their practical operation they have destroyed much of industry's capacity of flexible adjustment to changing conditions. Its demarcation rules have impaired both adaptability within an industry and transfer from one industry to another. And the employers' organisations which have developed as a counterpart have had a similar effect.

C R

These are only a few examples of the way in which the free working of the competitive system has been increasingly modified. In every form of human activity indeed there is an instinctive dislike of standing completely naked before the full blast of competition. The etiquette of professions like the Bar, medicine or the Stock Exchange; the growth of combines, cartels, monopolies and understandings as to prices, are examples within the sphere of private organisation. And this has been supplemented by an ever-increasing use of the power and mechanism of the State, which has given the protection of tariffs and the aid of bounties. The full flood of competition has been canalised, locked, dammed and diverted from its natural course. Over a very large range of articles the effective limit to the price charged is not the competitive cost (price understandings or monopolies having abolished that limit) but what the market will bear, that is, the price beyond which the customer would do without the article. In such cases the consumer has lost what the economist calls the 'consumers' rent,' the difference between what an article is worth to him and the competitive price based upon cost of production. In many cases the effective competition is not so much with those who make the same article as with those who produce substitutes; if oil goes beyond a certain point, marginal users turn to coal and so on. Or it is competition in salesmanship rather than in quality and price of production, in expensive shops and sites, and in advertisement, which do not bring any similar benefit to the public.

These changes are recited neither as criticisms nor laments. Many of them were obviously inevitable; some of them clearly desirable. But they all have one thing in common – and this is the essential point – they are exceptions to the premises on which it was possible to demonstrate, with the certainty of an axiom, that private profit could only be secured in return for a public benefit. Decade by decade the exceptions have accumulated till they have not so much modified as transformed the system.

In other spheres too, as we shall see, the working of the automatic system was dependent upon conditions which were assumed to be permanent but have proved to be precarious. The gold standard will only effect necessary adjustments in the balance of trade if it is worked according to the rules, inflowing gold being the basis of additional money and the consequent increase of imports not being arrested by new tariffs. Capital can only be forthcoming if sufficient people will save under the inducement of interest, and can only be well distributed under the guidance of differing interest rates if they will be in fact guided in their investments by this difference in rates. But if investors have in a recent past lost their money through a disorganisation of their country's currency, their traditional habits of saving may be changed; they may prefer to consume what they have rather than trust to an uncertain future, a variation in habit which no practicable change in interest rates may be able to reverse. So, too, the flexible distribution of capital throughout the world, under the attractive force of varying prospects of annual interest and return, will be completely arrested if there is serious fear of widespread insolvency or still more of revolutions or disturbances of the peace.

And the last safety valve of the old system which allowed the migration of men, where either a scarcity of national resources or the existence of impediments to the sale of their goods abroad prevented them from earning their living in their own country, has now also been destroyed; for immigration is strictly rationed and controlled.

A tolerable working of the automatic system depends among other things upon stable habits, upon a proper functioning of the general mechanism of currency and commercial policy, upon confidence in the maintenance of peace and of the absence of such general disturbances, whether political or economic, as to cause insolvency on a wide scale. These conditions, too, we were accustomed to take for granted — but can do so no longer.

Underlying all the confusions and complications of the present situation we shall find two major causes of disturbance. The first is the one sketched in outline in this chapter; the conditions no longer exist under which a freely working competitive system can secure an automatic adjustment of the world's economic activities to changing needs; and we have not yet found how best to supplement it by collective guidance and planned direction. And secondly, the authorities through which existing regulation is exercised are, with few and partial exceptions, national, whereas the range of the activities on which their action impinges is world wide. There is thus a constant clash between the normal development of man's economic enterprise, which is independent of national limits, and the national frontiers at which it is impeded and diverted.

We shall have in due course to trace the operation of these and other underlying causes of disturbance in successive spheres of human activity and organisation and to see the way in which, through periods of apparent prosperity, they were sapping the foundations on which it was built; and it will be convenient to work back to more distant causes after looking first at the recent phenomena of the World Depression and the World Financial Crisis.

But before we enter the tangled maze it will be well to have some idea of our direction and our goal. We have lost many of the benefits of the old economic system without securing the advantages of planned direction. We cannot return to the unregulated competition of the last century; an unwillingness to accept some of its social consequences and the development of modern industrial technique together make that impossible. But we need not therefore aim at a regulated world from which both individual competition and freedom of enterprise are excluded. To take either course is to fail in the specific task of this age. That task is not to find a middle way, but a new way, to fashion a system in which competition and individual enterprise on the one hand, and regulation and general planning on the other, will be so adjusted that the abuses of each will be avoided and the benefits of each retained. We need to construct such a framework of law, custom, institutions and planned guidance and direction, that the thrust of individual effort and ambition can only operate to the general advantage. We may find a simile for our task in the arch of a great bridge, so designed that the stresses and strains of the separate blocks which constitute it — each pushing and thrusting against the other — support the whole structure by the interaction of their reciprocal pressure.

CHAPTER III

IMPOVERISHMENT AMID PLENTY

THE WORLD ECONOMIC DEPRESSION

IF we are to keep a due perspective amid the disappointments and disillusionment of these last two years, it is well to remember the prosperity and progress of the years which immediately preceded them. When, in 1919, at the Supreme Economic Council in Paris, we surveyed a world shattered in over four years of the most destructive war in history; the grave shortages of food and raw materials; the breakdown in communications by sea and land; the loss by death of many millions of workers in their prime; the disorganisation of currencies and public finances; the staggering load of debts; the dislocation of the channels of trade and the mechanism of industry; the profound changes in the habits and desires of man; revolutions and actual starvation in several countries, and the grave impoverishment in many others; the inflamed passions and new political grievances which threatened new wars as soon as there were again the energy and resources to wage them – the most sanguine optimist among us would not have ventured to prophesy the advance that was in fact realised in the next decade. Many indeed of those best qualified to judge believed that the foundations on which the fragile, precarious, and soaring fabric of western civilisation had been built were fatally undermined; that the delicate and intricate mechanism of money and finance which alone enabled man to find a market for his goods in every continent, and enrich his daily life with the products of every clime, was irremediably destroyed. Prophecies of universal bankruptcy, of a return to the conditions of barter, of a rapid or gradual sagging of standards and modes of life to the levels of the days before the Industrial Revolution, were frequent and sometimes apparently authoritative.

And yet, within only a few years, man had restored the damage, and more than recovered the levels of prosperity he had enjoyed immediately before the war had interrupted his progress. He had shown himself scarcely less adaptable to the new needs of a period of reconstruction than he had been to those of the war period. Already by 1925, only seven years after the conclusion of fighting, world production had increased, as compared with 1913, by 18 per cent. As its population had only increased by 6 per cent. this rise meant a definite increase in the average production per head and, therefore, in the average standard of living. Every continent except Europe produced more per man than in 1913. The centre of gravity of economic activity seemed to be shifting to other continents. But even Europe had recovered her standards, though not her relative position, in the world. Her population and her production were alike, and about equally, in excess of those of 1913. Her international trade had indeed significantly fallen by 9 per cent., her exports by 14 per cent. Nevertheless even in Europe the average man already made as much, and consumed as much, in 1925 as he had done twelve years before.

The progress of the next four years was even more remarkable. The rapid and dramatic success in 1923 of the League of Nations reconstruction of Austria, whose currency and finances had reached the last depths of disorganisation, and whose people were starving, led the

way to an astonishing recovery in a few years. Nearly
every currency was again based on gold; and after the
apparent settlement of reparation in 1924, credit revived,
industry was reorganised, and there was a rapid expansion of production and trade in every direction. Europe
not merely shared in this recovery; she recovered much
of her loss in relative position. Her output in crude products increased at the remarkable rate of $4\frac{1}{2}$ per cent.
a year; but even this is an inadequate measure of real progress, for the value added in the process of manufacture
to the raw materials utilised was and is continuously rising; in four years, for example, France's industrial production rose by 30 per cent. While world trade definitely
outran population, increasing by 19 per cent. as against
4 per cent., Europe's rose to no less than 22 per cent. and
her pre-war position was regained. Within a decade of
the Armistice not only the world as a whole, but even
belligerent Europe, had a substantially higher level of
prosperity and average standard of living than in 1913.
Here in a few years was an astonishing recovery and advance; damage was restored; dislocation corrected; and
the effect of any remaining disturbance much more than
offset by the progress of industrial technique. And to this
regular advance was added the effect of the upward movement of a business cycle which reached its peak in 1929.

Already, by the summer of that year, there were in
some countries signs of a reaction. But in the U.S.A. the
optimism engendered by earlier progress prolonged the
business boom and added to it the most astonishing
speculative boom in history. By all previous criteria it
had seemed for some time that a reaction must come.
Productive capacity and output were increasing at a rate
which could not be maintained except by a continuous
advance of purchasing demand beyond all precedent;

but still the values at which shares were dealt in presumed not only the maintenance but an enormous progressive increase of profits. A public which could get 5 per cent. on the safest bond issues preferred to buy shares at a current yield of 2 per cent.; and would borrow short money at over 10 per cent. to speculate at those prices. Minor reactions occurred from time to time, but each time they revealed a 'cushion' of new investors or speculators waiting to come in, which broke the fall and started a new rise. A theory even gathered force, on the eve of the greatest depression in history, that a 'new economic era' had been reached; that progress would henceforth be continuous and that the oscillations of boom and slump belonged to past history.

Meantime, however, while this boom was at its height in America it began to precipitate reaction in Europe and to reveal some of the hidden weaknesses that had been masked by the earlier phases of the upward movement. For the fury of the speculative mania drove people to borrow money to buy on margins at fantastic rates; call money rose to over 12 per cent. Many Europeans joined in the scramble on the New York Stock Exchange; others lent to Americans for them to do so. The Federal Reserve Authorities tried to put a sharp check on the speculation by restricting credit and raising the discount rate. Their action, however, while it handicapped industrial borrowing and reduced purchasing power, failed to arrest the speculative boom. On the contrary, it created further trouble. It increased the attraction of high interest rates to the European who was looking for the most profitable short-term employment for his funds. Short-term funds flowed rapidly westwards and soon the drain endangered the currency reserves of all the principal central banks of Europe. Each of them tried to safeguard its position by raising its rates; and the process of competitive increases in discount rates throughout Europe raised the costs of overdrafts and loans, discouraged enterprise in marginal cases and started the depression. And then came the crash in America. The fall in values was proportionate to the precipitous rise. The depression spread rapidly, and throughout the world. The fall in rates of interest was no check to it. For while dear money can check a precarious expansion, cheap money as a stimulus is as nothing against the effects of falling prices and falling demand.

With a few illusory symptoms of recovery at different moments, this depression continued and increased till prices generally had fallen by nearly 40 per cent., those of agricultural products and raw materials by over 50 per cent.; till (by June 1931) industrial shares in the U.S.A. had dropped to about half their value; till unemployment had risen to unprecedented figures throughout the industrial world; till the ability of those engaged in producing food and raw materials to buy anything but the barest necessities of life disappeared; till international trade had fallen to half; and till the whole industrial machinery of the world was working at little more than two-thirds of its full capacity. It is possible that, so far as this depression was caused by the turn of a business cycle, aggravated by certain special factors of disturbance, it would have passed its worst point in the course of 1931, and that recovery would then have begun. But in June of that year came the financial crisis, whose origin and effects we shall look at in the next chapter. This both prolonged and deepened the depression which, in range and intensity, is already, and in duration may still prove to be, beyond all comparison the worst the world has experienced.

What is this depression in origin and in essence ? And along what lines must we seek to end it and prevent a recurrence ? It will be convenient to trace in general outline what we shall later have to fill in in greater detail.

The first thing that is overwhelmingly clear is that this is a world depression in the fullest sense. It is world-wide in the range of its effects; its causes, however originated, are clearly related to defects in the world system; and there is the strongest presumption that such remedial measures as may be possible will require the concerted action of many countries.

§ *The Business Cycle*

The depression seems to be due to the downward movement of a business cycle, aggravated, however, by a number of special factors which are either peculiar to our own time or of much greater importance than ever before, and which account for its greater intensity.

Ever since the Industrial Revolution there have been recurrent periods of prosperity and impoverishment but in spite of the long, patient, skilled and organised enquiries over many years, in the U.S.A., in Great Britain, in Germany and elsewhere, the nature of the cycle is still imperfectly known. The most vital and most urgent of the problems set to the scientific economist by the practical necessities of man is still unsolved.

Progress is indeed being made, and the better arrangements for placing at the disposal of the individual student the apparatus and results of collective laboratory work, and for interchanging the experience of those working in different countries, are likely to help. It seems that the varying distribution of current spending power to consumption on the one hand, and to savings and through savings to investment on the other, is a central factor. But it is certainly not the sole one. It appears that there are longer and shorter term cycles; the shorter completing its course several times while the longer is in progress; and it has been ingeniously suggested that the intensity of the present depression is partly due to the lower points of the two cycles happening to coincide. But the length of the periods depends on doubtful inferences. The periods of the movements, the intervals, the range, the incidence in different parts of the world, the dates of the highest and lowest point in different countries all seem to vary. The causes are certainly complex; no single discovery of a remedy is to be expected; and the problem itself changes with developments of industrial technique and organisation.

It is possible, however, without entering the more doubtful regions of controversy, to suggest the general character of the cyclical movement in very general outline. Under normal and stable conditions the growth of population and the increased purchasing power created by improvements in industrial technique lead to a natural increase of demand for all kinds of manufactured products. Each manufacturer planning separately under these encouraging conditions over-estimates the future market for the goods he is making and, with a natural human ambition, hopes to capture a larger share in that market than he does in fact secure. Output, and very soon productive capacity, outstrip the needs of current consumption. Increase in wealth, and in the means of creating it, should of course increase purchasing power correspondingly, since human desires are indefinitely expansible and will continue so to be until the last Hottentot lives like a millionaire. But the Hottentot must produce something that others want and find the purchaser before his desire can become 'effective demand.'

Output may therefore get out of line with demand and go in the wrong direction; and over a large range of industry there may be overproduction. Prices then fall in a competitive attempt to sell more than the public wants, and drop below a profitable level. Factories work short time, the demand for raw materials goes down correspondingly; all those concerned lose profits, or employment and wages; merchants delay all their purchases and use up their stocks, because they see prices falling and expect them to fall further. Capital work on the extension of plant or development of new enterprise falls off abruptly. And so purchasing power and effective demand fall over a constantly extending area.

In time the process brings its own remedy. Stocks run down and merchants and others can no longer hold back. As prices fall the marginal consumer who was not able or prepared to buy at the higher prices begins to be tempted. As a result of producers working short time, and the less efficient and less financially strong being squeezed out altogether, the supply runs down. Meantime, as the demand for capital falls, interest rates fall too and any who see a chance for new enterprise can get their capital cheap. The upward movement, once begun, proceeds as rapidly as the downward and in much the same way; and in time it leads to a boom, to excessive and unbalanced production, probably to Stock Exchange speculation on exaggerated values, with a reaction to follow; and the circle is complete.

This is the normal movement of the trade cycle as we have known it for a century. But it is obvious that there is more than this in the present situation. There are clearly changes and defects in our economic and financial structure which have aggravated an ordinary depression and indeed transformed it into something different in kind from what has been known before; and some of these are permanent tendencies rather than temporary and remediable defects.

There is one, for example, which comes from the very increase in prosperity over the standards of the nineteenth century. The difficulty of planning ahead for future demand is much greater because that demand is now more capricious. A larger part of the purchasing capacity of the world is now available for articles that provide the amusements, pleasures, and comforts of life after the bare necessities have been satisfied, and these articles are in their nature more subject to the fickle changes of taste and fashion than the great stable products needed to sustain bare life and health.

Then again, modern industrial organisation, with its large and financially powerful units, may sometimes tend to retard some of the corrective forces that earlier depressions brought into operation. When most of the output of the world depended upon the individual effort of small manufacturers, who were unable to continue after prices ceased to be profitable, output adjusted itself rapidly to any reduced demand. The same force does not always operate so imperiously or so rapidly upon the financially powerful organisations which now control most of the basic industries of the world; they can and often do continue without abatement to augment stocks which they are able to finance for a future hoped-for market. So too the semi-monopolistic organisation of large sections of industrial production obviously impedes the automatic adjustments of the old system.

To some extent indeed large-scale organisation

introduces a new method of adjustment, that of planned regulation and control. This may in some cases smooth out the fluctuations, and it might do so in many more. But too often, at the present stage, an understanding between the different producers in a given industry, while not checking the upward movement towards excessive production in a boom, retards the first tendency to slowing down as prices begin to fall, and then, at a weak point of the market, collapses and demoralises the market completely. Moreover, if prices are maintained by varying forms of regulation and control over some parts of the economic system and not others, all kinds of strains and maladjustments develop. And this is true not only of industrial organisation, but of state regulation, and of the rigidity caused by inflexible wage rates in sheltered industries, and so on. It applies also with special force to the schemes of restriction that have been applied to many agricultural products and raw materials.

§ *The Agricultural Depression*

Meantime quite independently of any business-cycle the mechanisation of grain production has in recent years begun to affect profoundly the fortunes of agriculture. In the world of 1919, with diminished stocks, sporadic starvation, and the sudden dropping out of Russia as an exporter, the danger confronting the world seemed one of a shortage of the staple foods rather than of any excess. But much has happened since then. The Argentine, Canada, and Australia have developed their export surplus of grain and more than fill the gap left by Russia. The British Empire as a whole, including Great Britain, now produces much more wheat than it consumes. Large scale production has enormously increased output, not so much by improving the yield per acre as by making new land profitable and cultivable with a smaller man power.

Demand shows no similar expansion. Mechanisation, both in industry and agriculture, enormously increases the output per man. Industry can, within limits, increase its market correspondingly. There is no limit to what man will buy if he has the money; the pedestrian will advance to cycles, the cyclist to automobiles, and a taste for radios or gramophones and similar luxuries recently unknown can develop indefinitely. But man's appetite is not similarly elastic. There are limits to the human stomach, as Adam Smith observed long ago. Demand, therefore, except in countries near the margin of starvation, does not grow with prosperity beyond the growth of population. More than that, the consumption per head of the big staple foods produced from the earth, like wheat, sometimes definitely goes down with increasing purchasing power, for more luxurious foods take their place. The *per capita* annual consumption of wheat flour in the U.S.A. fell steadily from 224 lbs. in 1889 to 175 in 1929.

Moreover, one great category of grain consumption has been almost eliminated. A quarter of a century ago the traction power of the world, in spite of rail and water, was predominantly grain-fed; now it is predominantly petrol. The same mechanical tractor or plough which increases the output of grain, and internal combustion as a source of transport power in a myriad other forms, replace the oat-consuming horse; and man's food, maize and rye and wheat, is grown instead.

Nor are the human adjustments to falling demand and increased *per capita* output made so readily in agriculture as in industry. Over a large part of the world the peasant is still rooted to the soil, with no practicable alternative employment. When, therefore, the full effects of mechanisation in the new countries began in recent years to pour into the older countries of Europe the choice seemed to be between social upheaval or protection. Everywhere the second alternative was chosen. In almost all the grain importing countries tariffs were imposed, and constantly increased, to protect the peasant from the results of falling world prices, to save the peasant and landowner from loss, and the land from falling out of cultivation.

Sometimes the protection went far beyond this and, at the cost of the community and to the loss of exporting countries, actually encouraged an extension of cultivation. The internal price of wheat in Germany and in France is more than twice the world price and, at a cost, has preserved to one privileged class an island of undiminished profits in a sea of depression. With their foreign markets thus blocked, the exporting countries, large and small alike, which had no similar means of protection at their disposal, threw their increased surplus at ever more cut-throat prices on a restricted world market; and so the process continued, in a period in which gold prices generally were already falling; till the wheat grower found himself getting less than half, sometimes only a third, of the prices to which he had been accustomed.

And what mechanics has done for wheat, genetics (or we might say eugenics) has done for sugar. When in 1914 the great sugar-consuming country Great Britain was cut off from its normal beet supplies in Austria Hungary, a great stimulus was given to cane sugar. Some far-sighted Dutch planters in Java had for some time been employing scientists to study the Mendelian laws of heredity and the intricate statistical calculations which show the results of selection and inter-breeding, whether in animal or plant, and to try to find some practical application to

Dr

cone-growing. A combination of practical experiment and statistical research succeeded beyond all expectation and by careful selection the sugar-content of the cane was multiplied several times without increase in man power or in cost. Seed-selection of wheat is also giving similar results to those obtained in cane-sugar, though on a smaller scale, and is adding to the effect of mechanisation.

The new Javanese sugar cane confronted beet-growing European countries with a terrible situation. So far as they could reserve their home market by protection they did so. And this was carried to the point at which the home consumer gave in effect a substantial bounty to the export of the surplus. The inducement to this was the greater because the greatest accessible importing country, Great Britain, now instituted one of the most foolish of new State development schemes which even the post-war decade has witnessed. In a world which clearly had an excess of sugar-producing capacity, and in which the existing beet countries had a very difficult social problem to solve in dealing with a peasant population dependent on beet, she chose to foster under expensive conditions a new industry of beet production, so expensive that the British taxpayer and consumer have paid more than an extra shilling for every shillingsworth of sugar produced.

There is an old Egyptian legend that wheat, instead of growing only in the ear of the corn, used once to grow all the way down to the ground; but a woman by the Nile seized a handful to clean her child who had fallen in the mud; and the gods, angry that mortals should so waste their gifts, said that scarcity should teach their value and struck with barrenness all the corn except the ear. It may be that with science we shall again wrest from the gods the gift they so withdrew. But, in this paradoxical world in which plenty impoverishes us, the recovery of the lost gift would at this moment only increase our troubles.

During the last few years, therefore, there has been a depression in grain exporting countries coinciding in time with the industrial slump but largely due to different and more enduring causes. Had there been no industrial or financial trouble at all the grain producer would still have suffered, not indeed so badly because his prices would not have fallen so far and the real burden of agricultural indebtedness would not have been so greatly increased; but he would have had to pay more than he does now for such manufactured articles as he needs. Largely by a coincidence, therefore, two separate depressions have come together, interacting in many ways but mainly different in origin, as they are likely to be in duration.

Raw material countries, for the most part the same as those producing grain, suffered equal hardship, though somewhat different in its origin. With output capacity expanding and, as in the case of agriculture, only capable of reduction with great difficulty, demand was not only stationary, but it fell in full correspondence with the industrial depression and as a direct result of it. When industrial recovery takes place, producers of raw materials will benefit at once as agriculturists will not; but in the meantime they are hit even harder.

But while these developments in the organisation of industry and of agriculture were preparing the way for a crash, it was changes in another sphere, that of finance and money, which precipitated the trouble – and have extended it.

§ *Speculation*

In time of boom, profits of course go up and the prices at which shares (or 'equities') change hands, rise too, and they go up more than proportionately because it is anticipated that the rise of profits will continue. But it is not only that those who are genuinely changing their investments do so on the basis of higher prices. Many people, seeing an upward movement, buy with the intention of selling out soon at a profit. It is a small step from this to dealings in which the speculator never acquires a real share at all; that is 'speculation on margins.' And the individual is not limited in his speculations to what he can spare from his current income. He can borrow on the security of any property he may have or, to some extent, on his future prospects.

In a country like America with an advanced financial organisation, this process of speculating on margins and on borrowed money can extend over literally tens of millions of people, if they are caught by the speculative fever. And in 1929 every condition tended to encourage this fever. The world had apparently made an astonishing, and unexpectedly rapid, recovery from the war; and was as a whole much richer than before. America had not merely participated in this progress but greatly improved her relative position. And the American investor had just learnt, under misleadingly attractive conditions, the habit of lending abroad. Always hitherto, America had been a borrowing, not a lending, country and her investing public had not acquired the psychology of those who by long experience expect losses to alternate with gains and are not unduly discouraged by the one or elated by the other. Moreover America, more than any other great country, has a mass psychology which is subject to moods and impulses of a range and intensity not known elsewhere.

These conditions account for the scale of the speculative boom of 1929. In actual folly it has often been more than equalled. Nothing in recent years, for example, has touched the wild frenzy of the South Sea Bubble in England. But in range and in volume, and consequently in its far-reaching results, the 1929 speculation has had no equal or rival in economic history. Never before in the history of the world has there been a public, to be numbered not by hundreds of thousands but by tens of millions, with both the will to speculate and the financial facilities to enable them to do so. It is a new and terrifying phenomenon.

Speculation has indeed a real economic function, as all the text books tell us. If, when some seasonal or temporary cause makes a share, or a currency, or a class of commodities, stand at either less or more than the price they would normally have, speculators who base their judgment on a longer view of the underlying factors, and back their judgment with their money, provide a steadying influence. When prices fall too low through a temporary cause or public misjudgment they 'bull' the market; and in the opposite case they 'bear' it. Transient fluctuations are mitigated; the waves raised by any passing economic breeze are smoothed out as when oil is cast upon waters.

But when a speculator bases his operation, not on a judgment of economic realities, but on a guess as to what other speculators will do to-morrow; when, for example, he 'bulls' shares not because he thinks they are undervalued but because, although he knows there must some time be a crash, he guesses that others will first overvalue them more, and he hopes to get in and out again before the crash comes, exactly the opposite result may happen. The trough of the waves is deepened, not smoothed out, the storm is both increased in intensity and prolonged. Speculation based on economic realities may be beneficial, but 'speculation on speculation' is definitely injurious. And when this happens on a vast scale, the results may be widespread and disastrous.

While the speculative boom was in progress in America the demand for money to speculate with was so great that money was attracted by high rates from all the principal countries of Europe. Their currencies were threatened by the sudden outflow of liquid capital. Their central banks increased their discount rates to lessen the drain – or divert it to others. The high cost of money in these countries discouraged enterprise that was just profitable, and depression began in Europe while the boom was still at its height in America. And then the crash came, the reaction sharp in proportion to the excessive upward movement which preceded it; and depression spread in extending circles of disaster. It is a first task for those responsible for the intricate and elaborate financial system without which popular speculation on margins would have been impossible, if not to cure what it has partly caused, at least to prevent a similar recurrence.

§ *Money and Credit*

It is no wonder that when values fell headlong the investor who had money to lend or invest should have swung sharply from excessive rashness to excessive prudence. And subsequent events prolonged and increased his timidity. He saw reputable firms going into bankruptcy; he became anxious about the solvency of debtors to whom, but for the world depression, he would have lent without fear. And unhappily he was further frightened by rumours of political disturbances which were often greatly exaggerated but spread rapidly in the pessimistic mood attendant upon impoverishment. His difference of mood expressed itself in several forms, of which one now specially concerns us. He became extremely reluctant to lend abroad; foreign issues ceased; and foreign lending was confined to short-term credits from the banks. Debtor and developing countries requiring new credits to maintain their balance of payments could only get them in the form of short-term advances, liable to be recalled at any moment if there was a shock to confidence.

The unwillingness of the investor in America and France to lend abroad in the depression caused an inflow of gold from other countries. For, when a country is owed more than it owes, and does not re-lend the difference, gold has to be sent in payment. But as America and France did not need this extra gold it became in part 'sterilised,' that is, it was not used as the basis of as much money as in the countries from which it had come. The net result of this 'maldistribution' of gold was therefore to reduce the total amount of money in the world, and thus to exert a depressing influence on the general level of prices.

These disturbances of the normal system were, as we shall see later, largely due to inter-governmental debts originating in war expenditure and war damage, to high and frequently increased tariffs, and to political anxieties, but these factors, like gold and credit, are so important that they must be reserved for separate and fuller treatment in later chapters.

Meantime, while trade between different countries was prevented from finding its customary adjustments by all these impediments, the remaining method of restoring a balance, by the movement of men themselves, has been made impossible by the new restrictions in immigration.

§ *The General Character of the Depression*

This depression affords the most striking example known to history of impoverishment in spite of plenty. An apparent over-production of everything means, and can only mean, that the vast system which stands between the producer and the consumer, which adjusts supply to demand, by which future production is planned, markets found and the means of payment provided, has developed grave defects and is failing to fulfil satisfactorily its part in the economic life of the world. Ability to produce is unable to translate itself into ability to purchase.

The reader who would see what follows as a connected whole must conjure before his mind a picture of the intricate, multitudinous and interacting economic activities of man. Let him take first a single article, a table or an automobile, and recall the long series of separate processes from raw material to factory, from factory to purchaser, that have to be linked together. Then let him imagine the reactions upon this single chain of processes of all the others that represent the myriad needs and desires of the consumer and compete for his purchasing power. In every process there is a specialised class of men, dispersed perhaps all over the world, competing with each other and seeking those who need their products. That the economic machine may work without waste or interruption, each process has to be exactly adjusted to every other that concerns it. In a stationary world in which population, human needs and desires and methods of production remained the same, the adjustments would be found; there would be neither waste nor progress. But the world is not stationary; and it is so linked together by modern facilities of transport and communication, that a change anywhere reacts quickly throughout the whole.

Every one of the myriad activities of man is therefore always falling out of adjustment with those to which it has to be related and needs a corrective mechanism to bring it back again. Changing prices, supplemented by some measure of deliberate estimate and direction, may re-adjust supply to demand; credit may bridge temporary differences between the reciprocal claims of individuals, or of countries; the monetary system may give, or fail to give, a stable foundation for all these interacting processes and claims, and it may secure, or fail to secure, such changes as are required. The rest of this book will tell how in this post-war period maladjustments have been increased by special causes, by reparation and war debts, ill-conceived tariffs, ill-directed and irregular lending, the alternations of confidence and anxiety about political relations; and how the corrective machinery of changing prices and of the money system has been inadequate for its now more difficult task. As we touch each particular subject therefore the reader will do well to think always of it as a cause, or as a possible means of correction, of these maladjustments between economic processes from which our present impoverishment results.

So far, we have followed in general outline the course of the depression until June 1931. We have now to describe how it has been aggravated by the financial crisis that began in that month.

CHAPTER IV

CONFIDENCE AND COLLAPSE

THE WORLD FINANCIAL CRISIS

In the early summer of 1931 a director of the Credit-Anstalt of Vienna asked that its assets should be revalued and the forthcoming balance sheet amended accordingly. He was probably thinking simply of his duties as a conscientious and scrupulous member of the Board of Management, with no realisation of the momentous consequences which were to follow.

The revaluation took place. The assets consisted largely of credits to industries and of securities which, like most securities throughout the world, had lost much of their value; and the financial institution most closely associated with the industrial life of Austria was revealed as insolvent.

A few days later I was in the office of the Governor of the Federal Reserve Bank of New York. He was turning from one telephone to another, speaking now to London and now to Chicago. He said, as I entered: 'I have been speaking to Montagu Norman. The position of the Credit-Anstalt is serious, and the consequences may be far-reaching.' It was as if, in another June seventeen years before, one had been in the Foreign Office of a great European power and been told of the murder of the Archduke at Sarajevo. And the consequences were as rapid, and as disproportionate to the immediate cause.

The Austrian State was at once involved, because the Government felt that it must give its guarantee to

§ *The Fall of the Pound*

Meantime, however, the 'standstill' arrangement had reacted seriously on the British position. Great Britain herself had very large short-term obligations, against which the claims on Germany now 'frozen' were a substantial counterpart. She remained indeed a principal creditor country, with assets enormously in excess of her liabilities, but her assets were mainly in the form of long-term investments, and loans not quickly realisable; on short-term she owed more than she was owed now that her German advances were no longer liquid. Anxiety as to her position was increased by the fact that her share of world trade, mainly because her wage and cost level had remained stationary while world prices were falling, had been going steadily down since 1925, and her invisible exports no longer gave her, as always in the past, a large surplus on her annual balance of payments, which was the foundation of her financial strength. Her budget was also threatened by the increasing charges of unemployment insurance and the falling off in revenue resulting from the depression.

For some time past there had been considerable sales of British securities held by foreigners. These now increased and the conversion of the proceeds realised into foreign currency weakened the pound, and speculation against sterling followed. This was a safe operation of the 'heads I win, tails I do not lose' kind, since the pound might fall far below its normal gold parity and could not rise similarly above it. Then a run on the short-term deposits in London began and reached formidable dimensions. It became necessary to support the Bank's reserves by new foreign credits; there was imminent danger of the pound being forced off gold; and a drastic effort to re-establish budget equilibrium was essential at the same time. Differences as to how this should be done led to a fall of the Government, and the formation of a 'National Government.' But this Government was not based on an equal partnership of the different parties: the great bulk of the Labour Party went into opposition. It perhaps came too late. In any case the drain on London continued. It was increased by a protest against proposed reductions of pay by some sailors at Invergordon, which was presented to the world in exaggerated reports as a 'naval mutiny.' The withdrawals proceeded at an accelerated pace; the recent credits were exhausted; and on September 21st the struggle was abandoned. The pound sterling ceased to have a legal value in gold.

The repercussions were staggering. It was my duty to announce it, on behalf of the British Government, at the Assembly of the League at Geneva, the best focus of world opinion at that moment. The impression made by this great event was unforgettable. It was felt that in a world structure already strained and endangered a main pillar had snapped. True, the pound had only gone back to what it was before 1925. But the upward movement of recovery was then in progress; currencies had gone off gold through the war, a great but temporary and past disaster; it had been generally expected that the pound would return to gold and at the old parity, the date only being uncertain; and any tendency to fall had been corrected by those who speculated on its appreciation. But in 1931, thirteen years after the war, the fall of the currency which was the principal medium of international transactions clearly reflected deep weaknesses in the general economic structure. And, after nearly two years of world depression, which had revealed grave dangers in the world's financial mechanism and situation, it was felt that the repercussions would be disastrous and far-reaching.

These repercussions were soon visible. Australia had already left gold and Canada had imposed an embargo on it. Now, not only other parts of the British Commonwealth and all the Colonies, but Scandinavian countries as well followed suit. As South American countries had left gold earlier, the Russian rouble had lost value, Spain had not stabilised since the war, and China remained on silver, gold soon ruled less than half the world instead of nearly all.

Unhappily nearly all the consequences of this crisis, threatening one country after the other with the dangers that its currency would be forced off gold, or that it would default on its foreign obligations, or both, have been to deepen the economic depression. This is true both while countries are still striving to keep their currencies on gold and when they have ceased to do so. When the strain of an adverse balance is draining the gold reserves, and when new credits cannot be obtained, the situation can only be relieved by a change in the balance of trade, that is by a reduction of imports and an increase of exports. The first is attempted by new tariffs and prohibitions which reduce the world market, and therefore cause a fall in prices, and evoke retaliatory measures which continue the same process. The second, an increase of exports, can only be successfully achieved, if at all and that with great difficulty, by a desperate selling on any terms, which again forces down world prices and again provokes new tariffs in other countries. These results are illustrated in the course of the creation of Germany's export surplus in 1930–31; a vivid picture of the reactions on neighbouring states was given by the Swiss delegate at Geneva in September.

Yet, disastrous as the general result is, it is extremely difficult to see what other course any single country can adopt in the emergency. We find, for example, even the League of Nations Financial Committee, which in 1924 had in striking terms advised Hungary to adopt a more liberal trade policy, counselling her in 1931 to restrict her imports in order to ease the strain on her currency resulting from large annual foreign obligations with no corresponding export surplus.

Similar results, moreover, follow when a country gives up the struggle to maintain its currency and goes off gold. This is shown by the consequences that followed when the pound fell in September. First, the British market is so large a part of the world market, and the pound so largely the medium of international trade, that in a great number of cases it was rather the pound prices than the old gold prices that remained when the pound left gold; that is, world gold prices fell, though not of course on the average to the full extent of the depreciation of sterling.

But that is not all. Great Britain, alarmed by the adverse balance of trade which underlay her financial weakness, thought she might reduce it by new tariffs, and also organised on a big scale a 'Buy British Campaign' which has much the same effect as tariffs except that it is purely 'protective' and brings in no customs revenue. A General Election in October resulted in the return of a Parliament with an overwhelming majority of supporters of the National Government, most of whom were in fact believers in protective tariffs for Great Britain though they had not been chosen on that issue. Already, however, before this happened the fall in the exchange value of the pound had had the protective effect of an import duty and the stimulating effect to exports of a bounty. This from the point of view of other countries was 'exchange dumping' and Canada and France promptly retorted by imposing additional duties against countries whose currency had depreciated.

Meantime it became increasingly clear that the central point of danger was in Germany. The Basle Committee in August had pointed out that a renewal of lending to Germany was essential but that this was impossible unless confidence were re-established by action which only the Governments could take. There followed the Hoover-Laval conversations at Washington which left the initiative to be taken by the European Powers (America apparently abandoning the lead which, to the great advantage of the world, she had taken in June), and in particular by France and Germany. After direct conversations between these two countries Germany formally applied for the appointment of the Advisory Committee contemplated in the Young Plan, and this Committee, appointed by the Bank of International Settlements through the medium of the Central Banks, met at Basle early in December. But any attempt at a real settlement was postponed till the summer.

Tariffs almost everywhere have since continued to rise; or they have been supplemented by prohibitions and 'quotas'. Most important of all, one country after another, especially in Central Europe and South America, have imposed restrictions upon foreign exchange with the object of not only preventing a flight of capital but also of restricting imports.

The effect of the financial crisis on the world depression was therefore in every way to aggravate it. As new lending stopped, the strain on gold led to further movements to countries which already had a surplus, reduced the amount of gold effectively serving as a basis for the general money structure, exercised a depressing monetary

E R

influence on prices, endangered the currencies of other countries and forced them to attempt to redress their balance of trade by measures which, in practically every instance, further restricted world trade and further reduced prices. Exports from debtor countries did not increase; it was their imports which were cut down.

The only way in which the balance could have been adjusted without this result was that countries with a positive balance and a gold surplus should have encouraged imports by a reduction of tariffs and a monetary policy designed to increase home prices. But the first effect of this, however salutary to the world position as a whole and in the end to the creditor countries themselves, would have been to injure home production already suffering from the depression; and this action was not taken.

Meantime the process continues. Some countries have declared 'moratoria' of their foreign obligations, others are likely to do so. Good constructive loans like those arranged by the League, or the Central Banks, are threatened with the bad. And as past loans fail, new loans become more and more impossible.

So almost the whole system of foreign credit on which the world has come to depend has become paralysed. And even that last and most crucial part of the mechanism, the discounting of bills of exchange and the supply of short credit through acceptances of self-liquidating paper, to bridge the period between the shipping of the article or commodity and its receipt, is now threatened. If that goes too, there may be a further fatal disturbance to the sale of even the basic food and raw materials, at even the present low prices.

In every possible respect except one the financial crisis is a most serious adverse factor in the depression. That one possible exception is that, since a lowest point must ultimately be reached, and things must take an upward turn even if natural forces have to work themselves out unaided, the very gravity of the effects of the crisis may accelerate the course of the depression, and thus shorten it, and where remedial action is possible the greater need may give the motive force for it. But if a lowest point must be reached, it is impossible to say what that point will be — or after what disastrous interval, after what consequences in impoverishment and social revolution the upward movement will begin.

§ The Nature of the Financial Crisis

What then is this world financial crisis in origin and essence ? It takes many forms; it has a myriad consequences. But at bottom it is simply this. Some countries (or rather people as a whole in some countries) owe more than they can pay and cannot go on borrowing to meet the difference. There is, that is to say, a gap in the balance of payments between debtor and creditor countries which is unbridged by new credit. Let us consider just what this means.

It is natural and normal that at all periods some countries in the world, for the purpose of their economic development, or for reconstruction after exceptional disaster, should require capital from other countries which, as the result of their current balance of trade and receipts from previous lendings, have a surplus on their international account, that is, are owed more than they owe. There is normally, that is to say, between one group of countries, which form a majority, and a few others, a gap in the balance of payments, which is bridged by new borrowings from the few creditor countries.

This is a process which may continue indefinitely to the advantage of all concerned, on two conditions, first that the money borrowed is utilised for productive purposes which on the whole yield more net return each year than the service and dividends of the loans and investments; and secondly, that creditor countries which have a surplus on their international account lend that surplus to other countries and lend it in an appropriate form, which means, in effect, on a long-term basis so far as the needs for which it is required are long-term needs.

The width of the gap which thus requires to be bridged each year by new foreign lending was last June authoritatively estimated by the British Committee on Finance and Industry presided over by Lord Macmillan.[1] On the basis of the obligations, and the distribution of world trade of that time, about two thousand million dollars of new lending by creditor countries was required each year.

Under normal conditions of course the balance of payments is maintained by a self-regulating process. Those who have claims to meet for which their current earnings are insufficient borrow the extra sums they need. If the individual cannot borrow enough, or finds it too costly, he reduces his expenditure; and so, through many individual transactions, a restriction on borrowings from abroad means for a debtor country that its power to purchase foreign goods is reduced, and it imports less. For a time small discrepancies are adjusted by movements of gold, but, under the normal system, these at once set corrective forces in operation; and to the extent to which an adverse balance of trade is not adjusted by foreign loans the balance of trade is changed. Thus the balance of payments is maintained, which is only another way of saying that people and countries pay what they owe, as

[1] Committee on Finance and Industry, June 1931.

the net result of individual transactions, combined with the operation of the gold standard, without anyone needing to know what are the total sums involved.

This system has now broken down, as a consequence partly of the economic depression itself, and partly of the causes which we have noted as leading to that depression. In particular, the gap to be bridged by new credit has been widened by the annual charges of reparation, war debts, and loans recklessly devoted to unproductive expenditure; by the fall in prices for which the fact that gold has failed to fulfil its function is in part responsible; and by high tariffs which have prevented the debtors paying in goods. This has set too hard a task for the credit system, especially as it has been weakened just when extra strength was required.

For, as we have seen, the normal flow of foreign investment was arrested in 1929. The disillusionment after the crash of the speculative boom, and the dangers of the insolvency of borrowers resulting from the depression, made the investor unwilling to lend abroad on a long-term basis. Borrowing countries, with immediate obligations to meet and with urgent capital needs, were forced in part to accept credits at short notice and to use them for purposes for which long-term money was needed, and in part to surrender some of their gold stocks. On these two resources, the one precarious (for a short-term credit might at any moment be called when it could not be paid), the other temporary (for gold stocks are soon exhausted), debtor countries had to live after the beginning of the world depression.

When political fears were added in 1931, the strain became too great. Short-term advances began to be withdrawn, and the consequences described above spread rapidly.

In some way or another the gap in the balance of payments needs to be bridged. But it must certainly be narrowed before it is bridged. Debtors' obligations must be reduced; and, if possible, their real burden must be lightened by an increase in gold prices. The balance of trade must be changed; debtor countries' exports must, if possible, be increased, and their imports must be reduced (as they are being); creditor countries, on the other hand, should import more and must lose exports (as they are doing). The much narrowed gap must then be bridged. This can only be to a small extent by further gold movements; for the rest, it must be by new foreign lending. Or perhaps it would be more exact to say that, to the extent to which new lending is not forthcoming, the gap must be narrowed by a change in the balance of trade till it can be bridged. There is *no* other method. An unbridged gap means, and can only mean, failure of the debtor to pay. And failure of one debtor drives other debtor countries (and indeed creditor countries too, if their assets are frozen and their obligations immediate) along the same path. So long as this process continues we shall be in an ever widening circle of disaster.

We have thus to consider what can be done to improve the working of the gold standard and the world's currency system; to reform the mechanism of credit and restart foreign lending; to lighten the burden of inter-governmental debts; and to reduce the impediments to normal trade adjustments which result from present commercial policy. These will be the themes of the ensuing chapters – before we proceed to consider still deeper defects in the economic and political structure of society.

PART II

Economic and Financial Reforms

CHAPTER I

GOLD: TYRANT OR CONSTITUTIONAL MONARCH?

THE WORLD'S MONETARY SYSTEM

MUCH of the reconstructive effort of the first decade after the Armistice was devoted to restoring gold to its monarchy. It was a reign of astonishing triumphs that was thus resumed. Silver has had a longer, but never so absolute, a sway. When Great Britain gave its allegiance to gold early in the nineteenth century most countries quickly followed, except those of the Far East, which for a time remained faithful to silver. But later, one by one, Japan, the Dutch East Indies, the Philippines, the Straits Settlements, Siam, Indo-China, India, all except China, turned to the more precious metal. The reign of gold was almost universal. It was a prosperous reign, for never did man's wealth increase so rapidly; and the reign was that of a constitutional monarch exercising authority within the rules and precedents, serving the public, and imposing only such restrictions on liberty as were required to prevent one man's activities injuring those of others. And the monarch was equal to the demands made on him; at the appropriate moment he drew fresh reserves of strength from Ballarat, the Rand, or Klondyke.

Then followed the interregnum of the war, and the

systems of 'managed' paper currencies, giving more freedom and liberty, bending under the pressure of the economic forces that gold had controlled and governed, for the time offering glittering attractions, but only too soon bringing anarchy and chaos. Man may some day become the master of his currencies, make them serve the purpose his reason dictates, and rely on his own deliberate action without any external compulsion. But in the confusion which followed the war experiments he craved for the order which gold had given. The rebellion was soon quelled. Within a decade of the Armistice the dominion of gold was as wide as ever. China remained in her original allegiance to silver – but over the rest of the world, with only a few minor infidelities and those mainly reluctant, gold prevailed.

But the monarch who came back had changed his character. Those who returned to their old allegiance found that he was becoming a tyrant, his exactions excessive, his conduct capricious. They are falling away again from their allegiance, some indeed involuntarily, but even these are hesitating whether they wish to return.

The responsibilities are divided between the monarch himself, his ministers, and external circumstances too difficult for them to control. In other words, gold itself is now showing signs of failing, revealing no new resources as in the last century; those who work the gold standard have failed to work it as satisfactorily as in the past; and above all, the economic adjustments which it is the function of gold to effect have become too difficult. Economic forces which formerly yielded to monetary influence have developed a power of stubborn resistance. Half the art of government, let us never forget, consists in the luck of having amenable subjects.

What man wants in the currency with which he has

to conduct his trade and conclude his contracts is quite simple. He wants it to be stable in value, and acceptable by all with whom he has transactions. Now these requirements can conceivably be met in two ways, each of which is subject to dangers of its own. A scarce metal, mined with cost and difficulty, such as gold, may be used. If it is forthcoming in such quantity as roughly corresponds with the increase in the demand for it, it will retain a stable relation in value to commodities; and, if there is confidence in its retaining this quality, it will serve the world's purposes. True, it costs human effort to produce. But it does not perish, can be used frequently and indefinitely, and can be made the basis of a volume of other money many times its own value, so that its cost is a small – though not negligible – proportion of the transactions it facilitates. More important than the cost is the fact that it is very much of an accident whether new production of gold does correspond with the increasing demand for it.

The other way in which a currency satisfying the above requirements might be obtained is that a public authority should issue notes, or coin with a small metallic value, but should maintain a stable value in relation to commodities by issuing just so many notes, and no more, as will keep the ratio between the supply and the demand for them constant. The value of money, metallic or paper, depends, of course, like that of any other commodity upon this ratio; cost of production only enters when, through competition in an open market, it determines the price at which a supply equal to the demand will be forthcoming. In the case of such a commodity as a paper note, however, demand is far from being simple and easily calculable. For it depends partly upon the extent to which people are confident enough in its future value to take it in exchange for their goods and services.

Nevertheless the difficulty in maintaining a stable value in a currency is not a technical one. It is one of human weakness. The issue of additional notes gives immediate financial resources to the issuing authority; and when increased taxation or reductions of wage-levels are the only alternative to inflation, the latter may be politically attractive. The depreciation of currencies during and after the war is only one of a long series of examples throughout history – a much more justifiable one than most. In these circumstances there is obviously a great danger that a managed currency, independent of a metallic basis, will lose its value.

Moreover, although, within a given country, legislative powers may secure its acceptance, trade looks largely to world markets, and legislatures are national. If it is difficult to secure confidence in national currencies at home, and to justify it by maintaining their value, it is infinitely more difficult to make them a tolerable basis of world trade and of the credit operations which it involves. The adoption of gold, on the other hand, as the basis of national currencies, gives the world the great advantage of what is in effect a single, and may be a stable, medium of exchange.

These are the causes which induced almost all the world to adopt gold before the war and to return to it afterwards. And in the last century gold served the world well. There were no intolerable changes in the general level of prices. As population and trade increased beyond the capacity of the earlier gold mines to serve them, new methods of payments by cheque reduced the demand on gold and new gold areas were discovered. The century that followed 1816, when Great Britain led the way on to the gold standard, falls into four periods of falling and rising prices; a fall till 1851, a rise from then to 1873, a fall to 1896, when the lowest point was reached, and then a rise again. At the end of the century the level was very much the same as at the beginning; and the maximum fall in the whole century was much less than has occurred in the last two years alone. Moreover the gold standard did much more than maintain a reasonable stability in the general price level. As we shall see, it automatically adjusted the balance of payments between different countries and, where necessary, the course of trade.

It is this delicate adjusting mechanism that has gone wrong; and it is worth seeing how it should operate when it is working at its best.

§ *The Working of the Gold Standard*

When a country adopts the gold standard it makes its currency worth a stated amount of gold. It assumes the obligation to give gold in return for currency, or currency in return for gold, at any time, on this basis. Where gold itself circulated as currency, as in England, it was constantly flowing into and out of circulation, sovereigns being melted down and bullion minted. The Central Bank had therefore to keep a sufficient reserve of gold so that it would always be able to give it on demand in exchange for its notes; and it is with reference to note issue that currency reserves were fixed.

Since gold has gone out of circulation as coins nearly everywhere, the real function of gold reserves now is, not to meet demands for internal use, but to adjust foreign payments, so that, as the Macmillan Committee in England has pointed out, the basis upon which reserves are fixed now needs re-examination.

The main operation of the system (if we omit refinements of it such as 'forward dealings') may be described as follows. Englishmen needing foreign exchange to meet obligations abroad (whether to pay for imports or for investment) would sell pounds in the exchange market for the currency of foreigners who needed pounds for similar purposes. If the demand on each side was almost the same, nothing more would be needed. But if, as the net result of both current trade and capital transactions, more foreign currency was wanted than pounds, the pound would slightly depreciate, that is, it would take a few more pounds to buy a given number of dollars, etc. The fall would soon reach the point at which it would pay an Englishman, instead of buying foreign exchange, to demand gold from the Bank and export it. If that went on for some time the Central Bank would be concerned at the loss of its reserves. Its remedy was to 'put up the Bank rate,' that is the rate at which it was prepared to rediscount bills presented to it.

As the result of the ultimate dependence of the whole money market on the Central Bank, the result of an increase in the Bank's rate would be to put up the rate of interest for all money lent on 'short term,' that is money recallable at short notice. The depositor would get a higher interest on his savings; the Deposit Banks would charge more for overdrafts and advances; the money market would be prepared to pay more for short-term money lent to it whether from home or foreign sources. The immediate consequence would be that the flow of short term liquid capital – the most sensitive element in the whole credit mechanism – was changed. Englishmen who had been sending money abroad on short notice found it paid them to bring it to London. Foreigners also found it paid them to send their liquid money to London.

These changes in short capital movements would tend to redress the excess of sales over purchases of the pound which had caused the drain on gold from London, for it makes no difference to these exchange transactions whether pounds are needed for payments or for loans.

In most cases the gold reserve position would be corrected in this way. But a high discount rate had a second effect. It set into operation forces affecting not only the balance of payments but the balance of trade itself. For the loss of gold would restrict the issue of notes. This would narrow the cash basis with reference to which the banks were ready to create new money by opening credits for their customers. The money in the country would be reduced and, commodities remaining for the moment the same, prices would go down. Dear and restricted credit and money in London would discourage new enterprise, expenditure on new plant, the engagement of new workers. The demand for goods and services would therefore fall, and as a consequence prices and wages would also be reduced. But the fall of prices, accentuated by the reduction in the costs of production through the lowering of wages, would make the prices of a whole range of marginal English commodities attractive to the foreigner; he would buy in England instead of at home and elsewhere; while at the same time the Englishman would, in similar cases, find it now paid him to buy at home instead of abroad. British imports would therefore go down, and British exports up.

This effect would be doubled by the simultaneous operation of exactly the opposite force in countries into which gold had been flowing. If, for example, gold had been flowing into New York, the creation of new money and the fall in the rate of interest would increase American prices and so shut off marginal exports and increase imports. This process would continue until equilibrium was reached.

The working of the gold standard would thus maintain the balance of payments, that is, assure that each country had the means to meet its foreign obligations, both by changing capital movements and by altering the course of trade. It needed skilful, intelligent and determined operation; but the intelligence needed only to be directed to the defence of the gold reserves of the currency. It did not require anyone to estimate either the balance of payments or the balance of trade. It operated in this sense automatically. And its signal merit was that it effected the adjustments with a minimum of disturbance. If the disequilibrium requiring correction was of a temporary nature, liquid capital movements would provide the corrective. Only if the disequilibrium were too serious to be bridged by such financial operations was the course of trade itself disturbed. But in such a case the working of the standard was powerful enough to secure the change needed.

Gold therefore adjusted the payments between one country and another, and so regulated the relative price levels in the different countries as to secure any changes in the course of trade required in order to prevent one part of the world from being unable to meet its obligations to the rest.

The process was automatic and completely effective. It was not, however, without defects. The attraction of a high Bank Rate to foreign liquid capital is admirably designed to correct temporary fluctuations, but this attraction reduces the effect of the Rate upon the national price level. When there is a serious disequilibrium, the result may be to pile up big recallable foreign credits, a source of danger for the future, while leaving the national price level unchanged. This is in part the explanation of the British post-war position. On the other hand, when a high rate does secure a change in the balance of trade by forcing down prices and wages through restriction of money and employment, both waste and distress are of course involved.

Gold was less successful in regard to the general world level of prices than the relative levels of different countries. Here also indeed an automatic force operated. If at any time the world's gold stocks, and therefore the money based on gold, increased too slowly to correspond with increasing population and trade, world prices would fall, it would pay to work gold mines harder, to exploit the less profitable mines – and to spend more in searching for new areas. Moreover a certain amount of gold would be attracted out of hoards. But the operation of these forces was both limited and largely accidental; and the deflationary movement of falling prices might last long and be very disastrous. This inherent danger was avoided in the prosperous period of the 19th century by the development of the cheque system, and by the accident of the discovery of several new gold fields in succession.

We must now see how this system which, before the war, worked well, with some inherent dangers but without disaster, has since gone wrong.

§ *Recent Defects in the Gold Standard*

During the war, and for some time after it, a large part of the world went off the gold standard. The pressure of war demands in belligerent Europe, which was buying largely from America, increased prices. Gold under these conditions flowed to America, and

since the Federal Reserve system had resulted in an
economy in gold reserves there was no such gold scarcity
there as would counteract this rising price tendency.
Gold prices after the war were therefore at a much
higher level than before and the same causes drove them
further up through the boom of 1920 and again, on the
whole, during the 'paper currency' period till 1925. The
available gold was sufficient to support these higher
prices. Indeed it was more than sufficient, and prices
would have risen further but for the fact that, under the
American system, the inflowing gold was not the basis
of as large a superstructure of money and credit as in the
countries from which it had come; and that it was thus in
part 'sterilised.'

From 1925, however, onwards, production and trade,
in Europe as well as elsewhere, began to expand rapidly.
Moreover, paper currencies were one after the other replaced by gold standard currencies, no less than twenty
countries coming on to gold in five years; and gold was
required for the reserves of these new currencies. Very
soon this pull on gold began to exercise a deflationary
effect on world prices which fell, not so sharply as they
had risen from 1922 to 1925, but steadily.

In 1927 the Federal Reserve Board tried to arrest this
process by making a freer use of the gold in America,
that is by a more liberal credit policy. While, however, a
Central Bank can increase money it is difficult (though
perhaps not impossible) to guide its uses. And the extra
money did not result in a corresponding increase in commodity prices and so arrest the general deflationary
movement in operation throughout the world. Instead,
it helped to increase the margin of free resources which
later encouraged the speculative boom in shares, though
perhaps Mr. Mellon's large refunding of taxes was a

greater factor. In other words, the increase in prices ultimately resulting was to a substantial extent an increase in stock exchange values, not in those of commodities. Just how far it would have been technically possible to prevent this is a very controversial question. It is, however, also of great importance because the limited experiment of 1927 has, perhaps unduly, discouraged attempts to correct a deflationary movement by the deliberate Bank action of pumping new money into the market.

The lesson to be drawn from 1927 and the later boom is perhaps rather that the extension of new credit must be exercised with some discrimination as to its destination; and that some restriction of speculation on margins and on borrowed money may be necessary. Both of these are difficult, invidious and repugnant to all the instincts of those who have been brought up in a self-adjusting system. But that system has failed to work satisfactorily; greater stability in the general price level is essential; and if the conditions of a freely working system cannot be re-established with a reasonable hope of satisfactory results, as they probably cannot, the only hope is in not less, but more, deliberate control.

The tendency of gold, under the general conditions outlined above, to be inadequate to support existing prices, and to encourage, or at least fail to stop, a fall, was mitigated, but mitigated only, by two methods of reducing the demand. Gold was withdrawn from circulation as coin almost everywhere (till in Europe it was only in Albania that gold coins were the principal currency). And the gold exchange, as distinct from the gold bullion, standard was adopted in most of the smaller countries who were returning to gold; that is, their legal obligation was to provide the currency of other countries

Fr

exchangeable for gold; so that a large proportion of their currency reserves were in foreign exchange and not in bullion.

The first of these measures, the withdrawal of gold coins, was certainly on balance a wise measure, though it removed a 'cushion' which had sometimes softened the effect of adjustments. The second, however, the gold exchange system, had a grave defect in that it reduced the power of the gold standard to regulate the relative price level and redress the balance of trade. If, let us say, Hungary needed to replenish her currency reserves she could secure sterling credits in London to form part of them. This would not, however, have the same effect on monetary action and upon money in England as if actual gold to the same value had been shipped. The potential inflationary element in the gold exchange system has of course had advantages in a period of falling prices and the reduction in the demand on gold has been valuable. The fact remains, however, that the regulative power of the gold standard over economic forces has been weakened at a time when those forces are for other reasons showing a more stubborn resistance to its influence.

It is not, however, so much the recognition of this danger that seems likely to end the gold exchange system and make gold standard countries wish to keep their reserves in bullion, as the fall of one of the principal gold currencies, sterling. Many central banks had a substantial proportion of their reserves in sterling. When therefore the pound depreciated and rapidly lost about one-third of its gold value, these banks suffered a serious loss and their reserves were weakened. They will wish to avoid the danger of a similar fate in future. If, however, this process of substituting gold for foreign exchange should be completed, the increased strain on gold will be very great. When the pound went off gold in September 1931, about one fifth of the world's currency reserves were in the form, not of bullion, but of foreign exchange; and if these had to be converted into bullion the amount required would be equivalent to the total new production of gold in the world for several years.

Meantime, apart from this new factor, a possible shortage of gold for monetary purposes had already become one of the world's problems. The League of Nations' Gold Delegation reported in 1930 that there was a prospect that in a few years' time the annual gold production would be inadequate to keep up with the increase of population and trade. This was without reckoning the new strain that a substitution of gold bullion for gold exchange standards would involve. On the other hand, it did not take into account the recent fall in the level of prices, which requires, of course, a smaller amount of gold to support it. Nor did it anticipate a new supply of gold from the hoards of India which, in the four months ending in February 1932, have disgorged about £40 millions.

The next factor which we must here note in this context, as another exception to the normal working of the gold standard, is the one we have already mentioned in passing, namely, that the extra gold that has flowed to the United States of America and France, has not been the basis of as much money as in the countries from which it went. In France the cheque system has not been developed as it has been in England, many more transactions are on a cash basis; and the Bank of France can only issue franc for franc in notes against newly acquired gold. In America, too, much of the inflowing gold is represented by gold certificates which circulate as currency with 100 per cent. cover. The effect in both cases is that the gold has been partly 'sterilised,' i.e. not prevented altogether from serving as money, but deprived of its reproductive quality, its power to create additional money.

The importance of this factor may be judged from the fact that by the end of 1931 about three-quarters of the gold stocks of the world were in the United States of America and France. Indeed the *extra* gold that has flowed into France alone in the last five years has been about equal to all the new gold mined from the earth. If we reckon also the partial sterilisation in America the effect is almost as if, in otherwise normal conditions, all the gold mines in the world had been put out of action by a catastrophe of nature.

The part which gold scarcity, whether absolute or as resulting from 'maldistribution,' played in actually causing the depression at the end of 1929 is not easy to state with precision. It must be remembered that, though the depression was immediately preceded by a period of falling world prices, this fall followed an earlier rise. Prices in fact rose between 1922 and 1925, sharply towards the end of that period, and then fell slowly, with some oscillations, till in the autumn of 1929 the level was about the same as in 1922. One symptom of a gold influence on prices is perhaps to be found in the curious fact that the stock boom, even at its sharpest upward movement, was not accompanied by an increase of commodity prices. When the crash came and the depression spread, prices fell sharply as a direct result of the economic causes we have described, and not of gold shortage. Since then gold has doubtless been a depressing factor; but there have been comparatively few signs of promising enterprise being restrained by dear money, and it would probably be more exact to say that gold has failed to correct and compensate for a series of reductions in some directions by increases in others; and has rather tended to consolidate and encourage a downward movement than to be the main initiating cause. But it is a serious matter that gold has lost its corrective quality, that the economic system has lost its elasticity and that gold is a drag on a downward process instead of a balancing element tending to bring prices back to a normal point of equilibrium.

Perhaps the most important cause, however, of the failure of the gold standard has been the greater resistance of economic forces to its influences. It can only achieve its purposes in a flexible economic system which allows its influence to permeate through prices; and if its action is not impeded through deliberate acts of economic policy. The change in relative strength of monetary and economic forces since the war is well illustrated in the sequel to English stabilisation of 1925 at the old parity. In a flexible system an increase in the exchange value would have transmitted an equivalent reduction in terms of sterling throughout the price, wage, and cost structure. Only in this way could the change have been effected without loss of competitive strength in the world markets. But at every stage fixed wages, based on wage agreements, and prices held up by semi-monopolistic organisations and understandings, resisted the influence of the monetary action. In the last analysis the fall of sterling in 1931 represents the victory of economic forces over monetary action. Instead of themselves yielding, they forced the currency to adjust itself to them.

This was a process which could be seen in operation throughout the intervening years, and it was reflected not only in the passive resistance of the price and wage level but in their direct effect upon British monetary policy. When diminishing reserves could have been replenished by an increase in the discount rate, if the defence of the currency had been the sole consideration, action was deferred because (with an inflexible wage and price level) it would have been adverse to recovery. When the ordinary working of the gold standard would have meant restriction of money, it was compensated by open market' operations, that is the purchase of securities by the Bank of England with the object of putting the money paid for them at the disposal of the market as liquid resources. Granting the economic facts and social forces, it may of course be argued that this policy was, on balance, in the national interest. Indeed it may have been better that the pound should ultimately go off gold than that the restriction required by the strict working of the gold standard should have been imposed. But, however that may be, the policy pursued tended to let gold drift away, left uncompetitive prices and costs untouched, and ultimately (as the world observed the process) impaired British credit and left it too weak to withstand the strain of the crisis. In the end the fall of the pound was due to capital withdrawals on a very large scale. The amount of the withdrawals, and the motives for them, were such that it is unlikely that an increase in the Bank Rate at the last moment would have had any substantial effect. Even so, however, it is perhaps regrettable that it was not raised, so that other countries, to whom such different counsel had been given in the past, should not remember that England went off gold with her rate at $4\frac{1}{2}$ per cent.

This is only one example of the weakness of monetary policy in relation to a more rigid economic system of which illustrations might be found throughout the world.

But, in a very important sphere, the mere passive resistance of economic forces has been rendered much more serious by deliberate economic policy. We have seen how it was one of the functions of the gold standard to adjust, not only the flow of capital, but also the course of trade, by increasing the prices, and therefore the imports, of countries to which extra gold flowed. This adjustment is of course rendered quite impossible if, when the process begins to operate, the inflow of imports is stopped by increased and new tariffs. The height, and even more the inequality, of tariffs increase the economic disequilibria that need correction; but it is their variations that are fatal, especially increases designed to check new imports that may be coming in as a result of the proper functioning of the gold standard.

We have thus seen that the gold standard will only function as an automatic regulator of price levels, of capital distribution, and of the course of trade under certain precarious conditions. Any large increases in the demand for gold may, in the absence of a purely fortuitous discovery of new gold areas, force down the general price level, with disastrous deflationary results. The gold standard cannot adjust the flow of liquid capital if a higher rate of interest attracts the investor less than fears of losing what he has lent discourage him. It cannot readjust relative national price levels, if economic organisation offers too stubborn a resistance. It cannot correct a balance of trade which is leading to disaster if it is deliberately impeded by commercial policy.

In this, however, as in every other sphere of economic and financial policy, our goal must be not merely to restore the environment in which the old system worked, but in part to adjust the system itself to the new conditions. So far as a restoration of liberty, with the automatic

adjustments which it allows, is impracticable or undesirable, we must supplement the automatic system by
deliberate direction.

II

In considering what reforms are needed we must distinguish between immediate action, designed to relieve
the present depression, and normal policy, designed to
retain and advance a prosperity once restored.

What the world needs now is an *increase* in the general
world level of gold prices, preferably till it reaches the
level of 1929.[1] What it needs afterwards is reasonable
stability of the world price level.

To achieve the first object monetary policy cannot do
everything; but it could do much. What is needed is
the creation of more money, and in a way which will
correct and not aggravate the present maldistribution of
gold.

The difficulty of suggesting precise measures is that
events are now moving so quickly that the action required
may change from one week to another. Within a few
weeks, for example, the strain on the Banking system in
America; the loss of confidence in it; the consequent
hoarding at home and withdrawal of short-term money
from the foreigner; the outward flow of gold towards
France or the Netherlands; the absence of good discountable bills; the sudden export of gold from the
huge hoards of India at the rate of £3 millions a week
(nearly twice the rate of new production from all mines)
have greatly changed the immediate position. The first
need in America in these conditions is that the internal
Bank position should be improved, money attracted back

---

[1] I should now say 'a point intermediate between the present level and that of 1929.'
(See new Preface, page xxx.)

from hoards, and the conditions established under which good discountable paper will again be available. America has initiated action for this purpose in forming the Reconstruction Finance Corporation. Action which would have been appropriate a few months ago may not be possible while this immediate task is in hand. It may, however, shortly become practicable again, and with this proviso we may consider in what way monetary action could increase prices and correct a maldistribution of gold.

Existing gold could serve as the basis of a much larger volume of money than at present. A policy of creating more money cannot be initiated by countries whose currencies, while still on gold, are supported by inadequate gold reserves, or their gold would be further reduced by shipments abroad and their currencies be quickly forced off the standard. Those countries, however, which have a gold surplus could create new money so as to increase first their own and then the world gold prices, and at the same time set in operation forces which would correct the present economic and financial disequilibria. Let us imagine, for example, that the immediate banking difficulties in America are overcome, that hoarding is stopped, and that discountable bills are again available, as a result of the measures already initiated; and that, as is probable, America then has an amount of gold stocks that would support more money. The Federal Reserve System could then pump new money and credit into the market by 'open market' operations, that is by buying bills and other appropriate securities. In time prices must go up; gold would begin to flow out (unless American stock exchange securities proved too attractive to the foreigner); the balance of trade would be changed so as to make the task of finance a more practicable one.

The effect on prices would, however, depend not only on this increase in the supply of money, but on the responsiveness of the demand for it. Recovery would therefore be more rapid if this monetary action could be accompanied by plans for the stimulation of productive or useful enterprise, including the extension of public works. If this action were pursued and allowed to have its normal effect on gold movements and the balance of imports and exports; and if action having a similar effect were taken by the other country with a gold surplus — France — so as to prevent gold flowing from one surplus area to another — a powerful stimulus to world recovery would be given. And even if France did not follow suit, the extent to which she can absorb gold is limited, and soon, though not so soon, the upward movement would extend also to French prices. It would not be necessary to go further than using the surplus gold as a basis for the amount of new money which it could safely carry; that is the existing gold parity of the dollar and franc would be in no way endangered.

The difficulties of this policy are of course great. It might require new legislative powers to carry it far enough, possibly in the United States of America, certainly in France. There are technical difficulties, not perhaps insuperable, in directing new money in such a way as to raise the price of commodities and not form a fund which would encourage speculation. Certain interests would be adversely affected, for an increase of imports would injure trades already depressed. But these difficulties could be reduced or compensated for by the simultaneous stimulation of schemes of useful expenditure at home. And as regards imports and exports, the fundamental fact is inescapable that a country's ability to draw more from the rest of the world in payment of past obligations and current exports than she spends in return for what she buys or has borrowed, is mathematically determined by her willingness to go on lending. The receipt of gold affords an apparent escape from this dilemma for a time (though it is strictly no exception, for gold is itself an import); but that time is past, for debtor countries now hold less than is legally required as the support to their currencies.

A country can combine several ambitions successfully; but four she cannot achieve simultaneously. She cannot be a creditor from the past; a reluctant importer; a great exporter; and a reluctant lender of new money. To the extent to which she fails to go on lending, one or other at least of her other ambitions must be frustrated. She must either sacrifice her claims from the past; or buy more; or sell less – or, more probably, do something of all these. This is not a matter of choice, but a mathematical and material necessity. The creation of new money, within the limits of safety to the gold parity of their currencies, by creditor countries with a gold surplus would, if it were practicable, secure an adjustment to this inescapable necessity by the most rapid and least disturbing and difficult method. It would also do what scarcely any other single act of policy would achieve. It would raise the general level of prices and relieve, perhaps end, the world depression.

Let us now turn from immediate remedies to permanent reforms. Here the goal of world monetary policy should obviously be a reasonable stability of the general world price level. This is not of course stability of the prices of particular commodities (for demand must adjust supply through changing prices). Nor is it stability of the price levels in each particular country (for national price levels must vary in order to correct disequilibria in the balance of trade). It is only the general world level that should remain stable.

There is an interesting controversy which need not long detain us. Technical improvements in industry are constantly tending to make particular articles cheaper. Should monetary policy aim at a compensatory upward movement of all other prices so as to keep the general world price level the same? Or should it only aim at preventing any increase in the general level which results from monetary causes, so that while industry would not be subject to a deflationary influence the cost of living would tend gradually downward? On the whole, I should be inclined to prefer the first of these goals. It would help economic progress; and if the creditor gets as many goods or services as he provided plus his agreed interest, and the consumer pays no more on the whole for what he needs, neither has any injustice to complain about.

How then should this goal be achieved? It would be necessary to get the main objective defined and accepted, and the main methods of procuring it agreed, at a Monetary Conference including the Governments and Central Banks of at least all the principal countries – a resumed Genoa Conference plus the Central Bankers' Conference then contemplated but never convened. Such a Conference could consider the following programme of possible action.

The Central Banks, consulting through their instrument, the Bank of International Settlements, could correct limited and temporary tendencies to deflation or inflation by the methods already adopted by each of them in regard to their national currencies. I do not conceive that they would aim at an automatic and exact maintenance of any particular price index level, restricting money every time the index went up and increasing money when it went down. Monetary action is not quick enough, or exact enough, to achieve any such result; nor is there any single index which could be devised for such a purpose. I imagine rather that they would from time to time consider all the evidence available, including varying indices and other facts as well, such as current production, to see whether over a substantial future period the general tendency of prices in the world as a whole was up or down, and would set in operation forces which would correct any serious tendency in either direction. Judgment, corrected and feeling its way by experience, both as to the extent of the tendency requiring correction and the effect of the remedial action, would be required; and no mere application of formulæ and a routine procedure.

Let us see, for example, what might be done in a period of gold scarcity. At such a time, countries with a gold surplus could first agree to use it as the basis of a larger volume of money. It might also be arranged that, beyond a certain sum, surplus gold should be lent to the Bank of International Settlements in such a way as to enable this Bank to relend it to Central Banks in other countries (under suitable conditions) ; or all Banks might contribute a fixed percentage of their gold resources to this purpose. Thirdly, a general discount policy (leaving latitude for national variations within it) might be concerted. It would, of course, be essential that national discount rates should vary in order to keep national currencies safe and to adjust national levels of prices, the international flow of capital and the course of trade. But the range within which these differences operate might be reduced. This would have many great advantages. When, for example, there was a serious drain of gold from

Europe in 1929, each central bank was, in the absence of a concerted policy, forced into trying to attract credit and gold by raising its rate.   There was a process of competitive increases in discount rates which was injurious to economic enterprise.   With a concerted policy, differing discount rates, required to secure a distribution of gold according to needs, might have been arranged within a lower range.   It is the difference of rate which guides the gold flow: it is the absolute height which affects economic activity.

Next, through the Bank of International Settlements, both as suggested above and otherwise, arrangements for reciprocal emergency aid might diminish the currency reserves needed.   Lastly, the Central Banks could agree to reduce simultaneously the customary extra reserves beyond the statutory requirements.

So far we have been within the sphere of action that is within the competence of Central Banks, with their existing powers, but acting in co-operation.   A continuing tendency of gold to fall behind demand might however need more than this action to counteract it.   In that case governmental action would be needed.

This might take the form first of a simultaneous reduction in the legal minima of currency reserves.   In case of a long-continuing and increasing gold scarcity, however, no practicable reduction of reserve ratios would suffice.   A more effective means of action is required.   If all the principal countries were determined to maintain stability, this could be found in a simultaneous currency devaluation; that is, a simultaneous and equal percentage change in the gold content of the standard of the different currencies.   Granted agreement and determination, any such variations in gold supply as would otherwise change the level of prices could be completely counteracted. Let us imagine a Monetary Conference resulting in a Convention binding all the Central Banks, in co-operation, to maintain stability in the general price level within the limits of their means of action, and if they found that either a scarcity or a surplus of gold was rendering their task impossible, to report by how much gold was deficient or in excess. Supposing they reported that world gold stocks were 10 per cent. too low for them to be able to discharge their task. A simultaneous equivalent reduction in the gold basis of every national currency would have the same effect (without the cost) as the extra production of gold, even if the latter were practicable. The chief difficulty would be to prevent speculative gold hoarding in anticipation of such action, but that should not be insuperable. This method would be equally applicable to a danger of inflation through gold excess, the legal gold basis of currencies, of course, being then increased instead of reduced. No injustice to either creditor or debtor would be involved, since *ex hypothesi* the object would not be to cause changes in prices but to prevent them.

It is, of course, possible to conceive, as an ultimate resort, the acquisition and control by an international authority of the gold areas of the world. This would, however, involve a measure of international agreement of policy, co-operation in action and mutual trust that, at the best, must take many years to develop. And in that event there need perhaps be only a brief stage of concerted control of gold production before resorting to the ultimate economy, a world currency whose value would depend only upon a rationed supply without a metallic basis of intrinsic value at all. Such a world currency, can it ever be attained, would express a world unity which at present appears distant indeed.

No international currency control, however, can be satisfactory in a world whose commercial policies are essentially national, and some control or direction of foreign lending also is probably an essential counterpart of it. We shall see in later chapters what reforms are needed in this environment of the credit system and commercial policy in which monetary policy must operate. Moreover, even if the requisite reforms are achieved in both these spheres, and monetary policy itself is directed wisely, it is difficult to see how it can function as in the past, if the structure of prices and the wage level is, as it is now in varying degrees in different countries, rigid and inflexible. This has certainly been one of the chief factors in again unseating gold from its throne, or depriving it of more than half its dominion. Monetary policy will in future, as in the past, prove incapable of compelling a change in a national price level and wages level against the determined resistance of both industrialists and wage-earners. Yet there must be occasions on which such changes are necessitated by the international situation. A country which does not make the change will first lose its export trade and then be forced off gold. The only solution, if a stable medium of world trade is to be again established by the restoration of the gold standard, is that both industrialists and the leaders of the workers shall understand the position, and co-operate in creating the conditions which will make adjustment possible.

So far we have been considering reforms designed to improve the working of gold in a world prepared to adopt it as the basis of its currencies. But the events of the last quarter of 1931 have created a situation which may make this assumption a false one, and render it necessary to contemplate another possible line of development.

Great Britain, Canada, Australia, New Zealand, the Irish Free State, India, the British Crown Colonies, Japan, the Argentine, Brazil, Peru, Chile, Bolivia, Sweden, Norway, Denmark, Russia, Spain and Portugal, are now none of them on gold; and other countries are likely to depart from it. The coat of armour in which man has lived safe from many dangers, but has been squeezed almost to death as he grew, has now suddenly burst and at once given him a new liberty and exposed him to new perils.

Some of the above countries are linked to sterling. Others are maintaining an approximate stability in their internal prices and thus automatically securing a reasonable stability in their mutual exchanges. If we add to them China, which remains on silver, gold has lost more than half its dominion.

The countries which have recently gone off gold are now, in one form or another, managing their currencies. They realise the dangers of which the chaos of the first few years after the war is a vivid warning. They know the inconvenience to world trade that is necessarily caused by fluctuations in the foreign exchanges when some countries have gold currencies and others nationally managed currencies not anchored to a precious metal. They would doubtless prefer for the most part to return to the gold standard, if the conditions can be established which would enable that standard to work reasonably and to secure a price level that is consistent with economic progress. They will, no doubt, do what they can to help in the establishment of these conditions. They realise, however, that the conditions are very difficult of attainment, and depend mainly upon the action of countries still on gold. They will presumably judge in the light of events in 1932 whether the prospects of gold

G R

functioning well in the future are good enough to induce them to return to it. If not, they are forced back to the difficult, but perhaps not insuperable, task of managing their currencies without gold.

The primary objective in that case would probably be the substantial maintenance of the currencies' internal purchasing value, with so much stability in their external value as is consistent with that primary objective. This does not mean the prevention of any increase whatever in internal prices. In Great Britain, for example, the cost of living might be allowed to rise about as much as it has fallen in the last two years. This would enable certain needed adjustments to be made without leading to an increase in the general wage and cost of production level. It is the latter that it is essential to avoid until gold prices rise. This is not an impossible goal, for the conditions which caused chaos after the war do not now exist.

If a concerted policy, based upon an identical objective, could be arranged between the countries so managing their currencies, half a world of currencies, with a reasonable stability on this basis, might deal with another half based on gold. And even the variations in foreign exchange with gold countries could be reduced to relatively small dimensions. The exchange could be managed at a given rate for substantial periods, the level being raised or lowered from time to time according to the movement of gold prices. This policy might conceivably be a more attractive alternative for the countries now off gold than yoking themselves again to a metal that seems likely to cause recurrent or continuous deflation. And the definite abandonment and release of gold to countries still on the gold standard would tend to restore gold prices to a higher level, to redress the injustice to debtors that the fall of prices has caused, and perhaps give a renewed stimulus to trade.

But if currencies so managed may conceivably be preferable to a return to an unreformed gold standard system, the great difficulties and perils involved must not be ignored. The temptation to secure immediate financial resources by inflation, the more insidious danger of embarking upon policies or allowing price and wage systems to develop which will ultimately force inflation, may be great. And even if a given country can resist these temptations, it is less likely that all countries within a system of managed currencies would be equally successful. But directly any of them succumbed, the remaining countries would be subjected to 'exchange dumping' and be tempted to counteract this by following suit. If this process once started world trade might again suffer from all the difficulties of fluctuating currencies, and if it continued even the internal economic structure of each country might be again destroyed, as in so many countries just after the war.

The goal at which to aim is therefore, I suggest, the creation of conditions under which the gold standard can again work satisfactorily, and the return to gold (at appropriate, not the former, parities) of the countries that have now left it. But the latter countries would do well to study how to manage their currencies without gold, both separately and in concert, not because this is the best system, but so as not to be left without any tolerable alternative if the conditions of returning to gold are inacceptable, and so as to be in a better bargaining position with the gold countries. They should, therefore, I suggest, negotiate and co-operate with the gold countries so as to secure a satisfactory working of the gold standard. It is, however, of great importance

that they should, in the last resort, have the alternative of
concerted managed currencies, safeguarded, as far as
possible, against their intrinsic dangers, since the difficulties of re-establishing the conditions under which gold
can function properly will in any case be very great and
may be insuperable.

What part does silver occupy in the problem of the
world's currency ? Many schemes have recently been put
forward which involve in some form or another the increasing use of silver. Before we comment on them one
preliminary remark must be made very frankly. Gold, as
a metal produced from mines, concerns a few people in
a few countries. It is only as the basis, till lately, of
nearly every currency that it concerns the world. Silver,
as a metal produced from mines, equally concerns only
a few interests in a few regions; and it is only the basis of
one great country's currency. If a Gold Conference were
called, those who use it for currency purposes, and not
the producers, would dominate the scene. If world
currency is to be changed, it must be changed to
be improved, and not in order to raise the value of a
metal. Bimetallism, the use of both gold and silver, as
the basis of currencies, might have some advantages,
on the principle of putting one's eggs into two baskets
instead of one. But it introduces new complications and
cannot remove the intrinsic risks of an uncontrolled
metallic standard. It would not therefore dispense
with the need for such measures as have here been
suggested.

The world needs, in order to escape from the present
depression, and then to have a basis for orderly progress
thereafter, first, an increase in gold prices, and then
stability. If it is agreed and determined it can secure
both. But to will the end is to will the means. And

the attainment of this goal involves not only monetary action but reforms in many spheres of policy which create the environment in which a monetary system functions.   These reforms form the subject of our later chapters.

NOTE. – (March, 1932).   Recent action in America, taken since the above chapter was written, has an important bearing upon some of the proposals there made.

The object of the Reconstruction Finance Corporation in January 1932 (supplementing the inadequate National Credit Corporation of October 1931) was to thaw the 'frozen credit' position of the Banks by enabling sound institutions to borrow from these two Corporations.   In the meantime, however, a new obstacle to the creation of easy credit conditions was caused by a large withdrawal of short-term French deposits in America, and a consequent outflow of gold to France.   In spite of the very large reserves of the Federal Bank System, the gold available for meeting a foreign drain was not great, since by law the note issue had to be covered fully either by gold or 'eligible' bills, and the supply of such bills was, as a result of the trade depression, very limited.   A new Act (the Glass Steagle Act) has therefore been passed to allow U.S. Government Securities to be held as against notes.   Its practical effect is to release a great mass of legally immobilised gold; the Federal Reserve System is, as a consequence, invulnerable against any withdrawal of foreign balances, and can allow gold to be exported without contraction of the note issue.   It has substantial further resources and is now equipped to pursue the policy of 'reflation' recommended above if it desires to do so.   An encouraging indication of its intentions is given in the reduction of the New York Rediscount Rate to 3 per cent. on the 25th of February.

LATER NOTE. – (January 1933).   See Preface for present position of 'reflation' and proposals.

CHAPTER II

GOOD LENDING AND BAD

THE WORLD'S CREDIT SYSTEM

THE function of lending in the economic system is essentially simple, though the methods by which it is discharged are intricate and varied. The human effort needed to produce an article and sell it is spread over a considerable time. When it is at last sold it will normally be at a price which enables the seller to command more human effort for his future needs than has been expended on it in the past. But time will have elapsed.

It is the function of lending to bridge over this time interval; to lend money for this purpose is to provide 'capital.' Without lending the expansion of the business of successful producers would be slow; and the new man could hardly start at all. It is upon this simple necessity that the whole credit structure is founded.

The reader who wishes to understand the working of an advanced credit organisation would do well to read the Report of the (Macmillan) Committee on Finance and Industry of June 1931, which describes the British system, with its deposit banks, issuing houses, the part played by the 'bill of exchange' and other bills, the function of the 'accepting houses' and bill brokers, and the relation of all to the Central Bank. He will there see how the bulk of the money of the country consists of credit created by the deposit banks, and how the Central Bank can cause a contraction of this credit by increasing the rate at which it will rediscount bills, and by the sale of securities in the 'open market.' The power of control varies greatly in different countries. It is at its maximum in London. It is in practice weaker in America because the industrial organisations have greater financial resources of their own. In France it is also weaker because there is no corresponding 'bill market,' and because the Bank of France is not legally able to engage in 'open market' operations. The credit which the deposit banks create is in the form of advances to customers against suitable security. It is these advances which provide 'working capital' to the active producers, that is the money they require to bridge the time which elapses in the actual process of manufacture and sale.

Industrial enterprise, however, has not only 'working capital' needs. A new business that is being started, or an old one that is being extended, requires to expend large sums on its capital installation (land, factories, machinery, etc.) for which it cannot hope to recoup itself by earnings for many years. 'Long-term' capital is therefore necessary. Capital of this kind cannot be supplied by the deposit banks without danger; for their primary duty is to see that they are always able to repay their depositors on demand, and they must therefore keep their resources liquid. In practice banks have drifted into what has become long-term lending, but for the most part involuntarily. It is a dangerous function for them to discharge.

Long-term capital is therefore normally raised by other means, and in two main forms. 'Shares' in the enterprise are issued, those who buy them dividing the net profits that may be earned, obtaining nothing in bad times, and an unlimited return in case of great success. Many investors however prefer a smaller range of risk; and to secure capital from them 'Debentures' or 'Preference Shares' are issued

which give them a prior right to a fixed or maximum rate
of annual return, before dividends on ordinary shares are
payable. If the concern goes to pieces altogether, they
may of course lose their money, but short of that they get
their return even when the ordinary shareholders, who
are the real proprietors of the concern, get nothing. If,
on the other hand, the concern is very successful, they
get no advantage except a greater security for the capital
they have lent and for its fixed annual yield.

So far we have spoken of private enterprises. But
Governments too need to borrow, partly to bridge the intervals between the times at which their current payments
have to be made and the time at which revenue comes in
(often irregularly or only at fixed dates) and partly to
finance capital expenditure on state railways, or roads,
etc. The first may be met by the sale of short dated
'Treasury Bills' in the market; the second by the issue,
and sale to the public, either at home or abroad of
Government Bonds.

The systems by which the capital is in practice raised
for these purposes differ greatly from country to country
and according to the character of the enterprise for which
it is needed and the borrowers, and the habits of the lending public. Established businesses with a successful record can, within their articles of association, easily issue
new debentures or share capital to the public. But new
enterprises present a special problem; and a body of persons have grown up within the financial structure whose
function is 'Company promoting.'

The business of company promoters is to persuade the
investing public, who have no direct personal knowledge,
that a new enterprise is one in which it is worth while to
venture their savings. The promoters do this by issuing,
in public advertisements, a prospectus showing reasons

for thinking the enterprise will be successful and giving the names of those associated with it, on whose reputation, with that of the company promoter, the success of the flotation will largely depend. This has been the least satisfactory part of the English financial structure, and has been associated with the worst scandals. The reputation of the company promoter, an essential part of the foundation of such a system of public issues if it is to be satisfactory, has proved to be unreliable. Too often he vanishes with his flotation commissions, and is replaced by another who, if he has a shorter, has also a cleaner, record from the past.

Investments in foreign enterprises stand on a different footing. So far as England is concerned they have usually been made through a system of long-established issuing houses, which has proved a more responsible, competent and successful intermediary between the lending public and the borrower.

The willingness of the individual investor to venture his capital depends very greatly on his ability to change, or dispose of, his investments at any moment; and this need has created the world's Stock Exchanges, in which existing securities are bought and sold at prices which are published daily. These prices reflect the varying credit of the different enterprises and borrowers. The mechanism devised for this purpose is not used only for actual changes of investment from one hand to another. It enables persons not only to invest but to speculate; to buy not in order to hold, but to sell at a hoped-for higher price; and even to speculate on margins, that is, to make a bargain under which they undertake to pay a forfeit if a security goes down which they thought would go up, or vice versa, while they make a profit if their guess has been right,

§ *Defects in the British Credit System*

Let us now consider what has gone wrong with this system in recent years.

As regards the financing of home industries by capital drawn from within the country, the course of events has varied considerably from country to country. In Great Britain something like the following development has taken place. Till late in the nineteenth century the expansion of industry was, as we have seen, mainly financed out of profits made by the owners of individual concerns being put back into the business, or by direct and personal arrangement with other individuals. Of some £200 million a year (out of the £400 million of total annual savings) invested in home concerns in the period just before the war, only some £18 million was found through the mechanism of the London market. The great bulk of home investment made in the last century came from those who had personal knowledge of the business; and it was, to the full extent needed, in a form which made the return for the capital vary with changing fortunes. Either the business was individually owned, or its capital was mainly in the form of share-capital of a joint-stock company. There was no excessive weight of fixed debt, involving an annual charge independent of profits.

Increased taxation, however, the growth in the scale of business, a period of falling trade and other causes, have completely changed this position. Industries have needed to acquire their capital for new plant, whether for replacement or for expansion, from unknown and more numerous investors, and therefore through a credit mechanism, mainly located in London. In recent years, instead of £18 million, about £170 million, out of a total of £200 million a year for new home investment, has come through the London credit system. The investor, thus knowing less of the concern in which he is putting his money, has preferred to a greater extent to limit his risk and to acquire a right to a fixed annual payment with a fixed charge rather than to more expansible but more precarious profits. A larger proportion of the capital of industry devoted to providing its fixed plant has therefore come to be in the form of debentures and preference shares, as distinct from ordinary shares or equities.

Even more important is the fact that the capital of industries in England has come to take the form of bank overdrafts. To some extent these overdrafts have taken the place of the 'inland bill' which industrialists used to draw to finance short operations; and this change (partly due to the larger volume of Treasury Bills in the market) is regrettable since the rates of interest payable on bills were more elastic, especially in times of depression, than those charged for overdraft facilities. With the continuance of the depression overdrafts have extended into another sphere. As new capital has been difficult to obtain, businesses have gradually been financed more and more by the banks. Such overdrafts, which are in principle for the purpose of providing 'working capital' and are legally recallable at fixed short terms, have gradually come to form in large part the capital required for longer needs, to be, in effect, long-term capital with a prior claim over other forms of such capital.

The consequences have been unfortunate from several points of view. Once an industry is living on recallable overdrafts which it cannot pay if required, its mastery has passed to the banks. The banks, however, are not equipped, and do not desire, to control the business, and their investments which should be 'liquid,' have become 'frozen.' Meantime the known existence of these frozen overdrafts makes it impossible to obtain new capital, and so the system perpetuates itself. There has thus grown up a grave disproportion between the ratio of short-term and long-term needs of industry and that of the short-term and long-term capital by which they are met; and between the fixed and flexible proportion of capital which industry needs, and that which it has.   Short-term capital (overdrafts) has encroached on the sphere of long-term needs; fixed-interest capital (debentures and preference) has encroached on the sphere of the flexible ordinary share.   And this disproportion has been rendered much more serious by the fall in prices, which has both diminished trade and profits and at the same time increased the real weight of the fixed interest charges which stand ahead of dividends distributable on shares.

Meanwhile, the investor, already discouraged by the cessation of the dividends of old established concerns during the present depression, and by his knowledge of the existence of large fixed charges in respect of debentures and overdrafts, which stand ahead of dividends, is further discouraged from investment in new enterprises by the unfortunate results of the many issues of recent years.

How discouraging to the investor has been the provision of his savings for new capital to industry is shown by some striking figures, published by the Macmillan Committee, for the year 1928. In that year the total amount subscribed for capital issues in Great Britain of shares and debentures of 284 companies was £117 million. On the 31st May, 1931, the total market value of these issues was only £66 million, a loss of 47 per cent.; and indeed the loss was really greater, since many of the shares were sold by the promoters at a high premium.

Moreover, of these 284 companies, 70 were already wound up, and the capital of 36 others had no ascertainable value, the issues of these 106 companies amounting to £20 million. Now it is true that the period of between two and three years which the Committee took, ending with May 1931, included a year and a half of a world economic depression. At the same time, May 1931 was before the world financial crisis and before the deeper period of the depression. A later date would doubtless show a much greater loss. With full allowance for the effect of the depression it is evident that these figures indicate a most unsatisfactory situation, and that even if the slump had not come at the end of 1929, an intolerably high proportion of loss would have been sustained.

Foreign investment from Great Britain was more carefully managed. Of the annual savings in the country of about £400 million, rather more than £200 million used to be invested abroad (or re-invested, as the amount coincided closely with the return on previous investments) mainly through a limited number of old-established issuing houses and business concerns of reputation, standing and experience. If the same date of May 1931 had been taken, that is, before the financial crisis of this year added its effect to those of the earlier depression, these investments would have had a much better showing than new issues at home. More than half were in the form of sterling debentures, bonds and mortgages, and these were then substantially intact; the remainder, in equities, had suffered some loss in the case of countries producing raw materials of which the price had fallen abnormally, but the loss was in most cases completely explicable by the world depression.

§ *Differences of National Credit Systems*

In America the position is very different. Until recently the financial world of New York devoted itself almost entirely to the development of American industry rather than international finance. America was a debtor country until the war, importing and not exporting capital. She has only been lending or investing abroad for a short time, and, while some of her financial institutions have developed their new functions with skill and prudence, there are others of which this cannot be said.

The home issues, on the other hand, have been better managed than those of Great Britain. All American industrial issues of well-known companies are sponsored by some responsible issuing institution, and the name of the institution appears prominently on the prospectus. In general the American banks engage their issuing credit in the eyes of the public for the soundness of the issues they support, and knowing this they maintain a close and intimate association with the industries concerned. They have thus given the public real guidance in their investments of a kind which is not available to the British home nvestor. The difficulties experienced by the American banks in 1931, to meet which the Reconstruction Finance Corporation was formed, were not due to their investing in industrial shares, but to other causes. Many short-term loans secured by collateral that would normally be quite safe (deeds of land, railway stock, etc.) had become frozen because of the altogether exceptional fall in values which made the borrowers insolvent; and adaptation was more difficult because of the multiplicity of independent banks, which take the place of the branches of large banks in other countries, and because of the rigid legal rules as to investment, enforced by official inspection, which often have results contrary to their intention.

In France, the investor has long had an unfortunate experience in foreign banking, much of his money having in the past gone, under strong Government influence, for purposes largely political, in Russia, or in countries of Central and Eastern Europe, and having been lost. And he has, of course, lost in addition by the less avoidable depreciation of his more prudent investments through the effects of the world crisis. At home, the capital market is distinguished from that of Great Britain, especially pre-war Great Britain, and of America, by the fact that it derives its resources mainly from the very small capitalist. He is unwilling to exercise an independent judgment and relies on advice from the big banks. These banks have made practically all the industrial issues and have assumed a measure of responsibility to the public for them. In addition some powerful banking institutions have been formed as 'banques d'affaires' with close and direct participation in industry.

In Germany the association between the banks and home industry has been even closer. Industrial development started later than in Great Britain. Capital and independent investors were scarce, except perhaps in Prussia; and partly for this reason, and partly through the absence of any other organisation, the banks were driven to help industry to obtain its permanent as well as its working capital. It has become customary for most new concerns to be formed with the close collaboration of a bank. The bank examines the prospects, secures reports from experts, and draws up a scheme of financing, including the amount and type of capital to be issued. Its reputation is therefore fully engaged in the eyes of the public; and sometimes it takes some of the shares itself with a view to issuing them later to the public.

The relation between Banks and Industry therefore differs widely. It is closest in Germany, where the system has been of special advantage to industrial development, but has somewhat subordinated the interests of the depositor; least close in Great Britain, where the function of safeguarding the depositor's savings by taking care to keep assets in a liquid form has been the first consideration, industry and the investor having to look mainly elsewhere for help and guidance; and in an intermediate position in America and France, where the investor has received more guidance, and industry more direct assistance, at some cost to the depositor's position. But in no case is the banks' independence of industrial fortunes at all complete. Indeed in Great Britain, as we have seen, where the principle of avoiding long-term investments has been most insisted upon, the grant of renewable short-term credits to industries, which have used them for more than genuine working capital purposes and could not repay them, has at once 'frozen' a substantial part of the nominally 'liquid' assets of the banks, and given them against their will the legal power of control over a large part of industry.

It is, however, especially, though not solely, foreign lending with which we are here concerned. The financial crisis was due to its sudden cessation; this cessation itself was due largely to the way in which it had previously been conducted.

We may roughly summarise the position of the three chief lending countries in the years preceding the slump as follows. Great Britain continued to lend abroad through the institutions built up during the period when she had by far the biggest surplus on international account available for foreign lending; and to guide her action by much the same rules and criteria. As regards loans to Governments, she supported strongly, under the lead of the Bank of England, international corporate action to diminish the risk of the money being improperly spent, and most though not all issues for Europe were discouraged except on these conditions. Thus, she participated in the League's reconstructive loans to Austria, Hungary, Greece and Bulgaria; in the German loans that followed the Dawes and Young Plans; and in the loans to aid the currency restoration of Belgium, Poland and other countries under schemes approved by the main Central Banks. In some cases, however, loan negotiations took place without these precautions (as in Jugo-Slavia) with unfortunate results both as regards the particular case and in encouraging other countries to act similarly elsewhere (France in Roumania, for example). There was also excessive and imprudent lending to Australia, where the first hint of possible default was among the earliest heralds of the more extensive trouble to come.

More generally, there was a tendency to lend, not imprudently in the particular case, but on rather too big a scale for the diminishing surplus on Great Britain's international account. London was still the magnet for short-term liquid capital from abroad; and the resources so obtained were lent to a large extent either on long-term or (as in Germany) in the form of what proved to be precarious short-term advances, liable to be frozen. The continuous fall in Great Britain's share of world trade from 1925 onwards was undermining her power to export capital; and as her long-term investment and lending were not correspondingly reduced there was an increasing strain on

HR

her gold position, which came to depend upon short-term investments of foreigners in London being always renewed or replaced. When her own short-term advances in Germany were frozen and a shock to confidence caused withdrawals from London, the pound at once collapsed.

In France the position has been almost diametrically opposite. The stabilisation of the franc at a rate which left French prices low in terms of gold gave an export bounty, which lasted long, as the upward movement of franc prices was slow. She began her debt payments to America and Great Britain later than Great Britain, and on the basis of much more favourable settlements, and had no outward flow on this account during the years when Germany was paying little in reparation. Later, when the Dawes and Young Plans came into operation, she received substantially more from Germany than she paid in respect of War Debts. Large amounts of money had been put abroad in dollars and sterling during the period of the franc's depreciation and these added to the strength of France's position on stabilisation.

Meanwhile France's industrial capacity was rapidly increasing and was followed by no corresponding increase in the wage level and in consumption; the margin of savings being available as disposable capital. Moreover, as exports increased, since her prices were for the same reasons attractive in the world market, and as in addition her imports were restricted by tariffs, the surplus in her balance of payments – the amount available for new investment abroad – was large and rising each year. She took part in the League of Nations loans, and those recommended by the Central Banks; and issued other loans herself. But this disposed only of a part of the surplus. There were considerable fiscal handicaps to foreign issues; but more important was the reluctance of the investor to venture again after his loss of what he had lent before in Russia and the Balkans. In these conditions most of the surplus found its way abroad in the form not of real investment but of deposits, recallable at short notice, mainly in London and New York; and the still remaining adjustment was made by the inflow of gold into France.

In the post-war period as a whole, America has been in the same position reached a few years ago by France, of having a large surplus on her balance of payments available for foreign investment. Apart from the sums due to her in respect of War Debt she has had more exports than imports, and has made the gap greater by her high import tariffs. In the early years of peace European countries were clamorous for new capital for reconstruction, and other countries, especially Canada and South America, for expansion. The need could only be met from America, which alone had a sufficient surplus and which in turn could only maintain her large exports, while impeding imports, if she lent her annual surplus abroad. Under this double stimulus a mechanism for the organisation of foreign lending developed quickly. It was based, to an extent not known elsewhere, not merely on public advertisement, but upon thousands of local agents working on commission throughout the country on behalf of a small number of large issuing houses, mostly operating from New York and Chicago.

These agents for the first time taught the small investor in a hundred small provincial towns, and in the countryside of the Middle and Far West, to link their fortunes with those of the Governments and enterprises of distant lands whose very names he often scarcely knew. It was an astonishing achievement of modern organisation, and for its first purpose of inducing the investor to lend his money, and making this money available in the continents which most needed capital, it was extremely successful. But, as we shall see, at the other end of the operation, namely, the examination of the character and purposes of the loan, the capacity of the borrower and the likelihood of his using the money productively, the methods adopted were less satisfactory. There was too much competition and too little caution. Unhappily the more prudent bankers were, during the most sanguine period, embarrassed by the competing offers of less responsible issuing houses, who were content to sell the bonds to the public, whether at home or on foreign markets, take their very substantial commissions, and leave the consequences to be borne by others. And too often the competition tended to laxer conditions rather than lower rates.

While America is a creditor country, and during the post-war period as a whole has been lending on a vast scale to the rest of the world, there has been one very important period, the eighteen months before the crash in 1929, when she was a short-term borrower under very dangerous conditions. The operation of her banking system makes her short-term money rates, the counterpart of the bill rate in European centres, much more volatile than the corresponding rates in London and elsewhere. During the Stock Exchange boom of 1928 and the first part of 1929 the demand for money with which to speculate drove up the short-term money rates to a fantastic height, and made them a dangerous magnet for European short-term funds. European liquid money was pumped into New York with a consequent strain upon European currency reserves which has been described in the preceding chapter.

The main course and volume of the movements of

post-war capital can be shown in a few global figures. In the years 1924 to 1929 inclusive the United States and Great Britain each invested abroad a total net sum of between $2,500 and $3,000 million. Germany borrowed during the same period a total of just over $4,000 million, and very significantly borrowed more than half of this in the two years, 1927 and 1928, which immediately preceded the depression. Australia borrowed £260 million and South America took about $1,600 million from the United States and £100 million from Great Britain.

Such total sums do not, of course, in themselves prove that trouble was being laid up for the future. So far as loans are used for productive enterprises yielding in annual return more than the loan service, they are to the benefit of all concerned. But even the figures as they stand would suggest the improbability of this condition being fulfilled. An expanding country like Australia, or those of South America, should normally be borrowing capital; but it was unlikely that Australia, with a population of only about six millions, was wise in borrowing as much as £260 million in seven years. Still less probable is it that it was wise for an already highly developed country like Germany to borrow from abroad in two years over $2,000 million, two and a half times the amount payable in reparation.

When we turn to the available evidence as to the actual conditions under which loans were made in the years 1925–28, and as to how they were utilised, the inferences suggested by the above statistics are abundantly confirmed. Lending and borrowing were, in a large proportion of cases, reckless, extravagant and wasteful.

§ *Loans to Governments*

Among these foreign loans those made to Governments and public authorities are by far the most important; and it is on these that the main attention should be concentrated. Between 1920 and 1925 the vast majority of new foreign capital issues to Europe, and both then and afterwards a very high proportion of all foreign loans, whether to Europe or to other continents, have been of this character. Apart from the high proportion of such loans, however, they obviously have special dangers and need special precautions. An individual company usually borrows with a careful consideration of the consequences, which must fall directly on those who direct it. The lender is also more cautious because his security depends on the limited and calculable resources and prospects of the borrower. Moreover, if the transaction proves a bad one, the consequences are restricted both in range and in time. The individual dies and no heir is legally saddled with a net liability; the company goes bankrupt and its insolvency does not destroy the credit of others.

But when the borrower is a Government, default affects the credit of the whole nation and every individual concern in it. Moreover, there are the dangers of both a short and a long expectation of life. Too often the contracting Minister thinks largely in terms of his probable tenure of office, which is usually short, rather than that of the loan. But if political life is shorter than personal life, the nation which bears the burden is immortal, and the charges of a rashly negotiated loan may extend over generations. More than once when urging the unwisdom of concluding a long-term loan of thirty or forty years at a time of high rates, without at least a redemption clause after ten years, I have been unable to avoid the impression that ten years seemed a long time to an Eastern European Minister faced by the exigencies of his current budget. He was instinctively thinking in terms of a shorter period than if the effective responsibility were going to remain with him for the rest of his life.

This is not all. When a large loan is dangled before a weak Government by the representative of a powerful foreign financial institution, perhaps competitively by several of them, all sorts of political consequences, all unfortunate, are likely to result. They begin often with the process of negotiating the loan. The evidence recently given before the Finance Committee of the American Senate is instructive. It was admitted (says a despatch of January 9th in *The Times*) that '$415,000 has been paid to Don Juan Leguia, son of the deposed President of Peru, for his assistance in floating loans of the total value of $100 million for the account of the Peruvian Government.'

Then the borrowing Government may be tempted to peculation of the loan itself, to wasteful expenditure, or to increased military preparations; or an unconstitutional adventurer may be confirmed in power; or special associations may grow up between different lending countries and particular groups of politicians in the borrowing country. This last danger is greater when the accredited Ministers of the lending countries have conversations with members of the borrowing Government – as they do – about a proposed loan which is being competed for by different issuing houses. If, for example a Governmental negotiation is in progress at the moment about the funding of a War Debt, it is very likely to become a factor in the conclusion of the new loan contract.

So much have I seen of such dangers that I would go so far as to assert that when a large loan is being negotiated from a big country to a small one, political consequences and dangers are practically always involved, and that the political aspects of the proposed transaction ought to be considered by a body, preferably international, competent to consider them. The offering of money to public borrowers on tempting terms by persons with no political responsibilities can constitute a grave public danger, and in the years immediately preceding the depression it has done so on a scale not realised by any but those who have seen it at close quarters.

When hostilities broke out between Bolivia and Paraguay, both League members, in December, 1928, their recent financial history was naturally looked into in view of the possibility of financial pressure being needed in accordance with Article 16 of the Covenant. An interesting fact emerged embodied in a dispatch of March 24, 1928 in the South American Journal, which stated that President Siles had authorized publication of a conversation with Deputy Solarez in which he explained that a fund of $4,000,000 set aside in the loan to Bolivia for a railway from Potosi to Sucre had been used in the first place for national defence purposes and only in the second place to pay off certain bills due in connection with the railway. The point of this incident is not that it is exceptional but, on the contrary, that it is difficult to say that it contravenes generally accepted standards. In this particular case hostilities were stopped under the joint influence of the League and the Pan-American Congress, which happened by a fortunate coincidence to be both in session at the time. But fate cannot often be tempted thus with impunity. When a Government is tempted to rash adventure it is easy to realise how greatly the temptation may be increased if, at the crucial moment, a large loan is dangled before its eyes by foreign financiers.

The investor is now suffering from the Brazilian Moratorium. He would find it instructive to enquire where his money had gone. Since the war, the Brazilian Federal Government, States and Municipalities have issued long-term loans abroad amounting to about $800 million.

These include $8,000,000 in 1922 for electrifying the Central Railway of Brazil, which has not been electrified; $20,000,000 or more for a (Rio Claro) water supply scheme which has to all intents and purposes been abandoned in favour of another scheme.

The record of Colombia is even more instructive. Between 1924 and 1928, it borrowed about $153 million. A large part of this was devoted to constructing a railway to connect two valleys separated by a range of mountains about 9,000 feet high. There was no commercial justification for it, since both valleys had their own outlet to the sea. A very expensive tunnel through the top of the mountain range was begun and then abandoned; and while the Federal authorities were driving a tunnel through the mountains the local authorities were making a costly road over them. I have had a vivid account from one who was in Colombia at the time of the way in which the offers of competing lenders resulted in the public authorities incurring greater and greater obligations for these extravagant ventures.

One of the worst features of such loans is that the good lender is involved with the bad. There are of course responsible and prudent issuing houses in every great financial centre. But they are liable to be both blacklegged in negotiating their business and to have sound transactions made unsound by subsequent extravagance. Supposing, for example, that a modest and useful loan has already been issued to, and on the credit, of a

particular country, and utilised for the most productive
purposes; the subscriber will still lose if later and
wasteful loans disorganise the public finances and compel
default.

Numerous operations of a similar, or worse, character
could be quoted from the financial history of Europe in
the last decade. It is of course impossible to measure
statistically the evil of wasteful expenditure by public
authorities of funds obtained from foreign loans. But it
is very great indeed and will remain a cancer in the whole
of the world's financial and political system until it is dealt
with. I venture to challenge a denial from any responsible person acquainted with the public borrowings of the
years 1926–28 of the assertion that, with the exception
of loans recommended by the League of Nations and the
Central Banks, the *bulk* of the foreign loans in these
years to public authorities in debtor countries would better
not have been made.

If this is true, it is clearly a grave indictment of the
world's credit system as regards the immense sphere of
its operations comprised by foreign loans to public
authorities.

Nor is this all. The deadweight of these wasteful
loans, involving an annual charge represented by no adequate yield of a public enterprise, was a major factor in
causing the financial crisis of the same kind as reparation
and war debts, and may in future years prove a heavier
and more enduring burden upon the world's economy.
And the end is not yet. The defaults which have taken
place, and those which will come soon, will have largely
destroyed the confidence of the investor in foreign lending of all kinds, including that which is most sound
and most vitally needed. When the turn in economic
depression is reached, some of the resiliency of the

recuperative forces which should come from new foreign lending will this time be lacking.

Commercial loans do not involve the same dangers as public loans; and when they are unwise the consequences usually extend only over a limited range. This is not the case, however, when the banks of a country assume responsibility for loans from abroad. When this practice extends the whole of a national banking system may be endangered; and a substantial part of the difficulties of some Central and Eastern European countries has been so caused.

II

So much therefore for the principal defects in the world's credit system. What can be done?

§ National Investment

We can say little as to specifically national faults and remedies, so far as they affect chiefly the internal economy of a country. These, however, now represent for each country a most urgent national problem. The first step toward the revival of credit must be to encourage the investor to lend at home. Savings at present in every lending country not merely do not cross the frontier; they stay as idle deposits in a bank. More than that, so deep is the distrust, they are often converted into gold and hoarded in stockings, or back-gardens, or safe-deposits. In France a new business has grown up. An enterprising person has set up a shop just outside the Bank of France. He presents large amounts of francs to the Bank for the legal obligatory exchange into bullion, and then breaks the gold up into smaller fragments for the timid investor who distrusts his paper note. The same phenomenon has also appeared in a different form in America. This, indeed, the last expression of distrust and despair, will probably not last long, and it must be the first to go. But the mobilisation of idle deposits to restart enterprise will be slower in face of the depression and the doubtful prospects of all industrial enterprises. It is at home first that Governments whose position enables them to do so could most easily and most effectively give a stimulus to the revival of credit. If, for example, the creditor gold surplus countries could, as we have elsewhere suggested, create more money within the limits which their gold reserves make possible without danger to their parity, the effect on prices of thus increasing the supply would depend also upon the responsiveness of the demand. The result would be greater if this measure could be supplemented by schemes for public works. This would absorb the unemployed, give a fillip to prices, and help any recuperative forces there may be. Though the effects would be primarily internal there would also be certain desirable reactions abroad, for example in an increased demand for raw materials.

In America measures have already been taken to restore some of the liquidity to the banks, which had been lost through the fall in values, by various forms of collective support. It is of the utmost importance that confidence should be restored to the investor in the soundness of his country's banking system, and that the evil of private hoarding should be stopped. Conceivably this will be followed by further integration of small banking units, by arrangements for more permanent collective support, by the legalisation of branches of great institutions operating throughout the country, by a revision of the rules as to their investments and the methods of enforcement. Beyond this, more radical reforms are probably required, now that America is a great creditor country, in order to make her short-term rates less volatile and a less dangerous magnet for liquid capital from other countries – a reform without which any effective international control of gold is likely to be impracticable.

In Great Britain, the problem of internal credit is involved with the necessity of reorganisation (both financial, industrial and commercial) of the basic industries, textiles, steel, engineering, etc., and is complicated by the extent to which they are working on debenture and nominally short-term advances and overdrafts. If, as is to be hoped, the pound substantially retains its internal value, it will be essential that the fixed charges in respect of their present capital should in some way be reduced. It may be possible, as part of financial reconstruction schemes, to arrange that ordinary share capital, whose return varies with profits, should be accepted in exchange for fixed interest rights.

The joint stock banks, whose overdrafts are frozen and cannot be called in, need to face the responsibilities involved by what is now their mastery of these industries. They could, by collective action, give a decisive impetus to some of the reorganisation schemes now being attempted. A great difficulty of these schemes is the resistance of individual industrial concerns; and where these are working on overdrafts that they could not repay, which is frequently though not always the case, the joint stock banks could compel them to come into any reorganisation which seemed desirable for the industry as a whole. It may also be necessary to establish central industrial corporations, with wide powers of control over each of the basic industries, or sections of them, before credit for re-equipment can be obtained. Another urgent need is the reform of the system under which new companies are promoted by public issues. But the whole British financial system has recently been exhaustively examined by the Macmillan Committee, and it is unnecessary to attempt here more than a mere mention in passing of a few possible reforms.

In France the first need is perhaps that the Central Bank should be given greater powers over the money market, and that some of the fiscal impediments to foreign issues should be removed. But it would also seem, now that France has become so important a creditor country, that issuing houses specialising in foreign investments would be a valuable addition to her financial structure.

In Germany the deposit banks would be strengthened by the transfer to specialised institutions of company promoting work; and a close Governmental supervision of municipal borrowing needs to be continued.

§ *Foreign Lending*

These are only given as a few examples to illustrate the range and variety of the internal problems of the chief industrial countries. But it was ill-directed, and often excessive, *foreign* lending that undermined the financial structure; it was the change in the form of foreign lending from investments to short-term advances that laid the train; it was the sudden arrest of this lending that fired the mine. And the re-starting of foreign lending is required to give resiliency to the economic mechanism, when at last the upward movement begins. To establish a sounder foundation for foreign lending in future is therefore one of the two or three most important reforms the world needs, if a recurrence of our present troubles is to be avoided.

I think, therefore, that those on whom the responsibility rests should meet at once and see what it is possible to do. They are a manageable number. Little more than half-a-dozen great issuing houses with the Federal Reserve Bank authorities in America; the Bank of England leading a few great houses in Great Britain; in France a few issuing houses with the Bank of France; could between them, in agreement, control the situation. Once they had decided under what rules, and with what precautions, foreign lending should take place, they could, each group in its own country by its collective authority and influence, secure that the rules were observed and the precautions adopted. They could make it impossible for any blacklegging house to tempt money from the public for less cautious loans. But to do so it is essential that action should be taken now, while the investor is reluctant. If, in future years, the public is again in the mood of 1928, and if no collective authority has by then been established, the forces will be beyond control.

Along what lines should progress be made ? For the moment at least loans to private bodies may be left aside. The dangers of reckless private borrowing are much smaller and its consequences less serious. Attention should therefore be concentrated on loans to Governments and to Public Authorities. The lenders of the different countries, even if united nationally, must act together or they will break down each other's standards. And they would most conveniently use the two international institutions at their disposal, the Financial Committee of the League of Nations and the Bank of International Settlements. These two institutions might usefully co-operate, or form a Joint Committee, the League specialising rather more on the Governmental side, the public finances, and the Bank on that of the Central Banks and on what touches currency. Such a Joint Committee might begin by drawing up a kind of Charter of Public Loans, the principles upon which such loans should be arranged, and the precautions desirable in different classes of cases. Let us try to imagine what would be the contents of such a document.

It might classify the different kinds of loans, lay down the general conditions which distinguish between the good and the bad, and prepare the appropriate precautions in each case.

There are first, for example, loans for financial reform, for re-establishing a currency, for giving a respite during which a budget can be brought back into equilibrium. Such loans, when they are required, must of course clearly be raised by a Government. But precautions by the lenders will often be desirable to ensure that they are well-devised and well-spent. These will vary very greatly in different cases. Where a loan is to a stable and established constitutional Government and represents a small percentage of its annual revenue no precautions by the lender beyond those now customary may be required. At the other extreme where there has been complete financial disorganisation it would be well that the borrower should always be required to consult the League (or a Joint Committee of the League with the Bank of International Settlements) and the appointment of a Commissioner with legal powers of control, for a period, as in Austria and Hungary, may be desirable. In an intermediate class of cases, which will perhaps form the great majority, it will be well for the League to approve the general scheme and to arrange for periodical consultation with its Financial Committee, without having actual powers of control. The method can easily be flexible and adaptable to every need. Often the rôle of the League would doubtless be merely to examine a scheme, the borrower, whose reputation would be at stake, being solely responsible for its execution.

Then there are loans for unproductive expenditure, on

municipal buildings for example. These should probably be rare, as capital for such purposes is best raised internally, and the expenditure kept within what can be so raised. In any case certain criteria might be required in considering whether the public finances on which the charges of the loan must fall can safely and properly bear them.

Thirdly, there are loans for productive work, such as the extension of state railways. Here the position would be much safer if the enterprise were organised either on a private basis, or at least on one which secures business methods of management and a separation from the general machinery and finances of the State. In other cases there must nearly always be danger. In any event, adequate evidence should be given that the earnings of the enterprise, or the increased earnings on the proposed extension, will be greater than the annual service of the loan.

Two general comments may be made. In some cases, and these will include most loans for serious financial reforms in small countries, the political factors involved are so important that it would be desirable for the Council of the League to examine each proposal. It would have been impossible to reconstruct Austria and Hungary successfully, or even to establish all the refugees in Bulgaria, without providing against political dangers by a convention to which neighbouring states were parties.

In the second place, substantial loans need consideration in relation not only to the particular purpose for which they are destined, but also to the general economic structure of the country. If a country's economy is on a fundamentally unsound basis, if it is not 'viable' because of the commercial policies of neighbouring states,

I R

an inflow of new capital may only perpetuate and increase the underlying weakness and make the ultimate process of reform more difficult. This indeed is a remark of very wide application, not limited to loans to Governments. A large part of the present difficulties of Europe are due to the fact that capital for reconstruction has flowed in, and the reconstruction itself has proceeded, while the framework of commercial policies has been such as to create wasteful, unbalanced, and finally impracticable, national economic structures.

The League might also do very valuable work in securing an accepted doctrine on another problem of great importance, namely the relation of the Governments of the *lending* countries to foreign public loans arranged by national issuing houses. Hitherto the practice has varied and has often been such as to involve great dangers of political complications.

I would suggest a few obvious principles. Either there should be some examination of the loan scheme, at the time it is proposed, by an impartial public authority – the Government, or preferably the Governments acting through an international body – or no public responsibility whatever should be accepted for the subsequent execution of the loan contract. It would be intolerable if (as has happened in the past) private bankers were to arrange a loan, charged on public revenues, and later, when the public of the borrowing country became indignant because the loan had been applied to personal luxuries, and refused payment, should be able to call upon the armed forces of their Governments to enforce their claims. If a loan has not been certified by an impartial public authority as being desirable, the risks should, I suggest, rest solely upon the lenders, who have doubtless made the terms proportionate to the dangers of default involved. And this rule should apply not only to the refusal to use the armed forces of their Governments to enforce a loan (which is now less likely), but to the exercise of pressure by Ambassadors. Any official representation at all to induce a borrowing Government to observe its loan engagements should be reserved absolutely for cases in which the public interest has been recognised when the loan was first negotiated and some certificate obtained from a public authority. In other cases the sanction ought to be simply the credit of the borrower, which will be impaired by default. The relation between bondholders' associations, the stock-exchanges and the issuing houses makes this sanction an effective one without the aid of Governments being invoked.

The mechanism for securing that desirable foreign public loans are recommended by a public international body, and thus distinguished from those which are undesirable, is not difficult to establish. What is less easy but equally essential is that the issuing markets should so discipline themselves that this mechanism is utilised; that they should co-operate in reaching agreement upon principles and rules, and then in securing their observance. Joint action of a dozen or so institutions in the three principal lending countries could easily achieve this if they act before the foreign investor again becomes eager. They have many sanctions. What American investor after his recent experience would be easily tempted again to subscribe to a foreign loan which contravenes principles endorsed collectively by the chief issuing houses of New York and Chicago ? And, after the debts of the past have been dealt with in one way or another, by scaling down, and more or less mitigated defaulting, bondholders' associations themselves may in future find it in their interests to be more discriminating in the support they give to particular claims and so to strengthen any mechanism designed to make new loans sound at their origin.

Foreign public loans must certainly in future be based upon a procedure which is both selective and collective.

It may seem that undue space has been devoted to discussing precautions against reckless and improper lending, when obviously the urgent need of the moment is to stimulate not restrict foreign investment. But we are concerned not only with immediate measures but with permanent reforms in the world system, and this is one of those most needed. In addition, however, a selective machinery which will create confidence in the prevention of future abuse is the first condition of attracting the lender again, and when he does begin to lend, it is essential that what is available should be directed to the best purposes. If negative in method this policy is an indispensable condition of positive results.

More than this, however, will certainly be required. There is room for central institutions designed to put the credit and borrowing capacity of selected classes of those needing capital on the soundest foundation.

An institution is now being founded, on the basis of a scheme devised by the Financial Committee of the League, to serve this purpose for agricultural mortgage loans. The high rates charged by local lenders to peasants and small proprietors for their working capital, amounting sometimes to about 18 per cent., have greatly aggravated the agricultural distress in Eastern Europe. It is of course quite impossible to equalise borrowing terms under very different conditions. The Roumanian peasant must not expect to borrow as cheaply as the Dane can do. But many remediable causes have increased the difficulty. Land legislation varies and may prevent the conclusion of a mortgage acceptable to a foreign lender. A collective responsibility between the peasants of a given district may enable each of them to borrow on better terms. A Government guarantee may be a further help. A certificate by a specialised external institution as to the facts which bear on the adequacy of the security may do still more. A foreign bank or issuing house, or individual, cannot separately investigate distant conditions requiring for their appreciation local or specialised knowledge. For all these reasons a central Mortgage Institution may greatly improve the terms on which new capital can be obtained, when it is obtainable at all.

There is probably also an opening for other such specialised institutions, varying in constitution with the character of the responsibility assumed, to deal with other classes of borrowing and to stand between distant lenders and the borrower. With far greater economy and efficiency than separate and remote financial organisations can show they could secure the services of the necessary experts to report on the technical merits of a proposed scheme for the construction of railways, roads, or for reclamation work and other enterprises.

It is extremely desirable that such specialised institutions of this kind should be founded in accordance with schemes approved by a responsible and public body such as the Financial Committee of the League – as was done in the case of the Agricultural Mortgage Bank – or the Bank of International Settlements.

All this would be to the good. But we deceive ourselves if we think that these measures, or those which are usually recommended to establish the conditions under which foreign lending will recommence, will by themselves restart the normal flow of investment. Loans in the

form of the supply of goods on credit may be possible
under the strong inducement which industry has to enable
its customers to take its goods.   But ordinary foreign
issues, subscribed by the private investor, will be more
difficult.   It is all very well to say, as the Basle
Committee of August 1931 did, that the Governments
should create political confidence and reduce reparation
to within Germany's capacity, so that the investor will
lose his apprehensions.   But if the utmost progress
conceivable were made in restoring good international
relations; if reparation and war debts were not only
reduced but cancelled altogether; it would still, I
believe, be long indeed before foreign investment revived again on anything like the scale upon which the
world's balance of payments had come to rely before the
crisis.

We have still inadequately realised how deeply the
foundations of the system of credit have been undermined; how deep and lasting a wound has been inflicted
upon the investor's confidence. It was a miracle from the
first to attract the savings of the small shopkeeper of the
Middle West of America or the apprehensive peasant of
France into foreign ventures. But now that he has so
recently lost his money; as one default succeeds another –
and there are many more still to come – he will say, and
say for long to come, 'never again – at least abroad.' It
will require time and much encouragement to coax him
again into adventure.

Can nothing then be done, beyond what has already
been suggested, to restart considerable long-term foreign
investment in the near future ?

There is one way. It is that the Governments of
the creditor countries themselves should attach their
own credit to the operation – giving a Government

guarantee, either individually or (as was done for Austria in 1923) collectively. The French and American investor would even now lend his money if it carried the guarantee of his own Government. If money were so raised its use would, of course, need to be controlled by an institution with whose management the guaranteeing Governments were associated. It could be used partly for helping the finance of debtor Governments so as to diminish the risk or extent of default on existing obligations, and partly to restart enterprise by financing public works.

This may seem an extreme and impracticable measure to suggest. It may be both. But it is well to recall again the inducement and the alternative.

In 1928 the lending from creditor to debtor countries was $2,300 million, as, with some variations, it had been for years past. This was the sum which balanced international payments on the basis of past loan obligations and the current course of trade – or rather it did not quite achieve the balance, as some gold moved as well. The course of trade corresponded with this lending. In other words, the exports of the creditor countries were only possible because they lent on this scale. New foreign lending has now stopped; gold can flow no further, apart from the uncertain quantities coming from Indian hoards. The adjustment is therefore being made partly by cancellation or reduction on past obligations or default on them, and partly by a change in the course of trade. The latter means, and can only mean, either an increase in the imports of creditor countries, or a cutting off of their exports. The former is impeded by tariffs and further restricted by a laggard purchasing power. Creditor countries are so far indeed not buying more, but less. The adjustment therefore falls inevitably on their exports. As events are developing now it is hard to see how the creditor gold surplus countries will next year be able to sell any exports, except those few articles which can neither be dispensed with nor produced elsewhere. Cancellation or remission of Governmental debt would reduce the extent to which their exports must be cut off; monetary action tending to increase gold prices, and a reduction of tariffs, would do so too by giving them more imports. But new foreign lending can alone prevent a very large reduction, perhaps almost the complete cessation of their export of manufactures.

We have described how political debts, incautious lending, disturbed political relations, and impoverishment caused by the economic depression, strained the world's credit system and led to the financial crisis in which it broke. But one other factor, aggravating these and extending its effect beyond them, must be emphasised in conclusion. The fall in gold prices by about 40 per cent. in two years has made the load on the backs of debtors of every kind, private and public, national and foreign, insupportable. Throughout history lenders of money have been supplying it to borrowers on terms that were bound ultimately to be intolerable if the loans could not be repaid and discharged out of the current yield of productive ventures which they had financed. Sometimes the debts have been ended by bankruptcy or by revolution; often they have been lightened by progressive currency depreciation. But in this post-war period the world has had an unexampled load of debt, of every kind, both public and private, of which an unprecedented proportion is a dead-weight load representing war or wasted expenditure; and this mass of debt has recently been not lightened by currency depreciation but immensely increased by currency appreciation. Some cancellation, some remission,

large   default – perhaps   in   some   cases   a   deliberate
scaling down of interest – are inevitable.

If this process does not in all respects encourage the
investor to lend his money again, it should at least be a
help to those who are now trying to establish the world's
credit structure on a sounder basis.

CHAPTER III

THE DEAD HAND

REPARATION AND WAR DEBTS

(A) REPARATION

To tell the tale of Reparation, and the questions with which it is intertwined, would be to write the history of post-war Europe. With its weight, its uncertainty, the methods of its discussion and its enforcement, the passions which it has expressed and aroused, it has been like an Old Man of the Sea on the back of a continent struggling to get on its feet, after four years of prostration and enfeeblement. It has been a principal obstacle to every attempt at recovery. It has disturbed the relations of old allies no less than of old enemies. It is one of the two facets of the French demand – for payment and security – which has been at the heart of the relations between France and Germany, itself the central political problem of Europe. It has thus been a principal factor in the tendency of countries to re-align themselves into opposing groups and alliances, the alternative to the 'collective' system of the League and the Kellogg Pact, on which the future peace of the world depends. . . . The cash results have not been proportionate to these consequences.

In following the course of the reparation negotiations we have, unhappily, to make our way through a thicket of untruths and half-truths, originating in false analogy, fallacious principle and national bias. My own path through this encumbering growth I will indicate by a series of propositions.

The first characteristic of a reparation obligation is that it is a dead-weight charge. It represents damage done in a past war. It has no counterpart in a productive capital plant, such as a factory or its machinery, yielding an annual return out of which payments to the creditors can be made. It is thus essentially different from the capital obligation of an industrial company financed by a foreign loan. It is therefore a burden on the debtor state, requiring to be met by taxation, which has its normal result of reducing the taxpayers' standard of living and purchasing power, and the savings out of which domestic capital is formed; but, unlike normal taxation, it gives no service in return, such as protection of life and property and the provision of education or social insurance.

So far a reparation obligation is like an internal public debt representing war expenditure. In other respects however, it is very different from such a debt. The payments due have to be made abroad by the debtor Government. This has several consequences. First, the receipts are not a source of revenue to the Government on which the obligation rests; as are the dividends on war bonds. Secondly, the paying country must not only raise the sums required by taxation, it must convert them into foreign exchange. The sums remitted form an adverse element in the balance of payments, which must be met by either an export surplus or temporarily by foreign borrowing. A foreign debt, moreover, is specially subject to an increase in real weight in a period of falling prices. The world price index figure has fallen by about 40 per cent. in two years. This index is made up of the prices of commodities which enter into world trade; and except that food and raw materials have fallen somewhat more than manufactured articles, it measures the extent to which the real burden on Germany has been increased in these two years. The effect of a fall of prices in adding the burden of an internal debt is much less, for changes in internal prices tend to be on a much smaller scale.

In one further and very important respect reparation differs from an internal debt. It is resented as tribute to a victorious foe; and its justice is disputed. And the longer the time that elapses the greater is the unwillingness to pay out of current resources for such obligations incurred by others in the past.

Since the payment of reparation necessitates a surplus of exports over imports, except so long as foreign exchange is available through a net inflow of foreign capital, this involves a diversion of world trade and some dislocation. Just as when a change of trade occurs through other causes, some temporary loss may be involved to competing manufacturers both in the receiving and other countries, especially those who make the same goods as the country paying reparation.

It is not true, however, as has sometimes been argued by English and American writers, that in principle reparation brings no benefit to the countries receiving it because home production falls off to the extent of what is received. Additional imports do not, apart from temporary dislocation, involve loss. Moreover, reparation is a revenue receipt which enables taxation to be correspondingly reduced, and therefore leaves so much more purchasing power in the pockets of the taxpayer, who both improves his standard of living and creates a market for home enterprise by expending it. The only loss is the temporary one due to the dislocation which results from any diversion of trade, however caused.

A country, however, which like Great Britain is not only vitally interested in world trade, but which competes for it with much the same kind of articles as the paying country, Germany, and which itself receives only a small proportion, about one-fifth, of the reparation being paid, may well be worse off on balance than if all reparation were cancelled. This is still more the case since Great Britain pledged herself, in the Balfour Note, not to claim more in respect of reparation and war debt owed to her than she had herself to pay on her own war debt to America.

The foreign exchange required to pay reparation may, of course, be obtained for a considerable period not by an export surplus but by an inflow of foreign capital. And, in fact, though Germany now has a favourable trade balance, she has since the Armistice bought much more from abroad than she has sold. Foreign borrowing is, however, a very temporary and dangerous expedient, except so far as it is really devoted to productive purposes, for compound interest piles up rapidly, and in fifteen years or less the annual charge on the sums borrowed would amount to as much as the reparation annuities. It represents no solution therefore for an obligation extending over two generations. An inflow of foreign capital, however, which is used productively, and especially if it is in the form of investment in shares in German enterprises, is not open to the same objections. It equally provides immediate foreign exchange; but though it ultimately requires an export surplus it may itself help to create that surplus; and, so far as the payments due towards the end of the reparation period are concerned, the foreign exchange may be forthcoming in this way without an export surplus being necessary till after the end of the period.

It is not true, as has often been argued in England, that 'reparation in kind,' that is the direct delivery of actual commodities, has just the same effect, and involves the same economic strain, as the supply of an equivalent amount of cash obtained from sales in the open market. That would be true if the commodities would, in fact, have been sold, in the same quantity and for the same prices, had they not been delivered towards settlement of reparation. How far that is the case varies indefinitely with the class of delivery in question. It would be true in a world system functioning without friction, in which to make an article was equivalent to selling it. But it is the express characteristic of the present period that selling is often more difficult than making. It would, I believe, have involved no more economic strain on Germany in 1921 to build four houses in the devastated regions under direct contract than to sell extra goods on the world market needed to provide the finances to construct one such house by French contractors – with the world market and the French building trade as they were at that time.

Curiously enough the positions of the French and English about the element of 'transfer' (the difficulty of converting taxation receipts in marks into the foreign exchange required for reparation payments) are entirely reversed when we come to the main criterion of capacity to pay. Should it be the 'budget' (i.e. the limits of internal taxation) or 'transfer' (i.e. the possibilities of getting foreign exchange through an export surplus) ? Here the French say it should be the first. They argue that if the German Government raise the money in marks and sell them in the ordinary way, the normal working of the exchange and the monetary system will secure the necessary changes in the flow of capital and the course of trade and the foreign exchange will be automatically forthcoming. So it would be if the system worked as in theory it should, and as in practice it used to, but not now. The English on the other hand argue that payments can only be made so far as in practice foreign exchange can be obtained, and this may mean a sum much smaller than that obtainable in marks. This is also true in varying degrees of the whole period since the war, and notably at times of financial crisis like the present. It is clear that at such times a much lower limit than that of budget capacity must in fact be applied. It is also, however, true that a period of financial crisis is not one in which normal capacity to pay can be estimated without grave injustice to the recipients; for 'capacity to pay' approaches 'budget capacity' in proportion as the world financial and monetary system is working normally.

In practice we find that these two criteria have changed their respective importance at different periods. In the Peace Treaty, whose framers were curiously blind to the possibilities and consequences of currency inflation, the stress is on budget capacity, and no specific reference to the question of 'transfer' occurs at all. At the time of the Dawes Committee in 1924, the question of 'transfer' had become important and a special machinery was provided to deal with it in the form of a Transfer Committee who were responsible for changing marks into other currencies. Five years later the emphasis shifted back; the 'Transfer Committee' was dropped. Germany was made responsible for obtaining foreign exchange herself, though she was allowed to declare her inability to do so in times of special difficulty, subject to appeal to an Advisory Committee of persons nominated by the Central Banks. In fact, the main German case for moderation was in 1929 based, not on exchange difficulties, but a special aspect of the budget criterion, viz. the amount which would not unduly reduce the savings out of which home capital for normal investment was needed. And now, after the financial crisis of June 1931, the centre of gravity has, of course, shifted once more to the difficulties of exchange, which have for the time stopped all payments and must dominate any discussions of the near future.

Such are the main conflicting arguments which run through the first twelve years of this great controversy. Policies however have not been determined either by the intrinsic truth of these arguments, or the skill with which they have been presented, but first by the varied play of political pressure and passion, and then by the logic of accumulating strain.

A detached and impartial arbiter, could he have been empowered to settle the reparation problem on its merits, would have found it easy of solution. He would have recognised at once that there was one claim which in obvious justice was entitled to a natural priority. All belligerents had lost men and incurred expenditure in the conduct of the war. But, as a clear addition, the territory in which it happened to be waged had suffered devastation. Its houses were destroyed, its people homeless. Even if there had been a peace without victory, and an admission on both sides of equal responsibilities, these regions in France and Belgium would have had a special claim on the world for being used as the world's battlefield. The first necessity was to repair this damage. Germany had the men and the materials available; and for this work would willingly have provided both at once. Under large scale direct contracts the task could have been accomplished efficiently, rapidly and without financial difficulty, in two or three years. This reparation could have been supplemented by a delivery of ships in return for those submarined, by such deliveries of coal as were actually made, by reconstructive work which could not otherwise have been afforded (such as the new tramway system which Serbia had the wisdom to arrange that Germany should build in Belgrade), and by modest cash payments and bonds so clearly within Germany's future capacity that they could have been floated in the market.

Reparation of this kind Germany could have given at once; men, materials and management she had in plenty. This would have involved no strain on the exchange value of her currency; for she would have paid in marks. It would have been cheap because the German building trade was clamouring for work, whereas construction by French contractors involved inflated prices in a closed market already crowded with other orders. It would have meant no dislocation or disturbance of vested rights; for no business can be regarded as having a vested interest in the prospect of rebuilding houses destroyed in war. There would have been a similar advantage in the construction of such public works (electric installations, tramway systems, etc.) as countries entitled to reparation would have found useful, but, apart from reparation, could not have afforded. Work of this latter kind was indeed arranged – but as an addition to, and not in place of, cash demands already excessive.

Had reparation been so arranged, it could have been settled and finished in three years or so. The countries with war devastation would have received more real value than a decade of efforts were in fact to give them. The political, economic and financial recovery of Europe would have been relieved of its most formidable obstacle. The German currency need never have gone to pieces. The financial restoration of other countries would have been advanced by several years. There would have been no occupation of the Ruhr. Within less than a decade

KR

prosperity might have been securely restored; peace firmly established.

Fate or folly ruled otherwise. The scene in Paris has been often described, once in a classic of the English language. It was dominated by the passions of a war just ended, by the illusions of a war finance not applicable to peace. For a few years expenditure within a country, or an alliance determined on war, and making its own and each other's supplies at inflated prices, can rise to heights undreamed of before – and heights which are utterly impossible in other conditions. But men who had seen the world spend some £50 million a day, and were under pressure from their Parliaments to squeeze the last penny from a defeated enemy, listened with impatience to those who argued that such a sum per annum is not inconsiderable for a country to find from its current taxation.

Nor in spite of Mr. Keynes, Mr. Norman Davis and a few others, were 'expert' advisers wanting to counsel folly. Most men long trained in a special experience have a vision limited by the special character of that experience. A savage counts with difficulty beyond his ten fingers; the man in the street finds that £100,000 conveys a more or less intelligible impression: a pre-war Governor of a central bank might think in terms of £100 to £1,000 million. Beyond whatever may be the personal limits of imaginative apprehension, one figure is much like another. And when an ex-Governor spoke of £24,000 million, he was that most dangerous of counsellors, a man urging a policy born of passion with the authority of assumed expert knowledge.

The attitude of M. Clemenceau, with a ravaged country before his eyes, is intelligible – and was indeed inevitable. Mr. Lloyd George, within the limits of his power a passionate advocate of moderation, had robbed himself of half his strength by his armistice election. Like a jockey who, in a momentary panic lest he should be shaken out of his saddle, had loaded himself with unnecessary weights, without reckoning that they would handicap him fatally in the race, the British Prime Minister had secured a Parliamentary majority clamorous for the impossible.

France and Belgium were the countries principally interested in reparation; and their claims were extreme; Great Britain was interested in the inclusion of war pensions (permissible only under an interpretation of the armistice conditions which it would be charitable to call ambiguous) and the seizure of the German merchant ships; and she too obtained them. America urged leniency in reparation, but her counsel had the less weight because she saw no analogy between reparation, in which she was disinterested, and war debts, where she was creditor. It would perhaps be unjust to say that the policy of each country was determined by its self-interest. There was a real element of truth in each case – but varying interest certainly determined the perspective in which these different elements were seen.

The net result was that a list of categories of damage for which Germany was to pay reparation was drawn up; a Reparation Commission was appointed to assess this damage with power, by majority vote, to arrange the *mode* of payment according to Germany's capacity, but not to change the total except by unanimity; the members were to be appointed by the respective Governments, but once appointed the Commission was to carry out its task as an autonomous body independent of Government instructions.

The Commission was to have been a homogeneous expert organisation carrying out a technical work of collecting an agreed debt, and it was an instrument suitably designed for its duties on two assumptions, both of which were false. The first of these assumptions was that the total of the scheduled damage when assessed would be within Germany's capacity (and automatically divisible among the recipients in accordance with its constituent elements); the second was that the United States of America would ratify the Treaty.

The falsity of these two assumptions, especially of the first, foredoomed the Commission to failure from its birth. The total damage, ultimately assessed at 132 milliard gold marks (£6,600 million), was hopelessly beyond Germany's capacity. No reasonable scheme offering the prospect of the payment of this sum was practicable. In substance, therefore, the main problem of reparation had to be dealt with anew. It was impossible that the Governments should leave the responsibility for a negotiation so vitally affecting their budgets and their policies to an autonomous body outside their control. Moreover, it followed from the same fact that the division of such reparation as was obtained was by no means automatic. This, too, the Governments had to settle. The long drawn out wrangle on these two questions proceeded outside, but was reflected inside, the Commission.

The consequences of the second mistaken assumption are worth recording, if only as an amusing instance of the pitfalls that beset the framers of Treaties. The Reparation Chapter had been meticulously drafted so as to secure that there should always be an odd number of voting members, five, in order to make the majority vote effective. The failure of America to ratify (which meant that her representative was an 'unofficial observer' without a vote) automatically resulted in all these careful provisions having precisely the effect they were designed to prevent; there were always four voting members. For a time it seemed that there would frequently be a dead-lock. Then it was discovered that in a remote part of the Treaty, which was never thought of in relation to Reparation, and but for this accident could never have been applied to it, it was provided that any Chairman of a Committee or Commission appointed under the Treaty should, in case of deadlock, have a casting vote. France, whose Delegate was President of the Reparation Commission, therefore had a second vote; it was rarely if ever cast; but the knowledge that it was there in reserve necessarily underlay all the discussions.

Under these disabilities, especially the first, the Commission, instead of being all-powerful, independent and united, was in fact, impotent, dependent and divided; its powerful personalities a source of disruption rather than strength, its internal organisation founded upon what one member described as the 'sacred principle of international distrust.' Its relations with the Governments alternated between individual protests and collective compliance; its rôle in relation to the major issues of policy became to endorse formally, and to execute in detail, what others decided. For a year or two it retained at least some illusion of power; thereafter it remained, like the town of Trieste, a structure built too generously for a business that had gone elsewhere.

The centre of effective authority passed in four stages to the Governments in Conference (1920–22), to the military occupation of the Ruhr (1923–24), to powerful expert Committees (Dawes and Young), endorsed by the Governments at London and the Hague (1924, 1929). But it has now come back to the Governments directly under the lead, in June 1931, of precisely that Government which had been absent from all the earlier Conferences.

§ *The Balfour Note*

The interval between the first and second of these stages, between Genoa and the Ruhr, was marked by an important declaration of Great Britain's Policy in the Balfour Note of August 1922. Its basic principle was that she expected to recover as much (and no more) from the Allies to whom she had herself lent money for war supplies and from Germany, as she had to pay to America from whom she had borrowed. That is, believing that a cancellation of both reparation and war debts would be the best solution of the tangled problem of intergovernmental war indebtness, she offered to place herself in the same position as if this solution were adopted. For making this declaration Great Britain has been the subject of an opprobrious criticism of which it is easier to see the cause than the justice. Subsequent events have surely shown not only the liberality of such an offer as an element in a general settlement, but a far-sighted vision of the increasing strains on the whole world position resulting from these debts. The loans from Great Britain to her allies (even excluding altogether the vast sums borrowed by Russia) as funded in the later years, amounted with accrued interest to £1,300 million ; the corresponding debt to America, also with accrued interest, amounted to £945 million. Great Britain's proposal therefore amounted in effect to a surrender of all her claims on Russia, of all the large excess of her claims on her other allies over what she herself owed to America, and in addition, of all her reparation claims (amounting to 22 per cent. of whatever Germany should pay). On what country would general cancellation have imposed a greater sacrifice? The mistake made, and though it was serious it was surely not a discreditable one, was that the proposal was put forward when others were not yet ready for any such drastic and generous settlement. France and America considered the declaration as designed to leave all the odium and the moral responsibility of the future reparation exactions upon them. America resented this the more as she was not interested herself in reparation as a creditor, and refused to admit any connection between reparation and war debts, stating truly that they are legally independent, and claiming for the latter a superior sanctity, whose justice we shall discuss later.

Whether or not, however, a merging of the two, and a general cancellation, would have been just and expedient, it was natural that those who were not prepared for so drastic a step should have disliked the position in which they were placed by such a unilateral declaration. The resentment so caused has prevented any recognition of the generosity of the offer itself. Meanwhile however Great Britain was not content to make the proposal, or even to leave it open as a withdrawable offer. She unhappily embodied the principle in a pledge, and in debt agreements, binding herself unilaterally. She thus had a hampering commitment in later negotiations, which brought her no visible benefit, and indeed much unpopularity. On this occasion, as on several others, Great Britain undertook prematurely and unilaterally a commitment, which would only have been wise as a part of a general scheme accepted by others and comprising equal contributions by them.

§ *Mr. Lloyd George and Monsieur Poincaré*

For the first five years the negotiations were dominated in succession, in conjunction or in conflict, by two great personalities, who were the representatives, and indeed

the embodiment, of the two main divergent policies, revision and mitigation on the one hand, punctilious and
relentless exaction on the other.

It is difficult for a short-memoried world, familiar with
his diminished public position in recent years, to recall
the real stature of Mr. Lloyd George in the first period
after the Armistice. The symbol to his country, and to
the world, of the slowly gathered might of the British
Empire; the latest survivor in public life of the greatest
figures of the war; the only representative at later Conferences of the protagonists of Paris and Versailles, he
possessed not only the authority of his position but,
then at his prime, the qualities which had given him that
position.

Magnetic, eloquent, dominating, persuasive; with
gaps in his knowledge, but understanding so much
more than he knew; gathering his impressions from those
around him as if by unseen invisible antennæ; indirect
and unexpected in method, but courageous, skilful and
inflexible in the pursuit of his main objective; intolerably
irritating to the precise, the exact, the official – at every
meeting of the Powers of this period *incessu patuit* – he
was visibly the greatest personality of all those present.

In Conference after Conference, convened at his initiative at the pleasure-resorts of Europe, he strove to lead
Europe to a very different mood from the one which found
expression at Versailles; to rebuild the economic life of
the world on a basis of co-operation in which a Germany,
with lightened burdens, and a Russia, no longer ostra-
cised, would be willing and equal partners. He had against
him the Treaty which he had himself signed, the opposition of all those who wished naturally to retain the rights
they had thus so hardly won, and finally the hampering
commitments from his own past. There was between

him and the representative of France with whom he had
chiefly to deal an incompatibility of temperament which
caused an accumulating irritation and gradually robbed
him of some of his accustomed skill in negotiation. He
could 'handle' most people – but not the French, who
disliked him more and more with each year that passed.

With so many external and self imposed handicaps no
other living man could have won so near success. When
he rose to open the Conference of Genoa in the spring of
1922, it seemed for the moment that it was the voice of
Europe speaking. With Wilson shattered in body and
shorn of power, he was beyond question the world's greatest figure – and never was an English Prime Minister so
nearly Europe's chosen leader. Genoa was the climax and
the turning point of his fortunes – and a turning point too
for Europe's policy. When, in the weeks that followed,
the aspirations and ambitions with which the Conference
had opened failed, when Rapallo seemed to set the Germans and Russians outside the society into which they
were being invited, the way was opened for a different
policy, and the domination of a different personality.

Public life affords no greater contrast, in all its range
of personalities, than that of M. Poincaré with the leader
of Genoa. Precise, formal, unmagnetic, with an untiring
and inhuman industry; knowing all that can be known
from printed book or written document, but understanding little that cannot be so expressed; a human
machine working with a frictionless perfection. What he
saw he saw exactly, microscopically, what he did not see
thus he did not see at all; he pursued his path like a horse
with blinkers seeing clearly ahead, but looking neither to
right nor left. Above all he was a lawyer, exact, scrupulous, conscientious. To him the Treaty was the Law.
Whether as President of the Reparation Commission or as

Prime Minister, his duty, as he conceived it, was not to question or revise, but to execute.

And in this conception he was expressing a national characteristic. Even apart from national policy and interest there is a certain difference between the attitude of the Frenchman, trained in a codified law, and the Anglo-Saxon accustomed to a case-made law, which modifies the operation of a statute and adapts it to changing conditions. The Anglo-Saxon is inclined to give both more and less than the exact text of the bond – to look, as he says, to the spirit as well as the letter; to expect an engagement to change if conditions change beyond reasonable expectation. But to a Frenchman the conception that if the conditions in which an engagement was made change beyond a certain point the engagement does not hold, is destructive of the basis of law on which society is founded. It is a natural complaint of the French throughout these negotiations that the English seemed to think of the Treaty as something to modify rather than to enforce; and that they regarded each new engagement (sometimes even at the moment it was signed) not as a settlement but as a starting point for new concessions.

These divergences of policy were encouraged by one striking contrast between the interests of the two countries. Great Britain, as France realised with some bitterness, had automatically attained her main objectives at once. The German Navy, the great menace to Great Britain, was already destroyed and sunk – and a Navy cannot quickly or secretly be rebuilt. The German Army, which was France's danger, was also impotent for the time, but men can be trained and munitions can be made more quickly than ships can be rebuilt – and more secretly too unless supervision is vigilant and meticulous. The greater part of the German Colonies had gone, under mandate, to the British Empire; a smaller portion to France – as was perhaps natural since they were the spoil of the British Navy; Alsace-Lorraine was regarded as recovery rather than acquisition. Great Britain had no clamant need comparable to the rebuilding of the devastated areas; the deeper wounds to her economic structure were then less visible. Her admitted claims were less than half those of France; and for these she had some substantial immediate satisfaction in the acquisition of the greater part of the German merchant fleet, which at once gave her an earning asset, very valuable at the time, and temporarily destroyed her chief competitor. These facts certainly made it easier for Great Britain to subordinate the exaction of Reparation, in which her interest was secondary, to the recovery of world trade in which her interest was paramount.

§ *The Right and Wrong Methods of Collecting Reparation*

France had one method, and one only, open to her of equalising the account in reparation, and removing the grievance which was to poison her politics and the policy of Europe for a decade. She could have arranged for the direct and immediate re-building of the houses of Northern France by German labour. But against this, the one wise solution, trade interest and sentiment combined, the first exploiting the second. Germany was not only willing but eager to make reparation of this kind. Her trade unions urged it, the Government offered it. She had the men and the material, and the difficulty of foreign exchange would have been avoided.

To its enduring honour too, French labour adopted a magnanimous attitude, which has never been sufficiently known and recognised. It might have taken the narrow

and selfish view that employment and wages among French
workers would benefit if they were given a monopoly of
the reconstructive work. But, on the contrary, the great
labour organisation, the Confédération Générale du
Travail, led by M. Jouhaux, took the most active steps to
urge the wiser and more generous policy. It pressed
this policy upon the authorities in Paris early in 1921.
It organised a conference of the 'sinistrés' themselves in
the devastated regions, who made it clear (though not
without some dissent) that they would prefer German-
built houses at once to the hope deferred of French-
built houses at some later time. It supported the same
policy at the meeting of the International Federation of
Trade Unions at Amsterdam in March of the same year,
where the German delegates expressly recognised the obligation on Germany to carry out this reconstructive work.

The French building trade, however, supported by the
understandable, though regrettable, sentiment of many
in France, took the narrower view and pressed it more
successfully on the Government. We need not follow in
detail how this great and generous conception was slowly
killed in the long drawn out conversations of M. Loucheur and Herr Rathenau. Enough to note that the
great opportunity was tragically lost.

The combined efforts of successive conferences and the
Reparation Commission extracted coal and other deliveries in kind and some cash payments. The payments
were made possible not by an export surplus, which
with the disorganisation of her internal structure and in
the face of external impediments Germany failed to create;
nor at this stage by foreign loans, for which, in the absence
of any fixed reparation charge, there was no basis of
confidence; but by the persistent belief of the foreign
speculator that the falling mark would recover. It was

his losses that paid reparation. But the fall of the mark continued; the optimism of the speculator vanished; the foreign investor was not yet attracted; and with every fall the possibility of external payments in terms of gold became more remote.

France accused Germany of debasing the currency in order to avoid payment. Every country tends to attribute to others a greater singleness of purpose, and a greater power to achieve it, than is compatible with the swaying political forces on which representative Government is based. The truth may be more exactly stated thus. Every Minister of Finance, whether in France, in England, in Czecho-Slovakia, or later in Germany, who stabilised a fallen currency had to impose the most drastic sacrifices and to fight his way against strong opposing forces. No one of them could have carried his policy if, while the sacrifices would indubitably fall on the country itself, the advantages would have largely gone to foreigners — and foreigners not loved. Since the stabilisation of the mark in gold would have been inevitably followed by increased demands for reparation payments, this was the case with Germany — and no further explanation is necessary.

In these conditions, reparation payments small and diminishing, and Germany's unwillingness and inability to pay both increasing, events moved relentlessly to the occupation of the Ruhr, early in 1923, Poincaré leading, Belgium reluctant, Italy hesitating, Great Britain dissenting, America detached. There followed two years in which reparation payments, beyond what the occupation cost, almost ceased; and the resources out of which they must be paid diminished; but the will of France was exhibited implacable and potent and the spirit of Germany was bent.

Those who criticise Poincaré's action say, with truth, that he further impoverished a Germany already unable to pay what was demanded of her; that besides further embittering an old foe, he alienated an old ally; that he threw Europe again into turmoil. Those who defend him say, also perhaps with truth, that neither would Great Britain have so far complied, nor Germany so far yielded, as to make the subsequent Dawes Settlement possible, unless France had given an unquestionable exhibition both of her power and of her determination. *Il fallait passer par là.* But if Poincaré could create the conditions under which a settlement favourable to France would be possible, he was not himself the man to settle. 'There is no one like Poincaré,' said one to me who had long worked with him, 'for getting up steam in the engine, but he can't stop at the platform.'

§ *The Dawes Committee*

In 1924, after some eighteen months of occupation, Great Britain and France were locked – deadlocked – in their different positions, and Germany was in no mood to give a voluntary assent of any value to a scheme imposed by France alone. No country could, or would, give way; no Minister would yield to his antagonists' arguments or pressure, or could justify himself to his critics at home if he did.

Under these conditions a skilful and interesting way out was found. The Governments who could not agree on policy, agreed on method. They appointed (formally through the Reparation Commission) a powerful Committee of Experts, who met in 1924 under the Presidency of General Dawes and drew up a new scheme of reparation payments. The Committee consisted of experts of the highest qualifications and standing. But their work was diplomatic even more than technical; they were diplomats disguised as experts. The Governments held to divergent positions from which they could not move each other. The task of the Committee was to find a scheme near enough to these positions to make acceptance possible under the extra pressure of a unanimous report of the Committee itself. They succeeded, and their plan itself is much the most skilful in its technical provisions of all those which have yet been designed to make Germany pay very large sums.

It arranged an ascending scale of annual payments – subject to possible increase on an index of prosperity; it provided security for the payments by an elastic control of assigned revenues based on the precedent of League Loans, and it transferred the machinery of enforcement from a many headed Commission at Paris to a single authority *in situ* at Berlin. The payments were fixed at a higher figure than Germany was likely permanently to pay – otherwise France's assent would have been impossible. But the Committee made them possible for the time by restoring a confidence which brought foreign money flowing into the country and by placing the new mark on an assured gold parity. And it included two adjusting provisions of the utmost importance. If the foreign exchange position endangered the gold value of the mark, foreign payments would be stopped on the authority of a Transfer Committee and the sums due accumulated, and for a time invested, in marks; and if by the finding of an impartial authority, world prices fell or rose by more than 10 per cent., the gold payments were to be changed accordingly. The withdrawal from the Ruhr was waiting as the price of Germany's acceptance.

This skilful scheme, accepted by Germany and her creditors at the London Conference of August 1924, gave Europe a valuable respite of five years in which she could forget about reparation and proceed with reconstruction. And during this great quinquennium, as we have seen, she stabilised her finances, increased her production and trade, overtook the progress of the rest of the world, and at Locarno and through the entry of Germany into the League made good headway with a policy of conciliation and political appeasement.

§ *The Young Plan*

But the sudden influx of foreign capital made the early payments too easy — and was afterwards to make their continuance more difficult. In the four years, 1925 to 1928, which followed the Dawes Plan, the net import into Germany amounted to no less than 15,000 million gold marks (£750 million) about half as much again as all the foreign exchange Germany has devoted to paying reparation right up to the Moratorium of 1931. A substantial proportion of this had been used unproductively, and the annual charges soon began to reach a formidable sum. By 1928 it was clear that the time must arrive when there would be difficulty in securing foreign exchange for reparation payments. But the whole economy of Germany had now come to be precariously based upon an increasing inflow of foreign loans. An arrest of transfer would have stopped far more than reparation. It would have stopped renewals of short-term advances and new lending, and might, it was urged, have brought the whole structure of Germany's new economic progress toppling down. It was also thought that the time had arrived when reparation could be 'taken out of politics.' It was therefore decided to appoint a new Committee with the object of making reparation safe by making it lighter and, if possible, by the issue of a huge reparation loan in the world's markets, to convert the Governmental into a commercial debt – henceforth removed from the arena of Governmental negotiations and controversies.

The argument was plausible but, I have always thought, premature. It would have been much better if the self-regulating machinery of the Dawes Plan had been allowed at least to begin its work, and only been replaced if it proved inadequate. Had a difficulty of transfer in fact seriously affected the general credit structure of Germany, then would have been the time to convene a new Committee. The truth would then have been evident that all the creditors of Germany, America among the first, and not only the reparation creditors, were equally concerned. America would have joined, not as a kind of detached arbiter, but an equal and interested member. It would have been evident that concessions required to re-establish the situation should be made in fair proportions from all; and that war debts were, in justice and reality, an inseparable factor in the problem. The recognition of this truth was to be deferred, unnecessarily – and disastrously – for another two years.

Moreover, the conception of 'mobilising' the debt, attractive to France at the time (and if events had developed differently perhaps ultimately the right solution) was premature, impracticable and ill-conceived. It was impossible to float an immense loan on the markets; and if it had not been impossible it would have been disastrous, for it would have starved normal development of its capital, and poured capital into just the country that wanted it least – dragging after it new gold to add to an

Lʀ

existing surplus, and further dislocating the general financial mechanism of the world.

So much might have been said, and was by some urged, before the Young Committee met in 1929. But the Committee's Plan itself contained defects of its own. It introduced the complication of a distinction between 'conditional' payments, which were to be paid if they could, and 'unconditional,' which were to be paid in any event, and by allotting, outside the scope of its apparent competence, a disproportionately high proportion of the latter to France, started a train of disastrous frictions and controversies. Above all it dropped the provisions of the Dawes Plan for adjusting the gold obligations of Germany to variations in gold prices. It would, of course, have spoilt the prospectus of a mobilisation loan to include a provision so unfamiliar to investors; but the large loan did not mature as it was; and the omission was disastrous. Within two years falling prices had made the annual payments of Germany under the Young Plan, designed to lighten them, heavier than they would have been under the Dawes Plan.

The Hague Conferences later in the year endorsed the Young Plan with some modifications, after a protest from Great Britain against the proposed change in the distribution of reparation receipts. At this Conference a new figure emerged on the political scene of Europe. Mr. Philip (now Viscount) Snowden, one of the best known personalities in English public life, but hitherto, as a person, little known abroad, now voiced the long-growing feeling of the country that its rights had been too lightly asserted. Slight, fragile, and crippled; with character and features both refined and sharpened, both spiritualised and acidulated, by long years of physical disability; rigid and unyielding in his convictions; inflexible to pressure; definite and clear-cut in his personality; he had one of the bitterest tongues in politics. But his opponents – and his friends – suffered without rancour what they would not have tolerated from anyone whom they did not know so well and respect so deeply. Trained exclusively in a national parliament, and unused to the language and methods of conferences with foreign Governments, he now argued his case at the Hague exactly as he would have done at Westminster. He had not only the strong support of his countrymen, but the sympathy of many European countries, when he expressed the view that England had received something less than justice in the negotiations of recent years.

But unhappily he directed his strength, and this sympathy, to a disproportionate issue. He had been impressed by a calculation that the proposed variation from the percentage division of reparation payments fixed at Spa was equivalent to a loss of £2½ million per annum. It was a calculation based on the assumption that the Young Plan payments would long continue unmodified; for it did not apply to the early years. On a more reasonable assumption the sum involved was trivial. But on this minor issue he employed his full bargaining strength, and language to which diplomacy is unaccustomed. His long-remembered phrase, 'grotesque and ridiculous' trailed disastrously through Franco-British relations, and every sphere of foreign policy, for several years. And the visible relegation to second place of Mr. Arthur Henderson, in a Conference of Governments accustomed to a different precedence between a Minister of Finance and a Foreign Minister, weakened the position of one who, notably among British holders of his office, had held firmly to the straight and middle course between weak compliance with France on the one hand and bias or provocation on the other.

The Conference adjourned with its work incomplete, and with an inadequate consideration of what should have been its chief task, that of determining the conditions under which the new Bank of International Settlements was to be established.   At a renewed session, however, a general agreement was reached which, largely through the skill and indefatigable patience of M. Louis Loucheur, among other things settled many outstanding questions with the smaller countries entitled to reparation which had long been a source of friction.

§ *The Hoover Moratorium*

Payments continued under the Young Scheme for another two years, under greater strain as the economic depression increased and falling prices made the real burden heavier, and out of increasingly precarious resources of foreign exchange coming into Germany in the form of short-term advances.   Then, in the circumstances we already described, came the financial crisis which threatened not only reparation but all foreign claims upon Germany. Mr. Hoover took his sudden lead in June 1931 proposing a Moratorium of a year for both reparation and war debts. It was intended not only to relieve the international exchanges of the weight of these obligations but, in doing so, to restore confidence and arrest the crisis.   So seriously however had confidence now been shaken that even a short delay of seventeen days in the acceptance of the Moratorium destroyed any chance it had of obtaining the second of these objects; and throughout the ensuing months it became increasingly clear that the German situation was at the heart of the trouble; that reparation was an integral factor in that situation and inextricably intertwined with many others.   The Prime Ministers' Conference of

July 1931, the Wiggin Committee at Basle, the Bankers'
negotiation of a 'standstill' arrangement for short-term
commercial advances, the Hoover–Laval conversations of
October, the Meeting of the Advisory Committee under
the Young Plan in December, represent a series of efforts
to deal with this situation.   The outcome is yet uncertain.
What the policy should be as regards reparation we will
discuss later in this chapter when we have considered the
now inseparably related question of War Debts.

(B) WAR DEBTS

War (or 'Allied') Debts have several of the same
characteristics as reparation.   They represent expenditure incurred on a past war and not a productive enterprise yielding a return out of which they can be repaid.
They fall directly upon the public finances of the debtor
states who must raise in taxation what they pay.   They
involve payment abroad and therefore 'transfer,' and are a
factor in the balance of payments.   Also, for the same
reason, their real burden is increased to the full extent
of the fall in world prices of articles entering into international trade.

They have, however, certain special characteristics of
their own.   To a greater extent than reparation they are
directly applied to the service of internal loans raised in
the receiving country for the specific purposes to which
the debt is applicable.   This is a fact which needs to be
clearly realised in the debtor countries.   England is too
apt to think of what she pays America as just a windfall
to the American Treasury, in aid of general expenditure.
To the American Treasury and taxpayer the matter
presents itself differently.   War Loans were raised in
America and expended upon food and munitions for

England and the other Allied Powers, on urgent request and upon agreed terms. The loans remain largely outstanding; somebody must meet their annual service; either the American taxpayer whose country did not use the goods bought with the proceeds of the original loans, or the English and French taxpayer, whose countries did. It is not just a question of whether someone should be let off paying, but which of two bodies of taxpayers should pay, the one which owes the money or the one which doesn't; one of them must.

That is, of course, only one aspect of a complicated problem; but it is an important one.

We must in the first instance note that the same argument is true as regards that part of the British internal War Debt which represents loans to her Allies (amounting to over £1,000 million even excluding Russia), and that part of the French internal debt which represents loans for reconstructing the devastated area.

The principle of 'capacity to pay' has been to some extent recognised in the debt settlements but, as we shall see, inadequately and unequally. It is enough at this point to remark that the British internal debt, for example, is so great as to be a dominating factor in the whole of her public finances; it amounts to about seven times her annual public revenue, and half as much again as her national income. In contrast, America's public debt (State and Federal) only amounts to three times the annual revenue, and perhaps one quarter of her national income. In the years 1925–1928 indeed she was amortising this debt at a rate which, if continued, would have put an end to it altogether in a single generation. America, therefore, has a method of off-setting any loss through remissions or default on war debts by a reduction of sinking fund provision, which is not open to the debtor countries.

The origin of the loans is, of course, very different from that of the reparation debt, and as it underlies many later controversies it needs careful, if only a summary, description. When the war broke out, France, whose soil was invaded, and whose conscripted forces with their reserves included a very large proportion of all males in the prime of life, was able and was obliged to put into the field a much larger army than her own remaining industrial strength could adequately supply. England, on the other hand, with only small and voluntary forces, and unprepared for a continental war, could only raise and train a large army slowly; and her industrial capacity was able to supply much more than its needs. It was natural therefore that large supplies of all kinds of munitions and clothing should have been sent from England to France; while British ships were also required for shipments of food and raw materials from other continents. These goods and services were not supplied by the Government. The goods were bought and the ships were hired by France from private industrialists or shipowners, just as the British Government obtained its own munitions and ships from the same persons, though under increasing Government control, price-fixing, rationing and direction, the benefits of which were equally available to both Governments.

These operations were financed mainly by loans raised from the public in England on the British Government's guarantee; and those portions of the loans which were used for the purchase of goods supplied to France remained as a corresponding obligation from the French to the British Government. The same operations extended to the supplies of all the other allies, Russia, Italy, Serbia, Belgium, Roumania, Greece, etc. Even when British naval and military forces rose to a proportion comparable with those of France, the industrial strength of Great Britain, enormously increased by war organisation, her credit resources, and the fact that her soil was not invaded, enabled her to continue to play this rôle. But more was needed, and from an early date both Great Britain and France began to draw large supplies from America. These were financed at this stage partly by the sale of foreign securities but largely by loans from America which were raised, not by and on the credit of the American Government, but by and on the credit of Great Britain and France. When America entered the war in 1917 this system changed. Henceforth loans were raised in America by the American Government and on its own credit, to pay for both American and Allied supplies, the portions devoted to the latter purpose remaining as a debt from the Allied Governments to the American Government.

The statement sometimes made that Great Britain's debt to America represents an obligation incurred on behalf of her Allies, and not herself, needs careful examination. It is not true, as is sometimes said, that she 'underwrote' French or other Allied loans, that is that she made herself liable for an obligation incurred by France, or that she borrowed money from America and handed it over for the purchase of French supplies. Indirectly, however, a part of the British loans do represent supplies to the Allies. The position can be readily explained. British shell steel factories, for example, had been supplying French needs during the early years. If France had been left to get these supplies from America, either before or after America's entry into the war, men, plant and materials in England would have been available to meet British requirements, and Great Britain would not have needed to buy so much from America. This would have been uneconomical, however, and Great Britain continued to supply France throughout the war. Towards the end America recognised this position, and debited France and not Great Britain in some of these cases, but this arrangement was partial and was not retrospective. The same argument applies as regards a considerable range of other supplies.

Nevertheless even if Great Britain had done no work for her Allies after America's entry, and used the men released for her own needs, she would still have had to buy wheat, cotton and cellulose from America for herself in large quantities. She had, however, in the earlier years not only supplied British goods for the Allies, but also utilised some of her financial resources for Allied purchases in foreign countries, e.g. in Chile; and this, of course, increased the extent to which her own purchases from America necessitated loans.

The truth on this complicated controversy may, I think, be accurately stated thus. British productive capacity and finance supplied not only as much as, but much more than, the whole of the needs of the British military effort and the British civilian population. Great Britain supplied more to her Allies on the basis of British loans than she herself obtained by means of foreign loans. Had she not supplied her Allies her own purchases from America would have been less. Had she not provided them with some finance for foreign purchases, she would have paid for more of her American purchases without borrowing. And if America had completely financed the Allies after her entry into the war, paying for their purchases in Great Britain as well as elsewhere, it is probable that Great Britain could have managed without borrowing at all. All this is true; and it follows that the British loan from America represents to a substantial extent the needs of Allies rather than her own. But more cannot be said. It is not true that the whole British Debt represents expenditure incurred for the Allies.

So far we have described the way in which the War Loans originated. We must, however, add one category of these loans which stand on a somewhat different footing. Some American Loans, which were also raised by the Government on its own guarantee and transferred as a Government loan to another Government, were used after the conclusion of the war for peace and reconstruction needs. In some cases these were devoted to productive work with a real and enduring utility, so that they were different from the dead weight of a loan for past expenditure in war. In some instances loans were devoted to ordinary current Treasury needs; an interesting example of this is the purchase of American war-stores left in France, which was debited as a part of the French Debt to America, whereas the stores were re-sold and the proceeds devoted to ordinary Government expenditure in relief of taxation.

We must therefore make several distinctions in our mind in thinking of the debt; some was incurred between Allies engaged in a common war; some in respect of purchases in America while America was neutral; some in respect of expenditure after the war for reconstruction purposes or for the purchase of saleable goods with a realised commercial value.

Here then we have large intergovernmental debts, which for the most part have as their counterpart internal debts incurred by national Governments to the investors in their War bonds. On the face of it, here is a plain obligation. What reasons are there, in justice or equity, apart from questions of expediency or practicability, to suggest that this obligation should be cancelled or reduced ?

The first argument may be stated, in an extreme form as follows. Great Britain might have said to France in 1914 or 1915, 'We are engaged in a common effort in which our interests are equally engaged. Because of our concentration on naval as distinct from military strength, our remoter danger of invasion, and our voluntary system, the military burden must, for over a year at least, fall disproportionately on you. That is not our fault for which we should be punished; but neither is it a circumstance from which we wish to profit financially. Had we been militarily as ready as you, two out of four soldiers in the trenches would have been British; now there will only be one, and a Frenchman will take a British place at the hazard of his life. At least the uniform and the arms we will send freely, with regret that we cannot send the man with them.' And the British position in relation to France in 1914 and 1915 was the American position in relation to both France and Great Britain in 1917 and 1918.

In effect, on the principle of the Balfour Note, Great Britain did ultimately go as far as this, and indeed further; but considerations of the expediency and practicability of collecting intergovernmental debts were then involved. Considerations of justice alone would scarcely have carried so far. For indeed, the premise from which the argument proceeds irresistibly is itself faulty.

It is not true that the national interests of the different countries were equally involved. British interests, for example, were indeed affected; and it is arguable that these alone would have compelled Great Britain to fight, or have made it expedient for her to do so. But the interests were less direct and obvious than those of the country directly invaded; the claim on the people less irresistible. And this is, of course, even more true of America's participation. She had certain interests. She has indeed profited from her entry in developing a fuller sense of nationhood, and in the establishment of a place of great influence and authority in world affairs. But this is not what determined her action. Interests had their place, but the dominant motive was to save Europe and to save France. The countries who fought together in the war were thus engaged in a common effort, but they were partners with unequal interest. An argument based upon partnership must also take into account that inequality. It cannot alone support a claim for complete cancellation. But it does suggest mitigation of the original contracts, and it is not the only factor which does this.

The loans raised, for example, in America, were spent in America. They spread prosperity in extending circles throughout the country and a proportion of the profits so caused, directly and indirectly, flowed back into the National Treasury through every channel of taxation. This would have happened even if the prices of what was bought had not been higher than they had been before and have become since. But in fact, under the pressure of war demand and scarcity, prices became enormously inflated to more than twice their previous and their present level. The consequence is that a debtor country which paid in full would be paying more than twice in real value, in goods and services, what it received, in addition to interest itself similarly more than doubled in value and burden. Now when a loan contract is made what both parties intend is that an equal return should be made later for what is immediately supplied, plus the agreed interest. Neither intends that, through an accidental defect in the measuring rod, the borrower should pay back twice as many goods and services as had been contemplated in addition to interest.

In the early years after the war I used very often to

discuss, alternately with Americans and with Frenchmen, the reparation and war debt problems. At a certain point, as we were speaking of one, I would apply the argument to the other. There was always an immediate protest, couched in identical terms, 'You cannot treat reparation and war debts as if they are on the same basis.' They said the same, but their meaning was diametrically opposite. To the American a voluntary loan engagement in return for goods supplied obviously had a superior sanctity over an enforced indemnity. To the Frenchman the restoration of devastated regions obviously had a prior claim as compared with transactions between allies for the supply of the instruments of their common effort. I always held – and still hold – a middle course. The considerations are different, but they are not unequal. There is, I think on balance no reason in natural justice why reparation and war debts should be treated differently. Whether there is on grounds of expediency, we shall discuss later.

§ *War Debts and Disarmament*

In the meantime, however, it will be well to comment upon the connection which has been established in American public opinion, as expressed especially by Senator Borah, between the remission of Debt and Disarmament. Why, says the Senator, should we let off our debtors when they are wasting money on armaments, and by doing so enable them to waste more and so increase the general sense of insecurity in the world ?

America has realised that France reacts very strongly against such a suggestion; saying that it strikes at the heart of her sovereignty and treats her as a helot nation. But America does not perhaps fully understand why what seems a proposition of common sense, and a generous one withal, should be received with such anger. I have tried in a later passage to make France's attitude to her Army, and the question of security, more intelligible to English readers by connecting it with certain elements in their own national psychology. Let me now try similarly to speak as a French advocate to America.

Twice within living memory France has been invaded by a powerful neighbour, with whom her territory is contiguous along a lengthy land frontier. This neighbour is not less endowed with military qualities, or industrial resources, and has a much larger and more rapidly increasing population. She is embittered, smarting under defeat and loss of territory and numerous provisions of the Treaties which she considers unjust. She has an extreme national element in her political forces which, though not yet dominant, is very strong and may at any time seize power. Against this danger France has only four possible means of securing herself.

The first is the pursuit of such a conciliatory policy that the militant forces in Germany will lose support. Well, France would like to establish good relations with Germany, but she feels that no basis of conciliation can be anything but precarious in view of the public opinion and memories in both countries, and gravely doubts whether she can obtain security in this way alone. Some attempts have been followed by failure, understandable but nevertheless discouraging. When, for example, the Rhineland was evacuated five years before the Treaty date, the occasion was used for an expression of xenophobia in Germany, not of reconciliation. In any case France is unwilling to try to buy conciliation by disarmament which would leave her at the mercy of her bigger foe. Secondly, France has the support of the collective system established in the Covenant, Locarno Agreements, and the Kellogg Pact. She would like this system to be stronger and to be a main element in her national defence. But she does not feel certain that it would, in fact, save her; she is entitled to ask whether either America or Great Britain have really reckoned the prospect of collective support under any of these Treaties as a substantial factor in their own estimates of what is necessary to protect them against foreign invasion ; and there can be no doubt the answer would have to be in the negative. Thirdly, she has alliances, precarious at the best. And fourthly, she has her Army, whose definite superiority is due to the limits upon Germany imposed by the Treaty, and is unlikely to be permanent.

And then France looks at America which is incontestably, of all countries in the world, the most secure against external danger, and yet spends more than any other country on her fighting forces. She can understand her insistence on naval 'parity' with England, not as a means of defence against danger of attack, but as an assurance against being overborne in any negotiation where policies and interests differ; and she has no adverse comment except that, in the absence of pledges not yet given, it might always render incapable of application the League system of support for its members against an aggressor. But America has also an army, not indeed so great as her military budget would suggest, for the American Army, like the British, is voluntary and expensive by French standards, but still a powerful one. And the danger against which this army is needed is invisible to a Frenchman's eye. If, he says, the American Army represents preparation against such a remote and infinitesimal danger as, say, a Japanese invasion of California or a Canadian invasion of the north, what would give France on such a scale an equal security against her own danger ? — the enlistment of the entire male population of the country would not suffice. If, on the other hand, the American Army is a form of national expression, a legitimate luxury, perhaps, which America can afford, but a luxury, then it does not qualify America to understand what the French Army means to France; that is, an essential safeguard against a really vital danger.

No one can understand France's attitude who fails to realise that this is what her Army means to her. She may be mistaken. It may be that her security would be increased by the pacification that would follow a real reduction. But what she feels is that the first duty of the State is to protect its citizens; and it would betray its most sacred trust if, in the absence of another adequate basis of security, it failed to maintain the superiority of the Army. Other arguments may prevail; in particular if America would help to strengthen the collective peace system, France might feel safe in reducing her military force — but is it conceivable that, on a monetary inducement only, she would barter away her right of maintaining what, mistakenly or not, she considers an essential protection against a deadly danger ?

Yet, when all that is said, and when the French attitude to a possible bargain is understood and sympathised with, there remains an undeniable connection between debts and armaments. It is true that Europe would have more security and not less, if armaments were reduced; that at present the only effective limit (apart from the Treaty provisions as regards Germany) is that of financial resources; that there is hardly a country in the world which would not spend more on armaments if it were better off; and that, with a remission of all debts, expenditure would be higher than it would otherwise be.

How can the connection be made in such a way as to help and not to hinder disarmament? The best way would surely be this. Every attempt should be made so to strengthen the 'collective' peace system that it would be regarded as a real and important factor in every scheme of national defence. The Disarmament Conference, with this advantage, should agree upon a budgetary reduction and definite limitation, so that no new resources, whether resulting from debt remission or from returning prosperity, could possibly increase armaments. It should do this primarily in pursuance of its own task of using any improvement in security to reduce armaments, but with a further inducement in the knowledge that an agreement so reached would help in the subsequent debt negotiations.

In this way, and perhaps in this alone, can the connection between armaments expenditure and debt remission be used so as to help the Disarmament problem.

§ *The Debt Settlements*

So much then, in broad outline, for the underlying principles and considerations we must bear in mind. We must now trace briefly what arrangements have been made for the repayment of these war loans.

It would be tedious, and is unnecessary, to trace in detail the intricate war debt settlements and their relation to claims for reparation. A clearer picture can be given in outline. Germany, Austria, Hungary and Bulgaria owe reparation payments to Great Britain, France, Italy, Japan, Belgium, Czechoslovakia, Roumania, Jugo-Slavia, Greece, Portugal, and the British Dominions. All these reparation creditors owe war debts to America or Great Britain, in most cases to both.

Mr

When reparation and war debts are taken together it is substantially true to say that the bulk of what Germany pays goes to America and France, in the early years about $260 million to the former and $80 million to the latter.

The war debt settlements as they now stand consist of two series of funding arrangements made by America and Great Britain with their respective Allied Debtors. Those made by America covered a total indebtedness of about $11,000 million (including accrued interest). Taking interest at $4\frac{1}{4}$ per cent., the usual rate for the Liberty Bonds, the settlements as a whole amounted to a remission of 40 per cent. On the same basis the American settlement with Great Britain amounted to a remission of only 18 per cent. This allows nothing for the fall in prices, which are now about half what they were when the loans were expended. If gold prices remained as at present, therefore, the Allies as a whole would, in terms of goods and services, be paying more than what they originally borrowed, with full interest, and without remission. Great Britain would be paying over 50 per cent. more, with full interest.

The settlements made by Great Britain with all her Allies (except Russia) between 1925 and 1927 amounted (also with accrued interest at the date of settlement) to about £1,300 million. Taking the same rate of interest, $4\frac{1}{4}$ per cent., they amount to a remission of about 70 per cent. To estimate the burden in terms of goods and services it would be necessary to make the same allowance as in the case of the American settlements, but for one important fact, the fall in the pound sterling. The obligations are in pounds and therefore Great Britain has made an involuntary, but none the less effective, remission in terms of gold to the extent of the depreciation in her own currency, which at the present rate compensates for the greater part, though not all, of the fall in gold prices.

America may complain that, if the Balfour principle were accepted and applied, the greater generosity of the British settlements would be, in some measure, at America's expense. This complaint, technically valid in any case as regards form and procedure, would have had substance also if subsequent experience had shown that the debtors to Great Britain could in fact have paid more than they were required to under the British settlements. But there are probably few who would now maintain this.

II

In all these circumstances what would be a reasonable policy for dealing with War Debts ? Let us first put aside the special situation created by the financial crisis that began in June, and imagine that we are looking at the problem in the early part of 1931. At that time it would, I think, have been reasonable to take the later settlements, the French and the Italian, and those with smaller countries, as fair arrangements on the basis of the price level at the time at which they were made, and as taking into account adequately the general considerations set out above. It would then have been evident, however, that the earlier British settlement had been based on a premature estimate of Great Britain's superior capacity, which subsequent events had failed to justify. On the position as it then appeared, and on an assumption that the world depression was ending, that prices would not fall further, and that there would be no general financial crisis, a reasonable settlement would, I suggest, have been (a) to reduce the gold obligation of France and

Italy to the extent to which prices had fallen since the date of the first arrangement – thus leaving the real burden unchanged, and (b) to amend the British agreement so as to make it the same proportion of the original debt as the French. This would not have made any allowance for the fact that, in part, the British debt indirectly represented supplies to the Allies, and that Great Britain was claiming a smaller proportion of what France owed her than America, but in all the circumstances it might have been a fair and final settlement. It would doubtless have been observed by all concerned if, and so long as, after an equal and similar amendment of the German reparation claim, Germany had continued to meet the remaining obligations, so reduced, resting upon her.

The continuance of the depression, the fall of prices, and the advent of the world financial crisis have, however, now created an entirely different and much more difficult situation.

This situation has been considered successively by the Prime Ministers' Conference in London in July 1931, the Wiggin Committee in Basle in August, and the Advisory Committee under the Young Plan in December.

Several conclusions emerge very clearly from these deliberations. It is obvious that the Moratorium of German reparation payments, at present arranged till the end of June 1932, cannot and will not then end. The Advisory Committee say this explicitly as regards the 'conditional' payments, which were within their terms of reference, and not obscurely hint it as regards the 'unconditional' payments which were not. It seems certain too that there must be a Moratorium for several years, whether arranged at once or by successive negotiations;

and that any later payments must be on a much smaller scale than those of the Young Plan.

Whether the creditors agree or the debtor defaults is for the former to decide, but that is all.

Secondly, the connection between Reparation and War Debts is clearly now inseparable. 'The adjusting of all Reparations and War Debts,' say the Advisory Committee, which included an American member, 'is essential.' It is in fact not conceivable that one part of the complex system of war obligations will be fundamentally changed and the remainder left intact; that those who are owed sums from Germany in respect of reparation will receive nothing and will yet continue to pay, without reduction, what they owe in respect of War Debts. Here again, whether the creditors agree or the debtors default is for the former to decide. Canute might as well order the tide not to touch his throne as Congress to ordain that 'the indebtedness of foreign countries to the United States should not be in any manner cancelled or reduced.'

War Debtors have indeed perhaps no reason to regret that Congress should have passed such a resolution, and should have been unwilling to re-establish the Debt Funding Commission which was proposed by President Hoover, recommended by the responsible Ministers of the American Executive and all those whose business gives them an experience of America's international position and trade. Had the Commission been appointed it would have given America's responsible verdict as to what she considered due to her, having regard to the fall of gold prices and the reduction in the capacity to pay since the last settlements were made. Unless however this American Commission had shown a liberality, and an insight into the world's real financial position, altogether greater than we have seen in any Conference or Commission of European creditors of reparation, that verdict would still have involved an intolerable strain upon European debtors. But default in such circumstances would have been an extremely serious matter, ranging Europe against responsible America. It is different now. Failure to meet the full obligations which Congress refuses to reconsider ranges the debtor with all that is most responsible and best qualified by expert qualification to judge in America herself. Congress has done all that it could to exempt default from dishonour.

Yes, as debtors we may not regret. But as members of a world community we may again sadly note that here again is one more instance of Government failing in its task of wielding its power with due care and upon responsible and expert advice; one more instance in which brute facts have been left to force their own solution without the control of regulative wisdom; one more instance of legal obligations being set aside. A national society is based on respect for law, which is impaired whenever a law falls into desuetude because it is such that it can neither win the support of public opinion nor be enforced; the economic and financial life of the world is based upon sanctity of contract, which is impaired every time a contract is broken because it has been so framed or is so applied that it cannot be carried out; world order itself is based upon the sanctity of treaty, which is impaired every time a Treaty fails to be strictly observed.

We have discussed what might have been a satisfactory settlement of Reparation and War Debts early in 1931, before the financial crisis. What is necessary now? More drastic reduction is certainly now needed. All the reparation question has been a process of reason coming gradually – but always too late. Time after time the creditors were willing to accept one year what would have settled the question a year earlier. But in the mean-time events had marched. It is so again.

A further Moratorium for some years, say for four or five, and extending to both Reparation and War Debts, would certainly seem necessary. Should there be more ? Shall there be complete cancellation ?

Certainly, if we look at the world situation as a whole, without regard to the special interests of creditors and the political forces with which they are associated, com-plete cancellation would obviously give the greatest relief. The case for something less complete may thus be stated. The cost of rebuilding the devastated regions in France and Belgium (represented like other intergovernmental debts by internal loans on which annual payments are still due for many years) stands in some respect on a different footing from the rest, though the extra sum involved by the conditions under which the restoration was carried out at inflated prices in a closed market must not be for-gotten. Germany's capacity to pay the amount of the 'unconditional' annuity under normal conditions, as distinct from those of the depression and crisis, was not disputed in 1929. Nor indeed was any doubt thrown upon it by the Advisory Committee of December 1931, who anticipated a return of prosperity to Germany, and added that 'it would be unjustifiable to judge its prospects for the future on the basis of an exceptional period of depression.'

In the early editions of this book proposals were made for a settlement of reparation on the basis of a moratorium, a drastic reduction of subsequent annuities and the provision of certain safeguards to secure that even these reduced annuities would fall or stop in time of depression. These proposals have been rendered obsolete by the

Lausanne settlement, and it seems more profitable, instead of repeating them, to recite and comment upon this settlement, the most satisfactory single event of 1932.

The Lausanne Agreement gives a complete moratorium for three more years, beyond the Hoover year. It provides thereafter for the issue of bonds upon the market involving for Germany a maximum annual payment of 180 million gold marks — less than one-tenth of the average sums prescribed in the Young Plan, the remaining capital obligation being stated nominally as 3000 million gold marks. In addition, the issue of these bonds is dependent upon conditions which ensure that they can never disorganise either German finances or the exchanges of the world. These reduced and safeguarded sums are to be paid into a European Reconstruction Pool, so that they are divorced from the embittered controversy about 'war guilt.'

The Agreement requires ratification and is nominally conditional upon a settlement of war debts. It is obvious, however, that though failure to ratify by any of the creditors might affect their relations with each other or the negotiations with America; and might cause a technical default of Germany in relation to a nominally revived obligation under the obsolete Young Plan, the settlement as regards Germany is in fact final unless she herself destroys it. Unless Germany herself throws away this great instrument of release, by failing to ratify herself, no one else can deprive her of it. A technical default due to the failure to ratify by others would not substantially impair either her financial or political credit; and it is scarcely conceivable that any serious attempt would be made to exact payments beyond the modest sums prescribed at Lausanne.

At last therefore we have an end of this disastrous legacy

of the war, which has poisoned the politics of Europe and disturbed the finances of the world for a decade.

With reparation settled, war debts remain. Europe has, as a creditor, at length shown herself united and reasonable, and now wonders how she will fare as a debtor. The Lausanne Agreement was not only an indispensable prior condition to negotiations on war debts. In several respects it presents also in the principles which it contains a model for the analogous problem. These principles, as we have seen, include a respite, the commercialising of a final remaining capital obligation which is itself fixed at a sum that makes such an operation practicable and involves annual transfer so limited as not to disturb the world's finances. This is not cancellation; nor does it imply that those who have sacrificed nine-tenths of their reparation receipts expect to reduce their own obligations by the same amount ; but it does suggest a reasonable consideration of the factors which are applicable in both cases: the fall in prices, the difficulty of transfer, the reduction in the capacity to pay of the debtors, the disturbance to the world's general economy of large intergovernmental payments, and the adverse effect upon creditor countries' exports. And there is one minor principle that might well be recalled. The next war debts payments are due on December 15, 1932. The American political time-table makes it extremely difficult to expect negotiations to be completed by that date. Lausanne was faced with a similar difficulty, for it was convened only shortly before the expiration of the Hoover moratorium. The first decision taken in these circumstances was that, without prejudice to the future, no payments were to be regarded as due during the progress of the negotiations, which were to be concluded as soon as possible.

All the European war debtors will doubtless have in mind the principles and precedent of Lausanne. To that extent there will no doubt be some resemblance in their approach to new negotiations. But, apart from that, it is probably desirable that negotiations should be separate and not collective, at least in the first instance.*

If we bear in mind the special character of reparation and war debts as 'dead weight' debts, with no productive asset behind them, their importance as a factor in the accumulating strain which resulted in the financial crisis will be evident. They have widened the gap in the balance of payments, which new lending is needed to bridge, and they have made new lending more precarious by destroying confidence. They have therefore been to a substantial extent responsible for the drain on gold which has helped to hold down prices, and for the violent dislocations in the course of trade of recent years.

* See Preface to present edition for proposals as to War Debt negotiations.

CHAPTER IV

PRECEPT AND PRACTICE

COMMERCIAL POLICY AND TARIFFS

HISTORY records no contrast between an almost unchallenged doctrine and an almost universal practice equal to that which confronts us in the sphere of the world's commercial policies. The place which protective tariffs occupy in the world's economy and, regarded as a whole, their normal and inevitable effect, are perfectly clear. They are like the natural impediments of mountain range or other obstacles to transport which increase the price paid for the benefits and economies resulting from the interchange of products of widely sundered regions. The economic results of a new railway, a tunnel through the hills, a ship canal constructed at great cost, are offset by the counteracting impediments of tariffs at the frontiers. If, for example, France and England built a channel tunnel and then each imposed new duties to protect the trades affected, the net result — apart from saving the discomfort of passengers with weak stomachs — would be simply the loss of the capital employed in the construction.

The limited and temporary exceptions which economists admit do not substantially modify the truth of this general statement. Nor is it science only that speaks. The World Economic Conference of 1927 was composed of some two hundred persons of every kind of relevant qualification, in business, in agriculture in official life and so on, nominated by fifty Governments; and they agreed unanimously that the chief impediment to the growth of the world's prosperity was to be found in its tariff policies.

As to the world as a whole, then, expert opinion, scientific and practical, is unanimous. For a particular country, however, deciding its own policy in the midst of foreign tariffs outside its control, opinions are more divided. A free trade country in a protectionist world would have a lower cost of living which would be of advantage both to her consuming public and to her exporters. It is true, however, that such a country is sometimes exposed to special dangers. If, for example, the gold standard loses its power to adjust the balance of trade her currency may be threatened. If, in a period of acute depression, many countries try to get rid of their exportable goods at any price the effect of this temporary 'dumping' may fall unduly on a single and isolated free market.

The part which tariffs have played in aggravating the present crisis is due to special circumstances which need to be explained. America, which before the war had always been a 'debtor' country, buying more than she sold and borrowing the difference, has since been in precisely the opposite position. The world owes her large sums in respect of war debts, and at the same time she has been exporting more than she imports. There has therefore been a large gap between what she owed and what was owed to her. For a time she lent the difference. But there were elements of danger inherent in this situation from the first. The 'debtor' world was piling up obligations beyond its strength. Foreign lending was a new experience to the American investing public; it was not a deep-rooted habit, safeguarded by traditional caution; and it was therefore liable to become rash in a period of optimism, and to stop suddenly with a change of fortune or of mood. It was therefore obvious to anyone who looked at the world situation as a whole that it was important that America should, to the utmost possible extent, receive what was due to her in the form of actual goods; and that commercial policy should be designed to facilitate this. In other words, the American tariff needed to be the lowest in the world. In fact it was one of the highest.

Nor is this all. The normal working of the gold standard, as we have seen, tends to correct a balance of trade, when necessary, by increasing the imports of creditor countries. It will fulfil this vital function, though with greater difficulty, even if the imports have to surmount the obstacle of a permanently high tariff. But it cannot do so if it is impeded in its actual operation by new or increased tariffs, calculated to check just the extra imports which the normal correcting process is bringing in. This is what the new American tariff did in 1930, and it is for this, as for other reasons, that the ratification of that tariff was a turning point in world history.

What has been said of America has become true in recent years also of France, which has similarly combined a positive balance of payments with too little foreign lending to bridge the difference.

The crisis of 1931 has at least done one thing which may in future prove of great value. It has revealed the anatomy of the world's economic structure. Now that foreign lending has stopped; now that gold movements from debtor countries (except perhaps India) are reaching their limit; the need for debtors to meet their obligations if at all by supplying goods, postponed and disguised for the time, is no longer theoretical and ultimate, but

immediate and actual. And creditor countries who have
been unwilling to be paid by imports are losing both what
is owed them from the past and their current exports.

§ *Recent Course of Commercial Policy*

It is in the light of these underlying conditions that
we must consider the evolution of commercial policy during recent years. When the World Economic Conference
met in 1927, foreign lending was proceeding freely and
the strain caused by the disparities of trade balances had
not become visible. The situation was dominated by
four facts. New tariff-making authorities, and therefore
smaller economic units, had been created by the Treaties.
Very high tariffs were being claimed by national industries which had expanded under the 'protection' afforded
by war conditions. Duties were frequently changed at
short notice, so that exporting industries were liable to
be disastrously interrupted by a new impediment which
could be neither foreseen nor provided against. And
lastly, the natural development of industry towards large-
scale operations was obviously increasing the handicap of
smaller economic units; for large-scale production can
only proceed on the basis of an assured entry into markets
much larger than those comprised within most national
frontiers. It was under the impelling force of these conditions that the Conference unanimously recommended
reduction and then stability of tariffs.

The immediate effect of this recommendation was considerable. Early in 1927 the upward movement of tariffs
was in full swing. This movement was sharply arrested;
some duties were reduced; other trade barriers, such as
prohibitions, were removed. At the end of the year the
situation, instead of being as without the Conference it

would certainly have been, very much worse, was definitely better.

The following year, 1928, was a year of new commercial treaties. One pair after another of European countries negotiated new treaties, and these for the most part included some reductions of duty, the benefit of which was automatically extended to other countries by virtue of 'the most-favoured-nation' clause. After a time, however, this process was brought to an end, mainly by the operation of the clause which made it of general benefit. This clause is so large a factor in the present problems of commercial policy that we must consider very carefully just how it works.

§ *The Most-Favoured-Nation Clause*

In the nineteenth century the traditional policy of Great Britain as a free-trade country was to claim from a protectionist country the right of entry for British goods at whatever was the lowest rate of duty granted to any other country. This was willingly accorded since Great Britain admitted all goods free of any duty whatever. Very often a similar clause was inserted in commercial treaties between pairs of countries with comparable though not identical systems. With each extension of the clause, however, the attractions of bilateral bargaining tended to become less, because the obligation to give an advantage to those who had not been parties to the negotiations, and had themselves made no concessions, seemed onerous and unjust. More recently the benefit of the clause has been claimed by countries who have very high tariff systems and the situation has rapidly become impossible. When two moderate tariff countries can only negotiate reductions *inter se* if they are prepared to extend these reductions to countries whose general tariff is higher than even their own unreduced tariff, and who give them no advantages in return, two results must follow. Firstly, reduction by the method of bilateral agreements will be arrested; and this in fact happened in 1928; and secondly, there will be a growing feeling that some modification in the most-favoured-nation principle is both just and necessary.

At the same time it would be a disaster if this principle disappeared altogether from the world's economic policies. It may justly claim very great advantages. It is designed to avoid the dangerous complications and confusions of political and economic motives which arise when a country feels free to distribute its favours unequally. Its disappearance might result in a chaos of complicated and differentiating tariff systems, and innumerable occasions of friction.

The danger of the 'most-favoured-nation' principle ceasing to be operative is not however to be averted by making it sacrosanct in its extreme and unconditional form. The consequence of that course is likely to be to leave the principle stranded high and dry, while the real tide of actual practice sweeps by. The only practicable method is to try, by suitable adaptations to existing circumstances, to retain its essential advantages while making it sufficiently acceptable to countries now chafing under its fetters. Happily the history of the clause points the way. Exceptions, strictly limited and safeguarded, have from time to time been admitted in order to adapt it to special exigencies and circumstances. It is universally agreed, for example, that any countries bound by the clause are at liberty to form a customs union providing complete free trade with each other, while still imposing tariffs against others. In addition, certain groups of closely associated countries have sometimes been allowed specially favourable duties *inter se*; a 'Baltic' exception, for example, covering Scandinavian countries and an 'Iberian' exception covering Spain and Portugal and countries of Latin America, have sometimes been included in commercial treaties. A similar right of preferential treatment is of course enjoyed as between Great Britain and the Dominions, although all possess complete autonomy in commercial policy, by virtue not of an exception to the clause, but of their common political sovereignty. We shall see later how an extension of the same principle might remove the principal obstacle to the United States of Europe movement.

§ *Why Tariff Reduction has not been achieved*

The League of Nations made its next effort to secure freer trade in 1929. A Conference first tried to negotiate a Treaty for a 'Tariff Truce,' designed to prevent increases for a substantial period during which a more ambitious scheme of actual reduction might be prepared. To this Conference all countries were invited, but by a process of self-selection it became a European Conference for, with scarcely an exception, all European countries attended and no others. The convention which emerged was one in which the obligations had been so diluted as to be almost invisible; and though it was signed, it lapsed for want of ratification. A similar fate attended the attempts to secure a convention to remove 'prohibitions' and to secure 'Equal Treatment for Foreigners.' Reduction of trade barriers by convention therefore failed, though the process of negotiation had some influence upon practice, as is shown by the fact that the main increases in industrial tariffs during these years were

Nʀ

made by countries outside Europe who did not participate.

It is well to consider the causes and significance of these failures. In the first place the technical difficulties of negotiations between many countries on complex, heterogeneous and interdependent tariffs are very great. Modern tariffs are of different levels, constructed on different principles, based on varying nomenclatures; and the countries who are negotiating in a particular Conference are linked with other countries by their reciprocal trade relations and by commercial treaties which include the most-favoured-nation clause. They therefore fear that if they bind themselves they will be defenceless against those who remain outside.

Much more important, however, than these technical difficulties are the economic interests and the political forces inevitably created by a protectionist system. When the economic life of a country has been built on a basis of tariffs, it creates a situation which makes radical reform almost impossible. It is not just a matter of a few vested interests (as it is when new tariffs are first proposed); for a vast capital expenditure has been incurred which, if the basis were removed, might be largely lost. A mass of population has become trained and specialised in certain occupations, which they cannot easily change. A national psychology inimical to reform has been created. A prospect of greater but uncertain prosperity is weaker than the apparently certain loss of something already possessed.

I remember this being vividly explained to me by a French Minister of Commerce. 'What is the use,' he said in effect, 'of talking to me about radical reforms in the tariff system of France ? Perhaps France might have been more prosperous under a freer system.

But I am a Minister in a country with representative government. I have to deal with France as it is and the wishes of the French people as they are. The France that has grown up under our present system is more interested in its home trade than in its export trade. Most people are in fact engaged in the first and judge policy by its effect on the internal market. Of a hundred people who come into my office, eighty-five ask me for protection in the home market, for fifteen who ask me to help them in their foreign trade. What can I, or any other Minister who may succeed me, possibly do, beyond minor adjustments or concessions, when this is the fundamental structure of my country ?'

And the political expression of these underlying interests and desires is even more adverse to progress. After several years of trying to get into the minds of those who were nominally in control of commercial policies, I came to the conclusion that the secret calculation in most minds was one of the strength of political groups and political pressures on the Government. Nearly all of them were habitually thinking in terms not of the economic policy which they considered, rightly or wrongly, the best for their country, but in terms of the reactions of any given policy upon the groupings of parties and sections on which their political support depended. Nor is this a mere unworthy clinging to office; it is often the only condition under which it is possible to carry on the Government of countries in which preferential protection for sectional interests has become the reward of those who can organise sufficient pressure.

Few realise how great, how almost insurmountable, this obstacle is, for none living have been through the experience of changing from a protectionist to a free system.

The only hope of securing more liberal policies was

indeed that the national interests in each country which stood to gain from them would organise themselves and find articulate and effective expression. They failed to do so. Agricultural duties for example were in 1927 generally much lower than those levied on industrial articles; the agriculturalist complained with justice that he was selling cheap in an almost free market, and was buying dear in a highly protected one. But he preferred to agitate, not for reductions in industrial duties, but for higher agricultural duties and for subsidies. The result was subsidised over-production. The industrial exporter, again, was slower in seeing his interest than the manufacturer who wanted protection for his home market. For the most part he was passive or else he exercised his ingenuity in devising schemes enabling him to profit by a secure market at home so as to dump at lower prices abroad.

Unhappily, too, the danger of losing the almost free British market, which should have been the strongest force for reduction, counted for very little. It had been obvious for years that European countries would lose this great advantage if their own duties were not reduced. But because Free Trade versus Protection was a major political issue between the rival British parties it was never possible to make this consideration really effective in negotiations. The Labour Party in power was pledged to Free Trade; its opponents were equally pledged to Protection; neither party seemed likely to be free to change its policy substantially because of what happened elsewhere. True, a reduction of duties in Europe might increase the chances of the Free Traders being placed in power; but equally the election might be decided on quite different issues. European countries felt, not unnaturally, that it was difficult to bargain, not with a Government, but with an electorate. In any case, even the offer of a Tariff Truce for several years – perhaps attractive to them in retrospect – was refused. The expected change has come; and any bargaining in future will take place on less unequal terms.

It was in view of these circumstances that M. Briand, in May 1930 made an attempt on another basis. He initiated a specifically European organisation, within the framework of the League, to achieve the ideal of a 'United States of Europe.' But it has not yet seriously tackled the fundamental problem of the commercial policy of Europe. We shall consider what this involves when we discuss future policy.

§ *The Effect of the Financial Crisis on Commercial Policy*

We must now note the new factors introduced by the financial crisis which occurred in June 1931. As we have seen, the essential feature of this crisis was that foreign lending stopped, and countries which had come to rely upon borrowing therefore found it difficult to pay what they owed and to go on buying from abroad. All of them have been under pressure to redress their balance of trade and to create a surplus of exports over imports. This change is unhappily being entirely effected by reduction of imports, which can be stopped by new restrictions, and in no degree by an increase of exports which depend on the willingness of others to receive them. No country is selling more, or indeed as much; all are buying less. In some cases new tariffs have been imposed, in others actual prohibitions. In others, exchange depreciation operates like a tariff on imports; in others a rationing and limitation of foreign exchange operates as a new, and very formidable, impediment to foreign purchases. We are in

sight of the final development of this process in a practically complete stoppage of all international trade except
in such articles as cannot be either dispensed with or produced at home.

The losses involved in this disastrous process may at
last, however, create the conditions favourable to a new
effort to reform commercial policies.

II

To what goal shall any new reform be directed, and
by what methods will it best be achieved ?

As to the ultimate goal an economist could only give
one answer – the lowest possible, uniform, and stable
tariff levels. Apart from 'revenue' as distinct from 'protectionist' duties, there are perhaps two kinds of desirable
exceptions, one economic, one social. First, emergency
tariffs or prohibitions are justifiable against sudden and
temporary dumping, designed to kill a competitive enterprise. And secondly, for social or similar reasons some
countries might foster certain activities which they consider a desirable element in the national life. It may be,
for example, that it is worth while for a given community,
in the interests of a varied social life, to sustain some
economic loss in order to avoid the specialisation in a few
activities which complete freedom would involve.

But, if we believe in world trade at all, its economies
and advantages, a tariff to compensate for differences in
wage-level, or in cost of production, is mere nonsense.
Countries differ in natural advantages, in the skill and
industry of their peoples and in the efficiency of their
organisation. Of these varying advantages, differences
in wages and in the standard of living and general level
of prosperity are the natural reflection and consequence.

Without such differences trade could not take place; counteract them and it will stop. A so-called scientific tariff usually means one which is based on the principle of compensating for differences in costs of production. This either represents a mere fallacy, or it is a policy destructive of international trade in anything except the few things that cannot be produced at home at any cost however exorbitant – such as rubber in England or America. For why does anyone ever buy anything from abroad if it is not because he gets a given article at a lower price – or a better article at a given price ? Abolish this advantage and why should anyone buy from abroad at all ?

Indeed, if we believe in international trade, the only mitigating circumstance about what are usually called 'scientific tariffs' is that they never are in fact scientifically framed and applied, for if they were trade would disappear. But if this is not their principle, what is ? Let us face frankly the fact that the operative principle underlying the flexible, varied and changing system is usually just this, and nothing more; that those interests which are so organised as to exercise the strongest political pressure get protection, or the highest rates of protection, at the expense of the rest of the community.

The evil consequences are illimitable. Time, energy, attention, money that should be devoted to improving processes, are devoted to persuading politicians. The system offers the highest rewards, the richest spoils, to those who can most successfully corrupt the Government. The machine of Government itself – in the widest sense, including the Ministry, the Civil Service, the Parliament, and the Electorate – cannot under these conditions – and does not – remain honest and competent enough to perform its primary tasks. So long as our system is based at all upon competition, the first task of Government is to determine and enforce the rules under which that competition takes place.   It is a task of a policeman who maintains an equal law, or of an umpire who keeps the ring.   But if the police-man is to spend half his time in dexterously transferring money from one citizen's pocket to another, if the umpire is expected on sufficient persuasion to jump the ropes and administer a stimulant to one of the contestants and a sud-den blow or kick to the other, he will have neither the time, nor the character, nor the public respect, which he needs for his primary duties.   And the complexity of the essential tasks of Government under modern condi-tions strains to the utmost the limited resources of man's regulative wisdom, competence and public honesty; there is no margin to spare.

There is indeed one form of tariff which might better deserve the name of 'scientific' than those which usually assume it.   A strong and competent Government might stimulate and assist reorganisation of an industry by offer-ing a temporary and conditional tariff.   But the condi-tions would need to be clearly defined, and rigorously enforced, preferably with the aid of other industrialists who wanted the prices of the protected commodity to be low.   It is possible too that a tariff might be useful as the counterpart of other forms of economic organisation. Experience suggests however that incompetence is more likely to be buttressed up than efficiency encouraged.

The best kind of tariff is therefore one which (with the few exceptions mentioned above) is low and uniform; with no prizes for organised persuasion; stable for long and definite periods; and only not permanent so far as it is subject to reduction by successive stages.

So much as to an ultimate goal when we build up from the new foundations left by the present crisis.   But during the crisis itself, and as a help to ending it, a different goal

would be desirable.   Just as an ultimate goal for monetary
policy should be a stability in the general level of world
prices, but the first goal a return to the higher level of
1929, so during the crisis it would be a great advantage if
the inequality in tariffs could, before being abolished, be
temporarily reversed.   As we have seen, a big adjustment
in the balance of trade as between creditor and debtor
countries is inevitable, and is indeed taking place.
Creditor-gold-surplus countries can mitigate the prospective stoppage of their export trade to the precise extent
to which they will take more imports; and a reduction
of their tariffs would be one way of achieving this.

But what is the practicable way of progress ?   One
country after another, by independent and unconcerted
action, will doubtless modify its tariffs, or its foreign
exchange regulations, under the pressure of current exigencies or the conflicting considerations which we have
described.   Here and there, too, action will be modified
by bargainings or understandings between pairs of
countries whose action has been mutually injurious.   But
cannot anything be done collectively to encourage a movement in the right direction ?   The most ambitious and
interesting attempt of recent years is that of Monsieur
Briand to secure greater economic unity in Europe, and
we shall do well first to consider this.

§ *The United States of Europe*

The obvious meaning of the phrase 'The United
States of Europe' is that all countries within the limits
of Europe should form a single unit, as the United
States of America do, with complete freedom of trade and
no intervening customs barriers.   But it is evident that
such a conception has no practicable chance of realisation

merely as an economic policy and without a complete transformation of political relationships. Zollvereins have often been advocated, and sometimes attempted, but they have never been realised except where there has been an overwhelming political motive and an extremely close political association between the countries concerned.

A consideration of the principal factors involved will explain why this is so. A Zollverein means a common tariff, which requires a political instrument to determine it; it involves the distribution of the Customs receipts to all the constituent states, and again therefore, a political instrument to determine in what proportions, or on what principles, the distribution is to be made. But the commercial policy of the European states is a central and crucial part of their whole policy; half the questions that occupy a national Government turn upon the relations between it and the country's economic organisation and these are inextricably interwoven with its tariff system. The receipts from Customs again are a very substantial part of the public revenues, upon which policy in every sphere, including military preparations, education, and social insurance, are dependent. It is evident therefore that a common political authority which was empowered to decide what European tariff should be imposed and how the receipts should be distributed would be for many countries as important as their national Governments, which would, in effect, be reduced almost to the status of provincial authorities. In other words the United States of Europe must be a political reality or it cannot, in the complete sense of being a single free-trade unit, be an economic reality.

But this is not all. The main competition of every European country is in fact not with other continents.

but with other countries in Europe. Their internal economic structure has grown up, and taken its shape and form, within a system of tariffs designed as a defence against the competition of neighbours. A proposal to establish a Zollverein for Europe, complete at one stage, is scarcely more practicable than a proposal for universal free trade. For similar reasons regional Zollvereins between pairs or groups of countries within Europe are unlikely to be often feasible. Here and there a specially close economic interest and sufficient political sympathy, may make it worth attempting. But Latvia and Estonia, where chances seemed specially favourable, have after years of effort so far found the difficulties insuperable.

Where a close relation of sympathy or common political ambitions give a motive force for union, as between Germany and Austria, these very factors create political difficulties. The main political danger of Europe is the formation of opposing groups of alliances. It is of great importance that economic associations should counteract and not coincide with political affiliations; in other words, that the lines of economic union should cut across the lines of any actual or potential political union. A Danubian Economic Union which includes Hungary as well as Czecho-Slovakia would relieve political tension – but would present great internal difficulties. So would a union which included France and Germany. On the other hand, an economic union between Germany and Austria, or France and Belgium and Poland, while more possible as regards the internal relations of these countries, would present political dangers and evoke strong opposition.

Under these conditions the conclusions to be drawn as to closer economic union in Europe are clear.

Firstly, the reduction of tariffs between European

countries is essential, whatever may be done by other methods, such as international cartelisation, improvement in transport, postal facilities, financial institutions and so on. Secondly, closer economic union can only proceed, as Monsieur Briand has himself realised, hand in hand with closer political union. Thirdly, it is likely that greater progress can be made through associations of contiguous countries, which might in time extend and amalgamate, than through measures applying equally at every stage to Europe as a whole. It is essential, however, that such associations should be so formed as to counteract and not reinforce any tendency to political groupings for purposes of national defence. And lastly, it will rarely be possible even for a pair of contiguous countries to establish a complete Zollverein at one stage; it will never be possible for Europe, or any considerable part of Europe to do so. A Zollverein for Europe, complete in one stage, is impracticable, and almost unthinkable. Progress towards European economic union through commercial policy can only be achieved gradually and by successive stages.

This conclusion, obvious and even platitudinous as it may seem, is really of cardinal importance because it involves a consequence that has scarcely yet been fully realised. This is that, if progress is to be made towards an economic United States of Europe, European states must be able to have lower tariffs against each other than against the rest of the world. This at once raises the whole question of the most-favoured-nation principle. The difficulty would not arise if a complete Zollverein were in question, for that is an admitted exception; but progress towards a Zollverein by stages is inconsistent with the most-favoured-nation clauses now commonly inserted in commercial treaties.

What will be the attitude of non-European countries to this movement in Europe for a partial and progressive Zollverein ? One aspect of it is the reduction of tariffs between the negotiating states. The other is the retention of higher rates for the imports of other countries. The movement is too strong to ignore; perhaps too strong to defeat; and its defeat would involve the waste of a force that might perhaps be put to a good use. Will the rest of the world concentrate its effort upon opposing what may be the only practicable method of progress towards European economic unity; or will it co-operate in establishing the best safeguards and directing the movement on to the best lines ?

This in turn raises the question whether progress in Europe is to be desired and assisted by the rest of the world. Do other countries, America in particular, think of the countries of Europe primarily as competitors, or as customers and debtors whose increasing prosperity is to be desired ? Is it a good thing or not for other countries, and for the world as a whole, that Europe should acquire some part of the benefit which America enjoys in her large internal free market ? The whole of the purchasing power of Europe together is only about equal to that of the United States of America; and at the best Europe will only achieve a partial measure of what America possesses under her constitution. Freedom of trade in Europe will in any case be limited both in range and in extent; it will not comprise all European countries, and it will not be complete.

If, as I believe, a more prosperous Europe would benefit the world as a whole, it is surely worth seeing whether a scheme at once practicable and equitable can be produced.

I suggest, for example, that a plan based upon the

following principles would merit sympathetic consideration by the world as a whole.

Firstly, the object of the scheme, clearly defined in the preamble of the agreement, should be to promote freer economic intercourse between the contracting states, and to secure the substantial and progressive removal of economic barriers *inter se*.

Secondly, it must be made clear that the object is not to encourage monopolies, but equal opportunity. The advantage which Henry Ford in the U.S.A. has over Morris or the Fiat Company is not monopoly (for he has the most intense competition with other American manufacturers), but an assurance that over a very large market he will not be subject to a tariff handicap.

Thirdly, all the negotiating states should undertake not to increase tariffs either against each other or against non-participating states, unless the latter make such new increases in their tariffs as to change the whole situation.

Fourthly, the plan of progressive reductions within the negotiating group should be such as to make their tariff levels more equal (the greatest reductions therefore being where tariffs are now highest); and within the group there should be the most complete and unrestricted application of the most-favoured-nation clause, based upon a standard nomenclature and classification.

Fifthly, the association should be and remain open on equal terms to all countries of all continents.

Sixthly, countries who do not enter the association, but whose tariffs are as low as the lowest in the association, should be given the advantage of the lower duties without themselves being under any obligation to impose higher tariffs against outside countries.

A scheme so safeguarded would utilise the strongest force capable of securing greater freedom of trade in such a way as to prevent its being abused and leading to increased tariffs against non-European countries. It would reduce the inequalities in the world's present economic units, which are based upon political frontiers that have no relation to economic needs and cause loss and disequilibrium of many kinds. Other countries would have an inducement to lower their own tariffs in the prospect of thus securing the lower rates applicable within the association. Separate groups formed under such a scheme might coalesce with each other till a large part both of Europe and of other continents would enjoy some of the advantages which America has in her large internal free market. Their growing prosperity would in the end increase that of other countries also, including America – just as the expansion of America herself in the last fifty years, has undoubtedly, on a long and broad view, enriched Europe.

If, however, Europe or pairs or groups of countries within it are left to work out schemes for reciprocal preferences for themselves, while the rest of the world adopts a merely negative attitude, they will either fail or they will produce schemes which will not include adequate safeguards against abuse and will involve serious friction with other countries.

I suggest, in these circumstances, that non-European countries would do well to follow, and to some extent participate in, the European negotiations, in no merely negative spirit, and to aim rather at safeguarding than blocking. They might even take an initiative, offering to agree, upon clearly defined conditions, that goods should pass between countries desiring to form, for example, a Danubian association at specially favourable rates. In any case, if a scheme is produced, it is to be hoped that it will be carefully examined as a whole, attention not being focussed simply on one feature of it, the differentiation of duties.

§ *Alternative Policies*

A few months ago this looked to be not only the most promising, but the only practicable, line of progress towards greater freedom of trade. It may still be so for some time to come. But events are moving fast. Restrictions on foreign exchange are now more formidable impediments to world trade than tariffs. The 'clearing house' arrangements between certain countries for foreign exchange operations have made the most-favoured-nation principle inoperative. New tariff systems have removed some of the old inequalities. As the temporary factors pass away tariff negotiations will be resumed on a new basis and in a new perspective. Conditions that seemed set and unyielding are now fluid, obstacles that looked insuperable may soon prove less formidable. It may be that the time will soon come when a more permanent and general reform will be possible. There is no reason why the method of regional association should wait for the general movement. There is no reason why, if the wider reform becomes practicable, it should wait because regional association has begun. In a reform of tariffs on a world basis the aim should be, as already suggested, to make them as low and as nearly equal as possible; stable for definite periods, and subject to reduction by successive stages.

This is one, and the better, alternative. But we must not forget that there is another. World trade may be restricted to small dimensions, through every country excluding imports of everything which (at whatever expense) it can make or produce at home. Along this line of development, America might withdraw within herself, arresting and almost abandoning her foreign investments, sacrificing her export trade, and cultivating an isolated self-sufficiency on the lower level of prosperity which that would necessitate. As the world closed against her Great Britain might be forced to supplement such preferential trade with the Dominions and India as may be practicable, with a policy of exploiting and closing in her non-selfgoverning Empire from the rest of the world, against all the traditions and principles of her history. This line of development would mean loss to every country, impoverishment to countries like Switzerland which have no similar resources, and an organisation of the world into separate units and groups which would soon be dangerous and ultimately fatal to world peace. It is along this path that the world is now proceeding. It needs to reverse its policy deliberately if it is to escape the consequences.

Let us, in conclusion, note again the direct connection of commercial policy with the depression and the crisis. Not only have high tariffs reduced the level of general prosperity; their inequality has increased the disequilibria, which credit and finance have proved inadequate to adjust, for they have been highest where, if the strain was to be relieved, they should have been lowest. The sudden changes of tariffs have dislocated trade and have impeded the corrective function of the gold standard by stopping an inflow of imports just when it was needed. And now, with gold no longer available in debtor countries for export and with foreign lending stopped and unlikely for a long time to be renewed on its former scale, a violent change in the balance of trade is taking place. It may come through an almost complete cessation of the exports of creditor gold-surplus countries. It may come by their admission of more imports. Apart from an unlikely resumption of lending on a sufficient scale, there is no other alternative. The choice is not whether the course of trade should be changed. Changed it must be; but it may be adjusted by a different distribution of an undiminished total of world trade, or by the complete sacrifice of a large part of that total, with great loss to all concerned.

So much for the relation between commercial policies and the immediate crisis. But their importance is much greater when we consider the permanent foundations of the world's economic structure. So long as small countries, lacking the resources within their frontier to support their populations in reasonable comfort, are blockaded by surrounding tariffs; so long as over-production of particular commodities is stimulated by protection and by tariff; so long as the framework to which economic enterprise has to adapt itself is subject to violent and sudden change, the world can never hope for any steady progress in prosperity. The very facilities of an advanced world system which should assist that progress will make the interruptions to it more violent. Credit and loans, for instance, which can accelerate development when it is on a sound basis, will only aggravate the ultimate loss if the basis is unsound.

The worst feature of the present tariff systems of the world is that they have no organic relationship to general policy, whether national or international. They have been framed for the most part by successive concessions to sectional pressure. The tariff policy of creditor countries, for example, is not influenced by the fundamental fact that they need to be paid what they are owed by a world which can only in the long run pay by goods and services. And changes are made without consultation with other countries, often without warning, though every import shut out is, of course, a foreigner's export.

In some respects, at least, we may hope for reform. A part of the public support which those demanding tariffs have secured is due to the feeling that, under present conditions, there must be more deliberate and collective planning of a nation's economic life. Those who have given their support on this ground are likely to insist increasingly that it shall be better used for real public and social benefit. The maladjustments, which we have reviewed, in the monetary and credit systems, and in economic processes, all now enforce the moral that each sphere of economic policy must be related to the whole. Moreover, there is a growing recognition that, as the World Economic Conference said, 'tariffs, though within the sovereign jurisdiction of the separate states, are not a matter of purely domestic interest.' We may therefore hope that, to an increasing extent, whatever be their height and general character, they will be part of a deliberate, general, and reasonably stable policy, and rarely be changed except after consultation with all those concerned, consumers as well as producers at home, and the representatives of foreign countries, whose interests are affected, as well as home manufacturers.

CHAPTER V

THE GOOD AND EVILS OF CARTELS

INDUSTRIAL ORGANISATION

INDUSTRIAL organisation has many aspects, and might be discussed from several angles. We might consider how it has been, or could be, improved, in order that more material goods may be produced with a given amount of human effort and the level of human prosperity thus be raised. Or we might consider the special importance of the 'rationalisation' of certain industries in a particular country which, like Great Britain, has been losing something of its competitive position. Or again – and there could be no subject of greater interest – we might examine the social measures to deal with the unemployment which at once reflects the defects of organisation at any given moment and also accompanies the process of reform, and is thus in both respects essentially a 'problem of industry,' as Sir William Beveridge terms it in his classic work.

The provision of a form of insurance, which will prevent the loss, thus inevitably arising from both the defects and the reform of industrial organisation, from falling solely either upon the workers or public or private charity, has been recognised as a measure both of social justice and social necessity by many industrialised countries, and may soon be by the others. The perpetual menace of destitution has been the most intolerable feature of the modern industrial system.

It is perhaps unfortunate, since it is so difficult to realise imaginatively an experience not personally felt, that those who either direct industry, or study economic processes, since they themselves usually have either reasonable security or reserves of income, have not themselves known this menace. Certainly this evil will now no longer be tolerated. Abuses and mistakes in particular systems exist and need remedy; but the line of progress is not through abolition but through reform; insurance will remain and be extended. The task of maintenance during intervals of varying activity, and of absorption elsewhere when the number of workers required in a given enterprise is reduced through rationalisation, is thus an integral part of the problem of industrial organisation.

We can, however, deal here with none of these special aspects of industrial organisation. We are not now concerned with the way in which productive capacity can be increased, desirable though that is as the means of normal progress, but with the special defects which prevent existing capacity from being utilised. Nor is the particular position of different countries our theme; but the general world depression. The displacement of labour again, from whatever cause it arises, is also from this point of view a part of the general question of the elasticity, the expansive and adaptive quality of the whole economic mechanism. The organisation of industry here concerns us so far as it has contributed to the maladjustments which constitute the depression and may help to correct them.

We have seen how recent developments in the form and scale of organisation have in some respects impeded the working of the competitive system as it was known in the last century. Over a large part of industry, particularly that in which standardisation and mass production

give large economies, in all the most advanced industrial countries, the size of the producing businesses
has become very great; and by their size and by their
association with each other, they have often acquired
many of the characteristics of a partial monopoly. Several
consequences follow. When there is over-production the
natural corrective of elimination by falling prices and
profits does not necessarily operate, or it may operate more
slowly. For financially powerful institutions are able to
continue output for a time at a loss and to pile up stocks
for a hoped for recovery in demand. Or their reciprocal
arrangements may enable them to hold up prices, and so
prevent the tapping of new markets. And then a sudden
collapse in these arrangements may throw excess stocks
on the market and demoralise it completely. Moreover,
the possession by great industrial institutions of large
funds, and of a credit upon which they can raise their own
capital, may weaken the power of the financial authorities, under the direction of the Central Bank, to compel
any necessary adjustments through monetary policy. This
has very notably been the position in America. In addition, so far as any arrangement within a given sphere of
industry enables prices to be held above the competitive
price based on costs, there is danger of abuse and exploitation of the public.

   That, however, is only one side of the picture. Large
scale organisation is a stabilising, as well as in some respects a dislocating, factor. If it may both intensify and
prolong a serious depression, it may smooth out or eliminate minor fluctuations, saving industry from unnecessary
interruption, the consumer from sharp downward and upward movements of prices, and labour from periods of unemployment. Adjustments seen to be necessary may be
quickly made by deliberate decision over a wide scale.

So, too, industry's ability to finance itself without public issues through the financial institutions of the country relieves it of certain dangers; and in this respect the industry of America has in the last ten years enjoyed a substantial advantage over that of Great Britain.

The dangers of exploitation of the consumer too have many correctives. The experience of America has been instructive in this respect. When corners and combines first became practicable, the first instinct of those who formed them was to concentrate their attention on the attractive goal of making quick profits by raising prices against the consumer. The immediate consequence was anti-trust legislation, rarely and with difficulty applied, but so damaging when it was applied as to be an overhanging terror to all concerns whose policy roused public indignation. This created a very healthy sensitiveness to public opinion; and encouraged the industrial leaders to turn their attention to securing all the economies that are made possible by large scale production; to reducing prices and so expanding the market. Publicity, with a cumbrous penal law in the background, and the visible benefits of a constantly increasing number of consumers with the power to purchase, became more effective safeguards of the public interest than the actual enforcement of the law. Moreover, no monopoly can be permanent if its prices are so high above costs as to encourage new competition from outside; nor, even if it is complete within its own sphere, can it escape from the competition of alternative products to which the public can turn. Gas and electricity; coal and oil; road, rail and river transport, would thus compete even if there was a monopoly of each. On balance there can be little doubt that the public has greatly gained by large scale production, even when it has involved some restriction of competition.

More important, however, from our present point of view, is the opportunity which the grouping of industry into large units affords for general planning and direction. A few leaders in each of a number of great industries in a country such as America could, sometimes alone, sometimes in association with similar leaders in other countries, survey the situation of the industry as a whole; could decide whether the present or prospective situation required reduction or increase of output, or a change in its direction; and could do much to see that any desirable policy which so emerged guided the action of the constituent business units. Moreover, a manageable number of persons from the different main industries could authoritatively voice the views of national industry as a whole; and could in turn ensure by their collective influence that any national economic policy found, at a particular time, to be desirable should guide industrial plans and action.

A score or so of the leading industrialists of America, with less than a dozen leading members of financial institutions, associated with other persons of equal standing from other spheres including that of the Government service, might be formed into a national council of unchallengeable authority. If such a body decided, for example, at a given moment, that a boom was working up to a point at which collapse must follow, it might induce the banks and Stock Exchange to discourage share speculation on margin and on borrowed money; and the great industries both to refrain from using their capital-raising powers in such a way as to hamper a desirable restrictive monetary policy by the Federal Reserve Board, and also to diminish an output that, on a general review, would evidently soon be excessive.

The reduction of output would perhaps be most

difficult. The arrangement of quotas for individual producing units is extremely difficult, as well as being at present illegal under the Sherman Laws. I suggest one method which would leave the relative position of competing units unchanged, and so avoid impracticable and embittered negotiations; a method which would perhaps be within the law even as it stands, and would in most cases effectively put on the brake just as it was needed.

If the national council decided that it was desirable that output should be reduced, could they not secure a temporary cessation of new sales on the instalment system ? Instalment purchase has substantial advantages when prosperity is going steadily up at a pace and under conditions which do not involve a sharp set-back. If a man is assured of a margin of income for, say, the next three years which he would like to use for an automobile that he cannot afford to pay for at once; and if the automobile will be a source of enjoyment to him for as long as the instalment payments last; there are no sound economic objections to the arrangement and there are some substantial advantages. It taps a new form of credit, extends the market, and enables many to add a new source of enjoyment otherwise out of their reach. But in the period of a boom working up to its peak, the system obviously increases the dislocation. Just when output is too high for the prospective demand it further increases it; and when the depression comes and purchasing power is reduced, a substantial margin of the smaller incomes is mortgaged to paying for production that has already taken place and is no longer available to support current output. I can see no more effective method of slowing the pace of output just when that is needed than a simultaneous temporary suspension of instalment sales. And a national council composed as suggested might well develop sufficient authority to make such a policy operative throughout the industries covered.

§ *International Cartels*

In many cases it is obvious that the objects of the large scale organisation of industry, and the formation of associations, combines, trusts, cartels, etc., with some of the characteristics of a partial monopoly, cannot be fully attained on a purely national basis. We have thus seen a considerable development in recent years of 'international industrial agreements,' or 'cartels.'

In most respects international cartels have the same main advantages and dangers as national ones, but on a wider scale. They may bring great economies, and they may involve abuses; they may either smooth out or intensify occasional fluctuations. They are capable of being a foundation of collective leadership and useful control of policy. They require similar safeguards against abuse. But they have certain special features of their own.

The Report of the World Economic Conference of 1927, in a chapter too often forgotten, has a short but admirable summary of their limits, merits, and of the precautions which are desirable in the public interest. 'Their field of operation,' it points out, is 'usually limited to branches of production which are already centralised, and to products supplied in bulk, or in recognised grades,' and they can only therefore be a partial solution of the general economic problem. They may, under certain conditions, 'secure a more methodical organisation of production and a reduction of costs and act as a check on uneconomic competition and reduce the evils resulting from fluctuations in industrial activity.' They may, if the advantages of the economies are shared between the other parties concerned, benefit all of them, giving not only greater profits to the producer, but higher wages and greater stability to the worker and lower prices to the consumer. On the other hand, they may 'encourage monopolistic tendencies and the application of unsound business methods, may check technical progress' and exploit the consumer. They are 'a development which has to be recognised and must be considered as good or bad according to the spirit which rules the constitution and operation of the agreements, and in particular according to the measure in which those directing them are actuated by a sense of the general interest.'

The Conference did not recommend an international juridical régime for the prevention of abuse, but urged that the League of Nations should watch their development and publish reports as to their effects upon technical progress, the conditions of labour, and upon prices; and that the Governments should help in its task. They believed that if this were done abuses would be largely prevented, and the measures of safeguard provided in national legislation could be made more effective; and that their development upon lines conducing to the general interest would be encouraged.

Here in this authoritative report is a charter of the utmost value, if it could be adequately utilised. Careful, adequate, courageous publicity by a central international body, equipped with the necessary resources and impartial as between countries and classes, would certainly encourage all that is best in the movement and, duly related to the national penal legislation in reserve, would greatly reduce the dangers of abuse.

And if these dangers can in practice be rendered

negligible, international cartels can certainly play a most valuable rôle, surpassing not only in scale but in character that of national agreements.

In the first place, they afford the means of planning supply over the whole range of an industry and so securing stabilisation as no national agreement could do, except behind prohibitive tariffs. They could provide a vital constituent element in a General World Economic Council, related to the great private organisations of every country through its members, and to the Governments through the mechanism of the League of Nations. Such a Council could at once, with authority and with practical influence, discuss on a world range those questions of finance and control of output which we have described in speaking of the national councils. And a policy so emerging might, through the machinery of the national councils, and with the personal aid of the members, guide the direction of industrial planning throughout most of the world. It could do much to introduce into a system, which still left room for enterprise, variety, freedom and competition, the now essential element of collective planning. We shall see in the next chapter how such an extensive and flexible association of industrial leaders might be related to the general machine of government and be an instrument both of stabilisation and of the defence of the public interest.

It must not be understood from what has been said that this development, whether national or international, involves the establishment of monopoly or the elimination of competition. Large scale organisations and associations of a kind which can be used for collective planning are not incompatible with very keen competition. They limit the forms of competition, sometimes restrict it, sometimes turn it into special directions. But usually an area, and often a substantial area, is left where there is enough competition to restrict the limits of practicable abuse. This is certainly desirable, for the dependence of the public upon external safeguards is correspondingly reduced.

But the possibility of monopolistic exploitation always remains a danger. Since, therefore, large scale organisation and world wide associations are likely to grow rapidly, the public is vitally concerned in seeing that all practicable safeguards are available. Of these, publicity through the League organisation, which happily for economic purposes enjoys the collaboration of countries like America which have not accepted its political engagements, could easily be made one of the most effective. But it can only act with sufficient external support.

There is little indication at present that the big cartels are ready to give the information, not about secret processes or inventions, but about costs, price scales, etc., which is needed; or that the Governments will exert the pressure required to compel them. Actual legal powers, under national legislation, would be desirable. But even without these much might be done if the public, both through their Governments and through representative organisations and the Press, would urge and require the League to pursue the task entrusted to it. If the League, adequately supported, collected information from other sources and asked the cartels for what it needed from them, and then published what it could; pointing out clearly where its report was defective because information had been refused by such and such (named) cartels, rapid advance could be made. Unhappily, the general public and the consumers are everywhere inadequately organised for the defence of their interests. But the products of cartelised concerns are the raw materials of many industries, strongly organised for other purposes; and the leaders of these industries, if they would, could give an effective impetus to an impartial and vigilant watch over their interests, which would be of great value to them.

Another sphere in which the rôle of international cartels has been much discussed is that of tariffs and commercial policy. It has been said that the industrialists of different countries, having agreed between themselves as to quotas or the allocation of markets, will tell their respective Governments that tariffs are no longer needed. This is an exaggeration. As a League Committee has pointed out, 'combines are often concluded on the basis of the commercial possibilities resulting from the protection afforded by the existing tariffs, and a change of tariffs modifying these possibilities would be regarded as jeopardising the combine itself.' It is also misleading because, even if the partial impediment to trade of a tariff were removed, but only to make place for a complete impediment in the form of unconditional reservation of the home market for the home manufacturer, the situation might be made not better but worse.

It is true, however, that when the cartels are adequately safeguarded from abuse they may put an end to some of the evils of the present tariff system. An agreement made from outside the sphere of Governments, though safeguarded from abuse by them, may exempt Ministers and officials from the demoralising influence of competitive appeals for ever-increasing protection by the state; and may put an end to that especially vicious form of tariff which is designed to give the home manufacturer a home base from which he can launch a destructive subsidised campaign of dumping, in order to dislocate and destroy a foreign rival in his own national market. Even the mention of such an instance is a reminder both of the

need and of the difficulties of securing the necessary safeguards against the abuse of cartels. Nevertheless, the
task is not impossible, and the potential advantages are
very great. They may secure comparative stabilisation
for reasonable periods both of prices and employment,
prevent deliberate destruction by dumping and friction,
and provide the elements out of which a machinery for
world planning and world policy may be developed.

Finally, international cartels, when national associations
already exist, have a further significance and value of great
interest. They cut across national frontiers and help to
eliminate them as factors in the world's economic life and
competitive struggle. They thus create interests and forces
which will tend to counteract the competitive nationalism which is the world's chief danger. Every grouping of the world's activities and interests along lines different from those of the national frontiers is a help in this
direction. Whenever the citizens of different countries
meet on a basis of common interest that transcends and cuts
across frontiers, whether they are industrialists, or trade
unionists, or financiers, or scientists, or schoolmasters;
whenever organisations develop on lines determined
by their special purpose, — industry, labour conditions,
education or finance, — and draw their members indiffer-
ently from every country, the foundations of international
relations are broadened, and international amity no longer
rests precariously on purely political foundations.

CHAPTER VI

SAFEGUARDS OF THE PUBLIC INTEREST

COLLECTIVE LEADERSHIP AND CONTROL

THE world's economic mechanism has lost its self-adjusting quality. And never was it so much needed. New process succeeds new process; the public taste and demand alter incalculably; and every improvement in the transmission of news and in transport increases both the range and the rapidity of the reactions of every change. The mechanism which adjusts production to new demands; which corrects sporadic excesses of supply; which moves capital where it is needed; which stops, or directs or expands enterprise; which adapts every activity to this shifting environment, needs to be flexible and rapid. And everywhere we see that it is precisely these qualities which it has been losing.

We can perhaps, here and there, restore the frictionless self-adjusting quality of the old freely working competitive system. But in every sphere which we have examined we find that this alone will not suffice. We need to supplement it by planned direction, by a regulative control. In the sphere of money and gold, for example, we may perhaps remove some of the impediments to the traditional working of the gold standard, such as the sudden imposition of new tariffs, — but we can never have a tolerable medium of world trade unless Governments and Central Banks pursue the agreed objective of a stable general price level through deliberate and co-operative action. In the credit system we may gradually re-establish the confidence of the investor, but we can never avoid the disasters entailed by ill-judged loans unless there is at least a recognised standard of conduct and some accepted basis of policy by the great issue houses. Programmes of industrial production again need obviously to be based more upon collective estimates, and to be subject, where necessary, in their execution to some collective influence. And tariff policies will clearly lead to disaster if they continue to be the outcome of the competitive pressure of sectional interests, and to be unrelated to the world situation or even to a general national policy.

The defects of the capitalist system have been increasingly robbing it of its benefits. They are now threatening its existence. A period of depression and crisis is one in which its great merit, the expansion of productive capacity under the stimulus of competitive gain, seems wasted; and its main defect, an increasing inability to utilise productive capacity fully and to distribute what it produces tolerably, is seen at its worst. And, in the mood of desperation caused by impoverishment and unemployment, the challenge of another system becomes more formidable. No one can expect that even if we now get through without disaster, we can long avoid social disintegration and revolution on the widest scale if we have only a prospect of recurring depressions, perhaps of increasing violence.

We have indeed before us only the alternatives of collective leadership, collective control, or chaos—not indeed quite mutually exclusive; for in practice we shall have something of all three. We must do our best to eliminate the third, and make the best mixture we can of the first two. For this is no simple choice between two alternatives: 'Hands off industry by the politician' or 'Leave it to the Government'; 'private enterprise' or

Pr

'state control'; 'Capitalism' or 'Communism.' We evade our intricate and complex task if we think it can be solved by slogans instead of reason.

Let us try to tread our way towards our goal through a series of propositions – surely obvious, though rarely accepted equally by opposing extremists.

In almost every sphere of economic activity the general public interest is involved, but it is in a very varying degree. In many spheres, but not in all, and in differing measure, the public interest is safeguarded by competition within the framework of law. Of a maker of men's straw hats we may require no more than that his employees should work under proper conditions, defined in factory legislation; competition will secure that the public gets what hats its taste demands, and at a reasonable price. The public interest is greater where the product is, like coal or oil, a basis of industrial life; and if partial or complete monopolies are formed, safeguards can no longer be found in competition. It is even greater in the case of currency, which must be a monopoly, and the general mechanism of credit and finance, where competition may itself bring dangers and abuses.

Where the public interest is involved it must be protected. To some extent an internal code or traditions developed within a particular trade or profession may afford a safeguard. But this will not suffice. Individuals may refrain from exploiting a privilege to their profit, but no class ever does so for long. Neither industrialists, nor lawyers, nor bankers – not even Central Bankers of whom it seems sometimes to have been suggested – are by virtue of their office exempt from human frailty and folly; nor are trade unionists or politicians. Some form of external safeguard is needed, varying as the public interest is great or small, and as competition is effective or not.

§ *State Control*

There are many kinds of external safeguard. State management, or detailed state control, is only one. There are indeed certain spheres, certain periods and certain conditions in which it presents great advantages. Where a complete monopoly is needed, as for the delivery of mails, exceptional incompetence or corruption in Government would alone justify leaving the work to private enterprise. And in special periods, such as that of a great war, a very extensive state control is necessary and brings great economies.

The results attained in Great Britain, for example, were amazing. At a moderate estimate, between a half and two-thirds of the productive capacity of the country was withdrawn into combatant or other war service. And yet, throughout the war, Great Britain sustained the whole of her military effort and maintained her civilian population at a standard of life which was never intolerably low, and for some periods and for some classes as comfortable as in times of peace. She did this without, on balance, drawing any aid from other countries; for she imported on borrowed money less than she supplied on loaned money. She therefore maintained the whole of the current consumption both of her war effort and of her civilian population by means of current production. She used up some existing capital, but not much more than the new capital she created, which remained of value. Her internal loans do not enter into this account, for they are only a method of taxation and not of doing what is essentially impossible, making the production of a later age available for present use.

The substantial fact remains that, with more than half her productive effort withdrawn for war service in the field or the factory, Great Britain met the scarcely diminished necessities of her civilian population by current production. True, those who were before idle now worked; and others worked harder; in particular, women entered productive employment; demand was simplified, and the difficulty of finding a market eliminated, by the conditions of the time; patriotism enlisted in Government service men previously sharpened in competitive life. Hasty inferences applied to other conditions would be dangerous. But this experience is worth remembering when it is urged that a Government service must always be incompetent, and that the economies of state control are always illusory.

The fact is that the suitability of an enterprise for state control varies greatly according to its character. Where its development has already resulted in a practical monopoly, so that the public get the benefit neither of competitive prices nor of controlled profits; where such competition as remains takes the form of attracting the consumer by advertisement, costly shops, appeals of agents on commission, and not of reduction of price or improvement of quality; and where hazardous experiment is not greatly needed; there is a *prima facie* case for the state. The case is proportionately weaker so far as these conditions do not apply. A priority list of comparative suitability might be drawn up on this principle, and would be a good guide as to what should be socialised, to the extent to which socialisation is desirable.

But how far socialisation is desirable depends upon another quite different factor, namely, how far the forces that determine the personnel and conduct of those who control the public service are compatible with a tolerable level of competence and honesty in management. This condition varies greatly at different periods and in different countries; and depends very much on what are the other functions which the Government has to discharge. If Government is expected to examine the competing claims of organised private interests for public aid, in the form of variable tariffs or subsidy, it will not retain either the honesty or the time to undertake an extension of real public service – or even to discharge its present duties properly. You can get a policeman to control traffic, or act as an information agent to tourists, and still expect him to arrest a thief; but make him act in his public office as a sales agent for any tradesman powerful enough to secure this privilege, and you will leave him with neither the time nor the character he needs for his primary public duty. It is well to remember that when industrialists demand 'Hands off Industry' because Government is dishonest and corrupt, their charges are largely true because of the pressure they have themselves exercised upon it to give them more than a fair run in a free field.

Nor should we hastily accept the libel on human nature that it is only under the perpetual stimulant of daily fluctuations of loss and profit that man will do his best work. A penalty for failure that is more than casual or merely unfortunate, a reward for good work that is more than momentary or accidental; yes: but that is compatible with a public service, though not always secured in it. How few indeed of those who do the world's work do so under the conscious stimulus of constantly varying profit ! Entrepreneurs have this stimulus, but the men they direct work for wages and salaries which are stable for long periods and only differ from those of a public service in a somewhat greater insecurity, which is destined to be reduced. And such leaders of industry do themselves an injustice when they consider that their own motive is only or mainly that of unlimited profit, as the best of them always show when they have the opportunity of creative work under different conditions.

The best work can be obtained in the public service – if the conditions are favourable; if the task is constructive and obviously useful; and if the service itself enjoys a real but conditional public respect, so that professional traditions can develop. The competence of a Government service depends upon the character of government itself, of the work which it undertakes, and the forces which determine its policy. While and so long as the general public life of a country is at a low level, we must accept the special dangers of incompetence in state management as setting a limit to its extension. But we should not fail to recognise that whenever, whether within the public service, in the strict sense, or outside it, we can establish conditions which make the worker feel that he is the servant of the community and not of private individuals, we not only give him a new status which he now insistently demands, but provide a new stimulus to good work which may even be more powerful than the old.

However, for our present problem, direct state management offers no substantial solution, though here and there it could be profitably extended if Government could be relieved of some of the functions it had better not have assumed. We are now considering, not a complete substitution of another system for our own, with a dictatorship at its head, but the reform of a system which leaves room for private capital, private enterprise, and democratic institutions, and still safeguards the public interest. The extent to which direct and complete state management can with net advantage expand under present conditions is limited. And happily there are alternatives.

A much more fruitful line of development is that of

mixed forms of management in which private interest and public representation are combined. In England we have examples in the Central Electricity Board; the Port of London Authority; the Traffic Bill introduced by the Labour Government (which proposed a monopoly for London traffic and some control of rates and service, with the stimulus of a variable dividend – but variable within a fixed limit), while the British Broadcasting Company is an instance of a special form of public management.

The last of these well illustrates the advantage of public control if we compare the record of wireless with that of the cinematograph in England. Both are potentially instruments of public amusement, intelligent enjoyment, and adult education; the first has utilised its opportunities worthily; the second, under uncontrolled private management (except for a merely negative censorship) has outdone even the worst of the press in triviality. There are many examples of such mixed private and public institutions in other countries, notably in Germany. There is no standard type, and must be none. Flexible varied systems are needed, so as both to encourage the enterprise required and to prevent abuse and exploitation.

Central Banks present a special problem. The sphere of currency, banking and finance is, of course, of vital importance as the basis of all economic activity. Currency is and must be a monopoly. Its basis is determined by legislation. The responsibility for its daily management and control is however usually entrusted to Central Banks, who also control in a large measure the whole of the national money and credit structure. The public is well aware of the dangers of currency management by Governments after the chaotic disorganisation following the war. The exceptional strain of that period made the test not altogether a fair one, but it remains true that there is great danger of inflation in direct management by a Minister subject to the daily exigencies and direct pressure which any Government experiences. There was a violent swing back therefore to management by Central Banks. These institutions are sometimes, as in England, completely free of formal public control within their charter, and are managed by persons chosen by share-holders or nominated by private bodies. In other cases the Governor is appointed by the Government; and in many the personnel of the Board of Directors is nominated by representative national institutions.

The absence of public representation is sometimes com-pensated for by the growth of traditions corresponding with the responsibilities. Even its harshest critics, for example, do not allege that the policy of the Bank of England in changing its discount rate is guided by a calculation of the effect on the dividends of its share-holders. It is, however, more plausibly alleged that a Central Bank will tend to reflect the financial interests with which it is most in contact, rather than those of industry or trade whose fortunes are equally affected. Nor can it be assumed lightly that traditions such as have grown grad-ually in London will quickly develop wherever a new Central Bank is established, or that in a Balkan country a Board chosen by shareholders will necessarily pursue the straight path of duty more than a Minister of Finance, responsible to Parliament. Their temptations and their deviations from the strict path will be different, but may not be unequal. The wide range of the powers of Central Banks over the whole of a nation's life remains in striking contrast with the narrowness of the electing constituency from which most of those who direct them draw their authority; and cannot but increase the demand for reform, however this may be mitigated or postponed by exceptional individuals or traditions. Government control of finance, under extreme difficulties, failed after the war; private control of finance has also failed since. Neither can afford to throw stones at the other.

The problem of the constitution of Central Banks is indeed one with two aspects, and not one; that of avoiding the dangers of political pressure on the one hand, and that of safeguarding the general public interest on the other. The solution is not found yet, and will doubtless not be the same for all countries. It will probably involve more public representation in the case of the Central Bank than would usually be desirable for the rest of the Banking system, deposit banks, issuing, accepting houses, etc., or the rest of the financial system including the Stock Exchange.

In the latter cases, as already suggested, what is needed is collective leadership from within working inside a framework of some public regulation and related both to central economic policy and to the general interests of economic progress. We have seen how in 1926–28 competitive and irresponsible foreign lending, limited by no accepted standards or rules, ignorant and heedless of the political factors and consequences involved, created a situation that resulted later, as it was bound to, in disaster; and how limited is the number of institutions whose co-operation would be needed to remove this evil. Half a dozen large houses in America; the Bank of England exercising its influence over a few issuing banks in London; a few authorities in France, have the combined power to prevent all the worst abuses of undesirable foreign lending, especially to

Governments and public authorities. A collective leadership and an agreement upon certain rules and principles are needed within each of these countries; this should then be co-ordinated internationally; and through the appropriate institutions due account should be taken of the political factors, and the necessary safeguards provided. So too as regards the institutions concerned with the dealings in existing shares, the Stock Exchange on the one hand and the banks which provide facilities for speculators on the other; there is an urgent need for a collective leadership which would prevent such disastrous speculative excesses as occurred in 1929; and this again is a manageable, as it is a necessary, task.

In industrial organisation, now that integration has proceeded so far, it must go further. The scale is now such that it may impede the automatic adjustments of the old system and, so far as it does not eliminate competition, it may change the form. But organisation has not yet reached the point at which collective planning of production, or its control where it is proving excessive or unbalanced, is yet possible. It has developed no mechanism which enables industry as a whole to contribute to the formation of a general economic policy and secure its application when adopted.

Collective leadership, a continued process of integration, and increased planning within each main sphere of the national life, in finance, and in each main industry, are however clearly not enough. These are indispensable in themselves and the necessary basis of anything more. But more is needed if planned direction is to take in the world's activities the place that has become essential. For the major lines of policy, the leaders in each sphere need to be brought both together and into relation with the machine of government.

§ *National Economic Councils*

At this point we come to a very significant development of the last decade; the formation of national economic councils. These differ greatly in form; they work with varying success; they are still in an experimental stage; and the best methods and composition, which will not be the same for all countries, have yet to be discovered. Nor have the more specialised institutions from which they must draw their membership and real influence been yet sufficiently developed. But the spontaneous and independent movement for the creation of such councils in so many countries gives a strong presumption that such a development responds to a real and general need in the post-war world. Institutions, through which persons representative of the main economic activities of the country are brought into regular association with each other and with the Government, are in operation at least in France, Germany, Italy, Poland, Belgium, Czechoslovakia, Spain and Great Britain; similar proposals are under consideration in Greece; and I have myself during the last year been asked to prepare schemes for India and China. While no corresponding permanent institutions exist in America and Australia, there have been special enquiries serving in part the same purpose.

Experimental, often cumbrous, usually ineffective, as these councils are at present, they may ultimately prove an adjunct of great value to the machine of government. The worst danger of the modern world is that the specialised activities of man will outrun his capacity of regulative wisdom; that the mechanism of central direction and restraint will prove too cumbrous and too weak for the complex and powerful forces with which it has to deal; that the thrusting energy of individuals and organised sections will destroy and not extend the commonweal.

Certainly Government is everywhere now proving inadequate to the tasks which it has assumed. Government does not direct, it is pushed into action by those who have a concentrated interest and no general responsibility. Rarely indeed is there any guiding framework of deliberately formed policy, determining the character, priority, and due relation of its several measures. Rather we have a mere jumble of unrelated actions, each a concession to external pressure. There is only one line of solution. Government must rid itself of tasks for which it is unsuited; rule more by principle, by basic law and regulation, and less by meticulous provision. And since, even so, the task of regulating and directing activities so complex as those of the modern world will be too great for Government itself, it must ally itself with every practicable form of external aid. It is here that the National Economic Council may be of value.

In industry and trade, in banking and finance, in the professions, there are institutions which are capable of representing more than merely sectional interests. They may have been formed primarily for defence of a common interest against an opposing organisation, or against competitors, or the public. But they have, or may have, another aspect; that of preserving and raising the standard of competence and the development of traditions which are in the general public interest. This function of specialised voluntary institutions can be encouraged both from within and without; and they can then play a vital part in the regulative control of the world's economic life. They will of course need to be suitably organised and constituted. In particular if they are to fulfil the public functions here proposed, the workers must be given an appropriate representation. They will require further to be related to each other and also to the central guardian of the public interest, the Government; and this may be suitably arranged through membership of a National Economic Council.

The National Economic Council in turn needs, to the extent to which economic life is international, to be related to the similar institutions of other countries, and for this purpose a World Economic Council is required, drawing its membership from the National Councils, and associated with the League of Nations as a National Council is with its own Government.

Meantime, the efficacy of such councils must depend upon the character of the more specialised institutions on which they are based. Such a development will be gradual, unequal, flexible and varied in form. Here and there a particular institution, perhaps a Central Bank, perhaps a new form of Chamber of Commerce, will develop traditions and win a public respect which will secure, with no more than latent powers of external control, an adequate regulation of a given sphere of the national life. Here and there those who manage a monopoly, otherwise dangerous to the public, will develop excellent standards of practice, which will need no external reinforcement beyond publicity and their knowledge that any abuse would lead to new legislation they would prefer to avoid. But standing behind them all, the Central Government, the only ultimate guardian of the public interest, because it is the only one whose authority is drawn from the public itself, must watch, intervening when necessary, but only where necessary. Where internal standards and traditions suffice, Government is best passive. It should welcome whatever relieves it of its task. It must decentralise; it must delegate; but it must not abdicate.

So only can we build an ordered society, which will neither disintegrate into chaos nor yet deprive us of the freedom, the variety, and the enterprise, which has been the promise and, with all its defects, in a large measure the gift, of the system to which we were born. To drift into either chaos or communism is to fail in the specific task of our age, which is to reform — perhaps to transform — the civilisation we know, not to destroy it in despair at its defects, in hope of we know not what. A new civilisation might indeed ultimately emerge — but it would not be ours; and who can foresee after what intervening disaster ? We at least who, in whatever capacity, have had any share in the responsibilities of government in this century would have failed in our trust, would have betrayed our generation. Not ours the merit if others then build where we have allowed to perish.

PART III

The Political Scene

CHAPTER I

ARMAMENTS AND ALLIANCES

THE EUROPEAN SCENE

It would be hard to say whether the financial crisis of June 1931 was mainly precipitated by political or by economic causes, by the increasing tension of political relations in Europe or by the impoverishment of borrowers suffering from the depression. Certainly whether we look to the past or to the future, to the embittered disputes and rivalries of great nations, or to the deep feeling and differing psychology which explain them, the desire for security and the attempts to attain it must be essential elements in our enquiry.

We will begin by considering the course of events which immediately preceded the financial crisis.

The close of the first half-decade after the entry into force of the Treaties had been marked by a political *détente* which was expressed, and apparently consolidated, in the agreements of Locarno in 1925. The next five years marked a falling away from the level then reached. While Stresemann lived he was able to continue his collaboration with Briand and Chamberlain in a policy of appeasement. But his successes in obtaining visible and tangible benefits for Germany, while considerable, were not sufficient to get ahead of the growing discontent and disillusionment in that country, which resented the continued occupation of the Rhineland, the postponement of any fulfilment of the promise made at Versailles that German disarmament would be followed by that of other countries, and the fixation of reparation payments at a figure which was still too high.

Stresemann was powerful enough to prevent the expression of this national feeling in a form which could have compelled him to reverse his policy; but he could not stop its growth, and the restraint upon the forces so developing depended more and more on the strength of his own personality. When he died the danger was further increased by the distress, the disillusionment and even the desperation resulting from the economic depression. Never was his influence more needed than when the Rhineland was evacuated in June 1930. There was no one left to say then to Germany what so greatly needed to be said: 'This is the fruit of a policy of appeasement. What other policy could conceivably have freed German soil five years before the Treaty date ? Now the chapter of the war period is closed; henceforth let us live as neighbours with our neighbours.'

This was not said; only Stresemann could have said it; and the occasion was used for celebrations (as I well remember, for I was there at the time) not of reconciliation but a renewed xenophobic nationalism, which found its most alarming expression shortly afterwards in the sweeping success of the Hitlerite candidates at the election.

So great was the resulting anxiety that, although the other three principal events of the year should each have improved the political atmosphere, the general political tension was greater at the end of 1930 than it had been since the occupation of the Ruhr. The Naval Conference had settled the 'parity' question between America and Great

Britain and had arrested the danger of a new naval competition which might have had incalculable consequences. But the success of the Conference was forgotten in its failure. It failed as regards Europe and left the French-Italian problem aggravated and exacerbated. The Reparation Conferences had resulted in what purported to be a final solution and (quite apart from the German aspect) had removed a host of complicated and embittering disputes affecting all the belligerents in the war. But this very success released certain forces hitherto repressed, which almost at once created doubts as to its finality. And the evacuation of the Rhineland, as we have seen, was used as an occasion to exalt nationalism and to encourage the more dangerous sections of Germany to give freer expression to their feelings than they had hitherto felt it safe to do.

By the late autumn of 1930 the anxiety was intense and even hysterical. In the most responsible circles in Paris men were asking each other whether war was imminent. These fears were indeed, in their form and expression, both foolish and exaggerated. If there was real cause for anxiety there was no danger whatever of war in a near future. Gradually a more sober mood succeeded. The anxiety, though grave, was less febrile. But then, early in 1931, the sudden proposal of an Austro-German Customs Union caused alarm, as much by the procedure adopted as by its actual substance. It was felt that Germany, in her new mood, was perhaps about to embark on a policy of Treaty revision by successive acts of unilateral repudiation. In Europe the danger was now more truly appreciated; it was not of a sudden outbreak of war, but of an increasing division of the Continent into two opposing groups which would ultimately make a conflict inevitable.

Qʀ

Meantime, these apprehensions had spread to America, very largely in their earlier and more hysterical form. In June, as the conditions tending to a crisis developed, men were asking each other in New York, as they had been six months before in Paris, whether there was a danger of a new war in Europe. The addition of these fears to the existing doubts as to the solvency of debtors impoverished by the depression gave a fatal shock to confidence. Gradually for two years, as we have seen, the foundation of credit on which trade and the solvency of debtor countries depended had become the precarious one of short-term advances, hitherto renewed but legally recallable at short notice. A run began and the crisis was precipitated.

It is equally clear, if we extend our view to what must follow the financial crisis, that political security is at the heart of our problem. The re-establishment of the conditions of foreign lending, without which no creditor country can hope to maintain its exports, will be impossible unless there is assured confidence in the maintenance of peace. Nor can commercial policy be adjusted to the needs of world trade, if, apart from other retarding influences, national self-sufficiency is desired as an element in national defence. Nor can the world be rid of the burdens, and dangers, of excessive and competitive armaments while there is an acute sense of insecurity. Till that is removed the only effective limit to armaments, which successive conferences will be powerless to change substantially, will be the amount of money that can be extracted from the taxpayer; armaments will increase with every advance in the machinery of taxation, and will skim the cream off all progress in prosperity, and in the net result create still greater insecurity.

Europe is the real centre of the problem of security. It is true that the general system designed to maintain peace is now undergoing its most severe test in hostilities between Japan and China in Manchuria and Shanghai. It is true that great wars may arise from disorder or divergent interests in the East. But it depends mainly upon the position in Europe whether the peace system can, if America will effectively co-operate, be made effective. It is the European situation therefore that we must now consider, and especially the relations of Germany and France which are at the heart of Europe's disunion.

§ *French Policy and Psychology*

French policy has reacted to the changing moods in Germany and to the fluctuating course of events elsewhere; but though quickly changeable within certain limits, it is almost immovable beyond them. Post-war France is certainly not militaristic in the sense that she has aggressive ambitions. She does not want war; she desires no new territory; she asks no more than the maintenance of the existing Treaty situation, and would be glad indeed to be assured of that. But her outlook is militaristic in the sense that she sees no solution of a military danger except in the terms of military preparation. A little more than that perhaps. Conscious of having the strongest army, and the largest free financial resources in Europe, she desires to retain both – and to make both of them felt in whatever negotiations of current policy may arise. That is a position of vantage which no representatives of any country have willingly forgone – so long as it lasted. She desires to bankrupt no debtor or competitor – but is not unwilling that they should feel that she could if she would. She does not desire to conquer others; but

(like every country in its day of fortune) she would wish
to be obviously, both to herself and others, invincible.

The idea of removing a foreign danger by a political
penetration, by adopting a policy so conciliatory as to
make it unlikely that an aggressive policy in the potentially enemy country would receive sufficient internal support, is a difficult conception for the French mind. The
Anglo-Saxon, with a less contiguous danger, with some
safeguard in an intervening sea, and with a long experience of colonial and Dominion problems (such as that of
South Africa) finds it easier. M. Briand has indeed con-
sistently preached the political value of conciliation
for many years, but to France as a whole it is a supplement, not a substitute, for adequate military preparations.

Against any probable opposing strength France wants
to see a sufficient superiority of military forces on which
she can rely herself. These cannot be her own alone. She
must then, she thinks, have allies. Or, if she could feel
sure of the League system working and wielding adequate
strength in time of need, that might do indeed; but there
must be no loopholes; no danger of reluctant support,
or interference with the League's restraining action by
countries not members of it; the sure prospect of material
aid is essential; no promise of moral influence alone will
deflect her policy. The points within which French policy
moves are thus, reliance upon effective League support
plus conciliation on the one hand, and reliance upon alliances upon the other. At different times and in response
to different external events first one and then the other
has been the dominant aspect of her policy. The forces
behind the two are not unequal, and it does not require
much to shift the centre of gravity.

It is especially incumbent on an Englishman writing
in English to try to understand and explain the real basis

of the French outlook and policy. The world has lived too short a time within the collective system of Covenant and Pact to develop the feelings and habits of thought by which it must be supported if it is to comprise the real forces and control the real actions of those who have accepted it. 'Friends are we with all and enemies with none except those who break the Treaties by which we are all in common bound'; 'a judgment on the merits of any difference that may arise unbiassed by either predilection or dislike' are principles to which we may give an intellectual assent, but are far from yet giving an emotional and instinctive loyalty. We still, all of us, form national friendships and antagonisms, and colour our opinions and may direct our actions, by the feelings which they engender. And between the Anglo-Saxon, especially the Englishman, and the Frenchman, there are differences of national temperament which each finds irritating. We in England inherit a 'balance of power psychology,' and when a given country attains for the time a dominant position, we feel an instinctive alienation from it; we judge more harshly what we consider its faults, though they are not new, and a national outlook and policy, which have not changed; and a stronger note of righteous indignation, of the origin of whose greater strength we are not ourselves fully conscious, marks the expression of our disapprobation.

To the Frenchman, more retentive of his enmities and alliances, the rapid and instinctive shifting of our sympathies from a recent ally, as it begins to enjoy the fruits of our common effort, savours of perfidiousness. The Frenchman again might, like us, express a stronger moral disapproval of another's action when it touched his interest; but, more conscious than we of his mental processes, he would do so understanding better the origin of his feelings. To him our particular quality of moral indignation seems hypocrisy, not less exasperating because it is subconscious. To the Englishman on the other hand, the Frenchman seems to concentrate a fervent attention upon one aspect only of complex questions, to the exclusion of those which touch the interests of others. What these other aspects are, which he seems to ignore, it is better to leave to French writers to explain. The theme is not neglected in English, nor likely to be; but the field remains open for a writer in French. We should all of us, on both sides of the Channel, be more profitably, if less pleasantly, occupied in trying to understand the merits of the other's case, than in meditating upon our own.

The fundamental desire of France is for security. She may make mistakes, like all of us, in trying to obtain her goal. She may attempt security against war by methods which increase her danger; just as her investor may attempt security against poverty by living sparely, saving relentlessly, and investing in *rentes* which lose four-fifths of their value, or foreign bonds which lose all. But security is her goal. She has for the moment both a military and a financial predominance in Europe. Her statesmen may in their negotiations experience a pleasurable consciousness of that fact which evokes no similar feelings in the breasts of those with whom they are dealing. That is but human, and at least the English financial representatives of the time when the present position of the pound and the franc were reversed have no right to complain of such an attitude.

The root of France's policy is, however, not arrogance, born of a conscious strength, but a sense of insecurity, born of the knowledge that her strength is precarious. Her financial resources are not based upon a greater production of wealth than England's but on the fact that her people

have been content to expend on their comfort a smaller
proportion of what they produce, and so leave that
margin which means financial power to the financier
and the statesman. Her military dominance is not
based on greater man-power or industrial organisation
than Germany's, but upon a Treaty-imposed inequality,
in its nature not permanent. She has as her contiguous neighbour a hereditary foe, not inferior either
in industrial resources and capacity or in the art of
war, and with a greater and more rapidly increasing
population; and by this foe she had been twice invaded
within the memory of those still living. Her very temptation to abuse her strength comes not from confidence in
it, but from the sense that it may not last.

It is difficult for one country to realise imaginatively
the quality of another's national psychology. We know
intellectually the facts of France's position. We may have
visited the devastated regions; but our emotion though
sincere remains external to our deeper and permanent
springs of feeling; it rarely gives us a real communion
with the emotions, experiences and memories of the
Frenchman. For an Englishman to understand the
instinctive feelings of the Frenchman about his Army and
his national danger, he will do well to start with what is
nearest to it in the English national psychology, the sentiment that has attached to the Navy. Great Britain has
been immune from hostile foreign invasion for nearly a
thousand years. But, a little over a century ago, she was
only saved from it by a narrow belt of sea and by her
Fleet. Trafalgar has ever since touched a deeper chord
than Waterloo. For a century afterwards she enjoyed
a feeling of security which was based on a Navy which
was then, and which she hoped would remain, invincible.
When it was threatened by German building there was

a shiver of apprehension such as had not been known since the days of Napoleon. And yet the form in which this expressed itself, 'two keels for one,' and the knowledge that, at the worst, this was a practicable policy, shows how different was her case from that of France, whose man power could never equal, much less surpass, that of Germany.

But suppose that sixty-five years after 1805 another Trafalgar had ended differently; that England had been invaded and, without aid from others, had only rid herself of the enemy by indemnity and the cession of territory; that after another half a century, she had again been invaded and had indeed expelled the foe after four years, but only with the aid of others on whom she could not count certainly in a future war; and that then for the moment she had acquired a naval dominance which she could not rely on retaining. We should then perhaps be able to understand the deep-rooted psychology which underlies France's sense of insecurity, her feeling about her Army, and her policy. We should know why she wants the League to be so supplemented and so assured as to be certainly effective in case of need, if she is to make its safeguards an integral element in her national defence, and be content with other preparations which, without the League, would be inadequate; why she clings to the military predominance which she possesses for the moment and aims at solidifying alliances to support and prolong it.

We might still think that France was seeking a security by methods which may diminish it; that she would do better to convert an enemy into a friend than to try perpetually to cow him by superior force. We might still hope that she would realise that the latter policy is one of desperation, that not only may but must fail, as it clearly is on any cool and realistic calculation; and that not merely the best, but the only, way of safety is a combination of conciliation with a strengthening of the collective system of Covenant and Kellogg Pact. But we should at least understand; and should perhaps redouble our efforts to make the collective system, if America would aid, so strong that we could not only reasonably expect France to rely on it, but regard it ourselves as an integral factor in our own schemes of national defence, – as we do not yet.

§ *The Position of Germany*

Germany is a country with both explosive forces and others which make for order and stability. Her history for a decade after the Armistice was a miracle of representative government. In spite of defeat in a destructive war, the country was, on the whole, governed wisely and moderately, and both her President, Hindenburg, and her Foreign Minister, Stresemann, worked steadily for a policy of moderation and conciliation. Hitler's movement itself was mainly the consequence of economic disappointment rather than political resentment; he was supported less by veterans inflamed by the past than by young men concerned with their future. But it used material, found an expression, and has had consequences that concern external relations. And the growing intensity of the economic depression is strengthening the forces that make both for social revolution and a foreign policy of desperation.

The stresses and strains of Germany's experience were bound, sooner or later, to result in an internal political crisis. This was artificially retarded while there was an obvious need to maintain a united front against other countries in the negotiations about reparation.

When the need no longer existed Germany began to feel herself free to indulge in some of the luxuries of political life which before would have been too expensive. The Rhineland occupation, too, was like a weight holding down explosive forces which increased during the process and were bound some time to be released. The danger attendant upon Germany's conscious re-entry into full and free equality among the great nations would have been greater the longer it had been retarded; but it was unfortunate that it coincided with the exacerbating influences of an economic depression. Whether with or without revolution Germany will work out her new political equilibrium and her new policy; what that policy will be in regard to external affairs must largely depend on the way in which other countries react to the problems of the immediate future – especially disarmament.

The German position, with the psychology underlying her policy, need not be as fully described to English readers as that of France. It is much better understood, and the English feeling against what is for the time the stronger power increases the sympathy with her old antagonist. It is well, however, to recall some of the major facts which explain the German outlook. The forced admission of war-guilt in the Treaty still rankles, the injustice seeming perhaps greater as a generation succeeds those who held the power in the fatal days of 1914. On this question those in other countries who still believe that, in the period immediately preceding the war, the rulers of Germany and Austria have a responsibility which does not rest upon those of either France or Great Britain, may yet recognise that the methods, the principles, the assumptions upon which foreign policy was conducted in the nineteenth century by all the belligerents of 1914, were such as to involve some common responsibility for the deeper causes of the disaster. If we return to the system of that century, as we infallibly shall if we allow the Covenant and the Kellogg Pact to be weakened, the same result will follow sooner or later, and the whole world will be responsible.

And as regards Germany's two principal material grievances, about reparation and disarmament, there is this to be said. Whatever be the basic justice of reparation or its ultimate fate, the actual policy of the creditors, as we look back in retrospect, may be perhaps excused or explained, but on its merits is beyond defence. As to disarmament, the pledge which accompanied the Treaty remains – but remains unfulfilled. Germany's case before the world is not yet unanswerable – but if the 1932 Conference fails of results it surely will be.

§ *Italian Policy*

Italy's position is in some respects obscure, as it must be under such a centralized and censored system. No one can say with certainty what is her economic condition, the real public attitude to the Fascist régime, or what would happen if Mussolini died. In general, it is evident that the peace of the world must always be somewhat precarious if the policy of a great country, in the greatest crises, is determined by the judgment, or the caprice, of a single person, who is subject to all the accidents of mortal nature.

But it is not difficult to discern the real basis of recent Italian policy. Italy is a country with a rapidly growing population, conscious of a greater potential strength than her present place in the sun; she is young as a nation, and came late into the international race. Her outlook is therefore the opposite of the 'sated'

Empires or countries, who are content to keep and to develop what they have, and have everything to gain from an assurance of the *status quo*. Conscious at the same time of present weakness, Italy searches for associates, and has sometimes aimed at a power in diplomacy by an aggressiveness of language which outruns her intentions. She has been divided between a desire to avoid restrictions on a future expansion, and an equally strong desire to avoid isolation.

She has thus been an adherent, but a reluctant adherent, to the new peace system. This is the clue to her attitude to the League of Nations; to the Locarno Agreements, which she obstructed until it was certain that they would be concluded, and then signed; and to the Kellogg Pact, which she derided while its fate was in the balance, and then equally accepted. A favourable new factor has become visible in her policy during the last few years. She has fully realised, perhaps more fully than any other country, that the practical value of a country's armaments depends entirely upon their relative strength in comparison with others; and she sees that she would be likely to get a better ratio with France under any negotiated Treaty than her financial resources would enable her to secure by competitive expenditure. She is therefore working simultaneously for a ratio satisfactory to herself, and also very genuinely, through her able and liberal Foreign Minister, Signor Grandi, for a strict limitation of armaments.

§ *Other European Countries*

The rest of Europe need not long detain us. Poland has serious friction with Germany and is apprehensive of Russia. Jugo-Slavia has explosive forces engendered by

the relations between Serbs and Croats; but if they were
not members of a powerful alliance including France they
would constitute little serious danger to the general peace
of Europe. Austria has the makings of a social revolution, which may always involve external reactions, but
again its danger to Europe depends on her special relation with Germany. Hungary has a high temper, keenly
felt grievances, and leanings to the old Hapsburg allegiance; but any danger would be negligible if it were not
increased by association with Italy, and so perhaps with
Germany. The Balkans, if left alone except for a collective restraining influence should trouble arise, would
be no threat to the world. They are not so much the
powder-box of Europe as the arena in which greater countries have tried out their strength – and still do so. Russia
may be a later menace but her energies are now concentrated on her economic plan and her intentions at least
for the present are peaceful. Spain under her new constitution is a pacific influence. The northern countries,
except for some anxiety about Russia, fear little and
threaten nothing, and they form a substantial, contiguous
and largely homogeneous block in Europe desiring peace
ardently and pursuing policies which help it.

The specific policies and influence of the two great
countries Great Britain and America which, while not
themselves a part of the Continent of Europe, affect it
so vitally, will be most conveniently considered when
we trace the history of the attempts to establish a new
peace machinery.

§ *The Real Problem of Peace*

The real issue upon which peace depends emerges even
from so brief a summary. The particular disputes or

sources of friction, much advertised and over-dramatised, the Polish Corridor, a proposed Customs Union, a naval rivalry between France and Italy, even a quarrel about reparation or disarmament between France and Germany – though that goes deeper – will not be the causes of a great war, though one of them may be the occasion. The real danger is deeper. All these disputes and the national fears and animosities which they cause and reflect are tending to align Europe into two great groups. France, Belgium, Poland, Czechoslovakia, Roumania, Jugo-Slavia, – beneficiaries or creations of the Treaties, and desiring the maintenance of the *status quo*: Germany, Austria, Hungary, Bulgaria, Italy (with Russia as a possible adherent) defeated or disappointed and desiring revision. The character and range of the groups vary from time to time. They tend to harden and consolidate when the political horizon is dark. The first group is the only one that at present can be called an alliance; the second represents only certain common interests and aims, out of which an alliance might later be formed. The political associations between the countries named are slight, varying as between different pairs and shifting from time to time. Where any Treaty exists it is always legally subject to the overriding provisions and obligations of the League of Nations. Nevertheless, there can be no doubt that such groupings of countries for united support against danger from others, are in essence opposed to the 'universal' or 'collective' principle embodied in the Covenant of the League of Nations and the Kellogg Pact.

Not, of course, all regional or local groupings or Treaties should be thus described. Treaties between contiguous countries or those with close and interacting interests for the settlement of disputes *inter se* may be a definite support to the wider system. Especially is this true of such Treaties if they include those who are regarded rather as potential enemies than as potential friends. The Locarno Agreements for example, though comprising only a few members of the League, do not represent a cleavage from the League system, but a strengthening of it. Because they include both France, Belgium, Poland and Czechoslovakia on the one hand, Germany and Italy on the other, and also Great Britain which has no affiliation with either of the two groups, they are a microcosm of the League, a segment of the universal system, not an alternative to it. So it would be if any Danubian grouping, formed perhaps primarily on a community of economic interests, could include both Czechoslovakia and Hungary. Consultations, again, between countries with a certain community of economic outlook – such for example as commonly take place between Scandinavian countries in regard to League policy, or a customary mode of election to a body like the Council which takes such a grouping as its basis, may be useful and bring certain advantages without any danger.

But an association for the common defence of the specific national interests of the countries within it is a danger to the universal system just in so far as it does in fact influence policy or is believed to be likely to do so. If a dispute, let us say, between Czechoslovakia and Hungary comes before the Council of the League, will the attitude of France and Germany to it be determined by their judgment on the merits of the case, or by their prior sympathy with one or other of the disputants ? How far can countries which are hesitating whether to rely on the collective system as the basis of their national security feel confident that, if such a dispute developed to the point of hostilities, the attitude and action of the powers not parties to the original dispute would be determined by their obligations under the Covenant, and not by narrower treaties and associations ?   There have been occasions when the intrinsic merits of a case have obviously prevailed over any bias of previous sympathy or friendship — and the collective system has been at once strengthened; but there have been other occasions when the contrary has resulted.

This is the real issue upon which the peace of the world depends.   Will the collective and universal system gradually become stronger or weaker than the alternative one of national armaments and military alliances ?   This is not only a question of the League of Nations, but of the whole post-war system for the maintenance of peace, of which the League is one part and the Kellogg Pact another.

CHAPTER II

VERSAILLES AND GENEVA

A DECADE OF TREATY-MAKING

In the political history of the last ten years all roads in Europe lead from Versailles; almost every event turns upon some provision in the Treaty with Germany, or the subsidiary Treaties of St. Germain, Trianon and Neuilly with Austria, Hungary and Bulgaria; upon the conflict between the policies of execution and of revision.

This is not to say that the troubles of these years are to be ascribed to any folly, weakness or wickedness of the three statesmen who shared the main responsibility for framing the terms of peace. The Treaties were not just, but they were probably about as good as the complexities of the questions, and the intensity of the passions, left by the war allowed. A German diplomat once said to me, inverting the trite Latin motto, 'Si vis bellum para pacem – if you want war make a peace treaty.' There would be more truth though less wit in saying 'If you want a just peace, don't prepare for it by war.' Justice is a child of peace and not of conflict; and a just settlement will not, save by a rare accident, be wrested from an armed struggle. It is well that the world should recognise that war, by its very nature, arouses passions out of which neither justice nor enduring peace are likely to be born; that imposed terms will never be the same as an agreement negotiated between equals; and that statesmen whose power is dependent on those who, in the moment of victory after long agony, clamour for its spoils, will rarely if ever be allowed to act, even if they would, as impartial arbitrators. The sword once drawn will be thrown weightily into the scales of justice.

The world was indeed more fortunate than it might have been in the three statesmen who were in supreme office when the conflict passed from the entrenched field to the conference table; and it has since done them scant justice. Each was better than the prevailing majority of the public. he served. Wilson lost his power not because he agreed to conditions inimical to peace, but because he made the establishment of the League of Nations the first object of his policy. Lloyd George's Parliament (though it is true that his own action was partly responsible for its character and composition) was throughout putting pressure on him, not that he should be more generous, but more extortionate. Clemenceau was thrown from office, not because he had imposed a Carthaginian peace, but because he had not seized the Rhineland provinces for France.

Publicists themselves exempted from the agonies of the war by distance or extreme youth ; and others who have not learnt that, when the great stakes of war are played and lost, the forfeit cannot, in this world of human passions, be wholly remitted, have since portrayed the trio of Versailles as the arch-demons of a vindictive drama. To those who understand the passions and the problems with which they had to contend they will rather appear, on a sober retrospect, as the triune Atlas of a crumbling world.

True, there are grave defects in the treaties by a standard of ideal justice. Here and there, fragments of territory not great indeed, but enough to comprise much human misery, were allotted because of pledges extorted in a crisis of the deadly struggle. More often principles, each sound in themselves, self-determination on the one hand, the natural lines of trade and economic advantage on the other, were in conflict ; or, as in Transylvania, blobs and patches of different races were dispersed in a way which made any conformity of frontier with nationality impossible. Alleviating safeguards were provided for the protection of minorities, but no solution satisfactory by every test was practicable. Reparation was perhaps the worst defect; but even there a mechanism of adjustment was included which could have been utilised if the public temper of later years had been more generous; and the domination of the Saar, in effect a part of the reparation provisions, was an injustice which was at least to terminate at a specified date. It was not the fault of the framers of the Treaty but of their successors if the alleviating mechanism which they had provided was not more generously or more justly used.

When all is said, what settlement after a decisive result in war has been to so great an extent based on principles (such as self-determination) independent of that result ? It was not justice entire and spotless; but it was more justice than war usually gives. 'Do men gather grapes of thorns or figs of thistles ?'

§ *The Trio of Versailles*

And greatest of the trio of Versailles in history will loom the figure of Wilson – if, indeed, as we too hastily assume, posterity will disentangle truth from the conflicting and confused records of contemporaries. Strangest of all modern myths is the legend that Europe made peace without America, or that the most unshakable will of our age was guilty of a weak compliance.

Consider the facts. The war was one of Europe, into which America entered only in mid course. The presence, and still more the prospects, of her unexhausted resources exercised a potent influence at the end. But others had borne the heat and burden of the day. France lost more than thirty times as high a proportion of her manhood. The questions to be settled by the Treaties were four-fifths of them European. It was European countries which had to live with the consequences of the settlement, from which America was parted by 3,000 miles of inter-vening sea.

And yet, not only did Wilson exercise the chief influence on all general questions, such as the estab-lishment of the machinery for preventing future war, and on the problems of other continents such as China, but even in Europe his voice was equal to that of the spokes-man of any other great power. For good or ill, the prin-ciple of self-determination was potent, and the exceptions to its application not frequent or of considerable extent. In what other century would a war so ending not have been followed by the cession of the Rhineland ? In the Polish Corridor it is well to remember that there are a large majority of Poles; in ceded Transylvania more Roumanians than Magyars. The fate of Upper Silesia was left to a plebiscite – perhaps misleading in its verdict and misapplied, but that was the fault of others. The new sovereignties carved out of the Austro-Hungarian Empire had been formed by the spontaneous uprising of the con-stituent nationalities before the war ended; they were not created but only consolidated by the Peace Treaty. Perhaps in all these cases 'economic' considerations should have counted for rather more when they conflicted with those of nationality. But that suggests no weak com-pliance on the part of the apostle of self-determination.

If we wish to see the real quality of Wilson, proved already as President of Princeton and Governor of New Jersey, again displayed at Versailles, we can do no better than consider his successful fight for the inclusion of the Covenant of the League as the first Chapter of the Peace Treaties. He fought almost alone. The realists were against him – they wanted to get on with their business of concluding with Germany. Distant and impractical idealists, misdirecting a public opinion that should have helped him, were also against him – pleading that the 'holy thing' should be uncontaminated by the evil treaty. He was ill-supported while absent for a time in Washington and had to fight hard to recover ground ceded and almost irreparably lost. But to him this was the first and greatest objective of his policy. He won. And he was right – abundantly right. Let those who know what it has since meant to secure world acceptance of even the shortest and simplest Treaty to strengthen the foundations of peace, ask themselves what chance there would have been of establishing that comprehensive, skilful and flexible instrument, with its rigorous and detailed obligations and commitments, if the peace had been first and separately concluded. We should still be talking about it – if we had not ceased to do so in despair. There would to this day have been no League, nor any other alternative mechanism of peace that would have any chance of coping with its task.

This was the greatest decision, the greatest achievement of Wilson's life. It would have been impossible for one who did not combine the vision of the idealist, the practical insight into the conditions of success of a realist, and an unshakable will, unmoved by either the opposition of foes or the foolish counsel of friends. If the world does indeed prevent the recurrence of great wars, it will be to this great act of this great man, more than to any other person or event in history, that it will owe its salvation.

It was not in Paris but in Washington that Wilson met his first great defeat. Neither the Triple Pact (by which he secured the Rhineland for Germany); nor the League (which he had placed in the forefront of his policy); nor the Treaty of which his principle of self-determination is a principal pillar, was ratified by his own country. There was indeed a moment when that same impregnable will, which had brought him for some months to the highest eminence of world power ever reached by man, was his undoing. He would not stoop to conquer – he would not make the slightest gesture of inclination. It was an infirmity – but that last infirmity of a noble and unshakable mind which will break before it will bend. He preferred, when a slight concession might have won ratification, to fight for the last iota of the deed he had signed with the last ounce of strength he possessed. Even then he might have won if, at this last crisis of his fate, not his spirit, but his body had not failed him, just too soon. Like Stresemann, in the face of his doctors' advice, he made the better choice and, knowing well the cost, started on that last tour of persuasion from which he returned stricken, shattered and impotent.

Those who saw Wilson most nearly are not in all respects best qualified to appraise him. He neither gathered his knowledge, nor formed his decisions, nor exerted his main influence in personal contacts. He had not Lloyd George's sensitiveness to impressions, nor his lightning response, nor his personal magnetism. He seemed – I recall a first impression of a direct conversation – rather formal, academic, donnish. He was at his strongest in detachment from immediate personal influence; and often at Washington he seemed to shun contact with strong personalities around him, as if to preserve the integrity and independence of his own thought. His training was that of a historian and a scholar, and the chiselled phrase of the written word expressed him better than the quick repartee of debate.

His figure thus seemed less in 1919 than 1918. How could it not? For a few weeks he had wielded more power than any mortal man in recorded history. Throughout the belligerent world his voice had been stronger in nearly every country than that of its own Government. He voiced the better mood of a distracted world, vindictive and aspiring in turn, and throughout the subsequent reaction he still held something of that mood, and used it to build what was most worthy of it.

Such a man needs distance to be seen in his full stature. The flaws of temperament, the errors of judgment from which none are wholly exempt, the political passions which he shared and from which he suffered, loom too large on a near view; and the main outlines of his personality are unseen or seen out of their due perspective. The figure of Wilson will loom in history above his lesser contemporaries and across the valleys of intervening generations of lesser successors.

Clemenceau, the incarnate will of France to win and to reap the fruits of victory, immovable as Wilson but with a narrower range of vision and ambition, is known, as few are known, through his self-revealing apophthegms and conversations, and his writings. Unconquerable, inflexible, cynical but not inhumane, nor, by the standard of contemporary or succeeding spokesmen of France, immoderate in his demands, his was not unnaturally the chief influence upon that part of the settlement which directly concerns the relations between France and Germany. But those who think he used it to crush his foe to the limit of his power would do well to read his passionate attack on those who had wished to impose an alien domination on the Germans of the Rhineland.

Unlike Wilson and Clemenceau, Lloyd George remained a dominant figure in European politics for some years after the signature of the Treaties. His personal qualities have already been described in the account of the reparation negotiations; and it is enough to say here that he displayed the same qualities equally in Paris.

The first chapter of all the Peace Treaties, thanks to Wilson, consisted of the Covenant of the League of Nations; and the whole history of the subsequent years has been reflected in the fortunes of this new instrument of Peace.

§ *The League of Nations*

The League has now become an integral part of the world's political structure. It is the normal, though not invariable, instrument through which political problems and difficulties either of general world interest, or affecting two or more of its member states, are dealt with. It has a network of specialised committees and regular conferences covering a wide range of technical subjects, economic and financial, social, colonial, and legal. It comprises in its effective membership the whole of Europe, except Russia; the whole of Asia, except Turkey; all of Africa and a substantial part of Central and South America; Canada in the North, but not the United States. It has a triple mechanism; for its central organisation is flanked by the International Labour Office and the Permanent Court of Justice at the Hague. It has now no rival as a permanent international organisation; for the Conference of Ambassadors and the Reparation Commission have both ceased to exist. The only alternatives to it are the ordinary mechanism of national Foreign Offices and Embassies on the one hand, and improvised conferences on the other.

Both the United States of America and, to a less extent, Russia are, in effect, members for its technical work and for the negotiations on disarmament. It has enlarged its orbit both of subjects and of member states, in both cases with great advantage but at the cost of certain internal strains. The inclusion in one organisation of those recently at war, and still divided deeply by differences of interest, policy and sympathies, essential to its task of reconciliation and its character of universality, has naturally made unanimous agreement in policy more difficult. Its inclusion on its agenda of some of the most burning of national controversies has again extended its utility, but also increased some of its internal strains.

The League has had in its first ten years a full and varied record, which includes triumphs, half-successes, and some failures. In co-operation it has notable successes, as in its contribution to the reconstruction of Europe. In the political sphere it has stopped hostilities in several instances, and settled a number of disputes which might in time have become dangerous, while in other cases, the more difficult and important, such as disarmament, it has so far made little or no progress.

Its success and its strength have at different periods reflected the temper of the time and the mood of its members. Where these have rendered settlement and pacification possible the organisation has achieved it. But an international organisation, necessarily composed of the states themselves and requiring their assent, can at most encourage the mood and temper that make for peace and gather the fruits when they exist; it cannot itself create;

it must draw its strength from its constituent members and must work within the limits set by their policies and desires. The practical success of the League has thus fluctuated with the varying mood of Europe. The better temper and outlook expressed and, for the moment, consolidated at Locarno, enabled it to act with decisive and dramatic success when Greek troops invaded Bulgaria in 1925. In the next years a certain reaction in the European temper handicapped it. But under these fluctuations there has perhaps on the whole been an increase in authority. In any case, here is the instrument, tried and, within the limits of the strength given to it, proved effective; and the only one which the world has at its service.

§ *The Locarno Agreements*

The Locarno agreements of 1925 were an attempt to make progress more rapid by an intensive effort in a localised region of especial importance and difficulty. Led by three protagonists, Briand, Stresemann and Chamberlain, seven countries, France, Germany, Great Britain, Italy, Belgium, Poland and Czechoslovakia, entered into new engagements, additional to but entirely consistent with those of the League Covenant. An engagement was made to submit disputes to a pacific settlement and in no case to resort to war to settle them – thus going further than the League obligation which leaves a freedom of action in certain circumstances and after a prescribed delay. And the Treaties were in one respect fortified by an important additional guarantee. If either France or Germany attacked the other, Great Britain and Italy undertook to give military support against the aggressor, an engagement much more specific and onerous than the obligations of Article 16 of the Covenant.

The 'trio of Locarno' occupied a place from 1925 to 1929 comparable with that of the trio of Versailles in the first years of peace; and their personalities were an important factor in the history of Europe for several years.

Monsieur Briand was for six years the outstanding figure in European politics. Stooping and slow in physical movement, medium in stature, his shaggy and leonine head dominated any assembly of which he was a member; and his presence, like that of many great artists, grew upon his audience as his eloquence rose to its height. He was incomparably the greatest orator of our day, persuasive, magnetic, dramatic, with a penetrating wit and with a voice at once mellifluous, resonant and sonorous. Viviani had a voice no less musical, and a skill as great in using it. He was the perfect executant on a perfect instrument – but his theme was unworthy of both. Briand, at least on his great occasions, had something to say as well as an unequalled faculty in saying it. No one will ever forget who heard his great speech on the entry of Germany into the League: 'Both nations have reaped an ample harvest of military glory. Henceforth they may seek laurels in other fields.' And at such a time his spoken word was a real creative force, moulding and forming the deep feelings and sentiments of which policy and action are born.

A greater and a better man since his close association with the League, he was thereafter a consistent, sincere, and powerful supporter of the cause of peace, pacification and conciliation, and both the policies and methods of negotiation which help them. He had a depth of insight, a range of imaginative vision denied to Poincaré – though he had neither the exactitude of detailed knowledge, the relentless industry, nor the unbending will of his great antagonist. He represented the France that reacted against the Ruhr and Poincaré-la-guerre in the election of 1924, and his strength waxed and waned as that mood prevailed against its always waiting alternative – and in close relation to similar swayings of mood and policy in Germany.

Stresemann was a worthy complement and colleague in the task of reconciling the two countries. A nationalist in his earlier political life, and a patriot second to none in his ambitions for the ultimate strength and position of Germany, he had the vision to see that in the period when he was in office there was more to gain from a policy of appeasement than of resistance. With the choice before him of turning east to Russia or west to the League, he turned west – but in such a way as not to close definitely the alternative path. The evacuation of the Ruhr, the powerful influence of Germany in and through the League, the evacuation of the Rhineland five years before the Treaty date, the steady growth of his country's prosperity and standing until the day of his death, are the fruits of his policy.

Short, stout, with close-cropped and almost shaven head, in his appearance a typical German as seen by foreign cartoonists, he had a personality at once charming, dominant, irresistible. He had a passion in advocacy which could sway other men's minds and judgment, but never deflected his own. I remember a scene at Lugano in 1928, where the Council of the League was meeting out of consideration for his already failing health. A controversy arose with Poland. I was working in an adjacent room at the moment, when I suddenly heard a voice on a note such as I had never before known in an international deliberation, harsh, rasping, impassioned. I went in and found Stresemann in the midst of a torrential speech; his tone was that of a man whose temper had escaped his control; but every phrase he used was calculated, precise, and within the limits of permissible advocacy. The effect was decisive. The tendency to support friends rather than judge on the merits of the case, which has sometimes threatened the League and is its greatest danger, was no longer apparent; and Poland, on the immediate issue in the wrong, was isolated. Never was there a more passionate or potent advocate of the policies of moderation and conciliation. And while he lived he held down, by the sheer strength of his dominant personality, the explosive forces in his country that showed their strength as soon as he had gone. He fought till the last moment, preferring, as Wilson had done, to throw the last ounces of his strength into the cause for which he stood rather than nurse and coddle a few more years of impotent existence.

The essence of Locarno was the bringing together of France and Germany. Chamberlain, therefore, the third of the trio, had a different rôle from Briand and Stresemann. It was that of a mediating friend between two till recently estranged, or an officiating priest at their nuptials. He asked nothing except their happiness, and the tranquillity that it would bring to all who lived near them. He was the more acceptable in this rôle because he brought a costly wedding present – perhaps too costly – in the British guarantee of the frontier.

Formal; rigid; precise. Correct in thought, in manner and in costume (Max Beerbohm's cartoon portrays him, erect, monocled, frockcoated, immaculate, before a group of dishevelled foreign statesmen who whisper in admiration, 'l'amant, sans doute, d'une Duchesse ?'); with all the virtues of a good official, conscientious, industrious, competent; exact and meticulous within the limits of his habitual vision, not sensitive to what lay outside it;

retaining from the Victorian school of politics in which he had been trained its best traditions of scrupulous personal honour in public life, which on one side touched quixotry (as in his resignation over Mesopotamia) and on the other side gave him a sense of perhaps too conscious rectitude. Like Poincaré, without personal magnetism himself, he was, unlike him, susceptible to it in others, in Lloyd George, in Briand, in Mussolini. He served with a touching personal devotion under Lloyd George in the Coalition Government; his compliance with French policy (sometimes perhaps exceeding what Briand himself would have wished, as when some of Poland's claims were in question) brought an accumulating reaction in his own country; in dealing with Mussolini (though the limiting principle to the Duce's provocative speeches and gestures at his most flamboyant period was to go no further than was compatible with British friendship) Chamberlain seemed curiously to accept rather than exert influence.

But he did a great service to the League by his regular attendance at the Council as Foreign Minister; and established a practice of which we shall realise the value if it should unhappily be abandoned. He was loyal to his colleagues, his officials and his principles. He never shirked a responsibility or bent under pressure from home. Indeed, he was too little accessible to advice or sensitive to public opinion, and inclined to think, especially after Locarno, that the British nation had not only given him, as it had, a large cheque on its confidence, but that it was a blank cheque, which it was not.

Such were the men whose association was the dominant influence in Europe for four years. They worked through the League, whose regular meetings, in which they were the protagonists, set them on a public eminence, elevated not only more obviously above the level of their ambassadors, but in the eyes of the world above their respective Prime Ministers. Their constant presence at these meetings, and their use of them for both their formal and informal negotiations, made Geneva for the first time the indisputable political centre.

Locarno undoubtedly marked a real progress in the pacification of Europe and its results endured for some time. Those who participated in the negotiations clearly thought that they had constructed a new world and came away in an *exalté* mood which made it difficult to express the doubts that occurred to more detached observers as to whether the agreements did not contain the seeds of future weakness. The future unhappily confirmed these doubts, and as they are very instructive as to the difficulties which beset those who are attempting to construct the mechanism of peace, it is worth while to consider them.

Locarno was made by the association of three powerful personalities, and its results came to depend to a dangerous degree on the continuance of that association. The chances not only of natural life, but still more of political life, make such a basis a very unstable one for the enduring needs of international relations. Each Minister moreover suffered to some extent in his own country from his relationship with the two others, Chamberlain and Stresemann being both accused of undue compliance with Briand, and Briand with Stresemann, either in the negotiation of the agreements themselves or in the course of subsequent policy.

So powerful a combination also disturbed to some extent the normal equilibrium of the forces and influences represented on the Council of the League of Nations. The relationship of such a body with dominant personalities presents a peculiarly interesting problem of international government. The League must, if it is to be successful, incorporate the chief personal forces in the world; but it is important that they should be, both in reality and in appearance, its servants and not its masters. In the early days of the League the personal strength of the statesmen who helped to create it and were steeped in its traditions – Balfour, Bourgeois, Cecil, Benes, Branting – added to the collective authority of the Council. The Council's decisions represented more than the sum of the opinions of its members, or any compromise between them; '*l'esprit du Conseil*' was a clearly discernible influence. For some time after Locarno it was the 'Spirit of Locarno,' to a large extent consistent, but not identical, with the spirit of the League, that tended to be the dominant influence. The equal interplay of forces on which a collective authority depends was weakened.

Signs of some reaction from the Locarno mood were not long in appearing. The rather vague and nebulous aspirations expressed at the once famous Thoiry lunch of Briand and Stresemann confirmed the feeling in their two countries that they had a little 'got their feet off the ground,' and lost touch with the national forces. The reaction in Germany against Stresemann's policy grew gradually. It was restrained by his powerful personality until his premature death, but then found a dangerous expression which in turn reacted on Briand's position in France and weakened his authority. In England a somewhat similar resistance grew rather more slowly. It took the form of a feeling that Chamberlain was unduly compliant in his negotiations with France. The strong and spontaneous explosion of protests against the proposed appointment of Poland as a permanent member of the Council was one warning of the growth of this feeling, which found a less fortunate expression, on a change of Government, in the Reparation negotiations at the Hague in 1929, to which reference has already been made.

Locarno, and the developments which followed it, illustrate very clearly some of the special characteristics of Great Britain's post-war policy, and her attitude to the problem of strengthening the structure of peace, and it will be convenient at this point to add a summary of the British position to those already given of the German and French.

In the Locarno Treaty, Great Britain gives a guarantee of the Franco-German frontier. No similar guarantee, additional to the less specific sanctions of the Covenant, is given as regards any other frontier, or for the benefit of any other pair of countries. It was given because Franco-German relations were obviously at the heart of the problem of Europe. An assurance of the inviolability of the frontier between the two countries was thought likely to remove the main cause of the sense of insecurity which was impeding the task of pacification in every sphere. It was for this purpose that Great Britain gave her guarantee, as a contribution to the peace of the world, of which she would share the advantage with every other country, and in return for no more specific national advantage.

As a decisive factor in assuring peace, as the coping stone of the structure of the peace mechanism, such a guarantee – onerous liability as it is – would doubtless be justified; and as such it was welcomed and confirmed by the British Parliament. But it was, in effect, Britain's last card – and it was played too soon. Little by little it has been realised that a pledge, which would have been worth while if a part of a final and complete plan to which all the other countries equally concerned in the maintenance

SR

of peace were making a proportionate contribution, entails great disadvantages if made prematurely and unilaterally. It might be worth while to give such a guarantee even unilaterally as the last and decisive contribution to a plan which really settled all the main difficulties between France and Germany, including disarmament. It might have been worth while, even in 1925 when such a complete settlement was impossible, to give such a guarantee if the other parties to the Treaty had, as a counterpart, given a guarantee which Great Britain could have regarded as a comparable help in her own specific problem of national defence.

But the pledge was in fact unilateral – and as such it was premature. We no longer have it to give as a help to the disarmament negotiations. It was given and, as such, is taken for granted, discounted – and to all appearance little valued. It is impossible to discern any influence from this pledge on the French feeling of insecurity. I know nothing so disappointing in recent history as this fact. I have discussed Locarno with innumerable Frenchmen, in and out of responsible positions. Some of them defend it: 'We must base our relations with Germany on a policy of conciliation'; others regret it: 'It is a trap and a delusion; armed preparedness is our only security.' At that point I remind them of the other feature of Locarno – the British pledge. 'Ah, yes,' they say, 'that is of course a good thing.' They had almost forgotten it – at least it has become no vital element in the substance of their thought, no integral factor in the forces that form their policy. And yet here is the strongest and most specific guarantee – the help of the full military and naval strength of Great Britain – that has been possible since the withdrawal of America, for France's one vital and historic danger, her eastern frontier. It is the equivalent of what

Great Britain would possess if the American Navy were pledged to aid her if the sea-borne imports of her food and raw materials were ever assailed.

There is, indeed, a remarkable and very characteristic analogy between the Locarno pledge and the pledge about reparation and debts of the Balfour Note. Both would have been suitable elements in a plan accepted by others and fortified by equal contributions by them; both were given prematurely and unilaterally, remaining to hamper Britain's future bargaining power, giving an impression of an aloof, external, detached (and perhaps rather self-righteous) attitude, failing signally to achieve the desired results of conciliating others or encouraging them to corresponding offers.

§ British Foreign Policy

If we are to understand this action we must consider very closely the specifically British attitude to the League and the peace machinery. Great Britain genuinely considers 'Peace the first British interest' and with rare exceptions she has shown a genuine sense of world responsibility in all the post-war conferences. She desires no acquisition of new territory and wants nothing better than an environment in which she can deal with the internal difficulties of the British Empire. In thinking of the danger of war she does not normally think of one in which she would be one of the original disputants. She thinks of a war breaking out between other countries which might involve her as a later participant and which, in any event, would bring impoverishment to her customers and injure her world trade. It is primarily as an instrument for preventing the outbreak of war between others that she values the League.

The reason why it did not occur to Great Britain
to ask for a special pledge for herself at Locarno is
due to a slightly 'external' attitude in this sense; the
idea of collective action being an integral part of the
scheme of her own national defence has never worked
into the body of British thought or become a part of
her actual policy. She thinks of herself as 'making
contributions to world peace.' France, on the other hand,
as we have seen, has always been ready to regard the collective obligations of the League, if only she could be
sure that they would be extensive enough and would be
observed, as an element in her own defence – perhaps a
supplementary one, but certainly a real one. The merits
or demerits of the rôle the two countries have played in
the League correspond with this difference of conception.
France, her critics say, attempts to make her influence
dominant in the League and to use it for her own purposes. She is, of course, entitled to do so within the
limits of the spirit and letter of the Covenant and those
set by the compensating influence of other countries; it
is for the others to make the counterpoise. Great Britain,
her critics say, while urging that France should be content with the collective safeguards provided by the League
shows no sign that she would be willing to rest one of her
own feet on that foundation when she is thinking of her
own more vital dangers. This is certainly not to suggest
that the British forces are greater in relation to her needs
than those of France. On an assumption of a need for
self-sufficiency, they may well be too weak. But as a
description of an attitude of mind the criticism is justified.

The other side of the attitude, however, needs equal
recognition. Great Britain's 'contributions' to a world
peace have been far-reaching and onerous – and in some
respects perhaps dangerously unilateral. Great Britain

has the same interests in world peace as America. Her exports to foreign countries; her investments abroad and their dependence on continued peace and prosperity in the countries in which they are placed are about equal. She is, however, unlike America, not only bound by all the other obligations of the League but continues to be bound, without reservation, by the provisions of Article 16 which prescribes, under certain conditions, the duty of applying economic and financial sanctions against an aggressor. When she originally accepted these obligations she expected that America would accept them too — and they have become infinitely more dangerous and more onerous since America failed to ratify the Covenant; for not only has she no assurance that, even in the most flagrant case, America would give her active support; she has no assurance (however much she may confidently hope) that America would not interfere. She has not merely co-operated, without reservation, in the establishment of the Permanent Court of Justice, but — which is very much more — has accepted the optional clause which binds her to accept the verdict of that Court in any legal or justiciable dispute, and has thus in such matters voluntarily forgone in regard to even the weakest of possible disputants the bargaining powers of a stronger country.

And, as we have seen, in return for no specific national advantage, for nothing except a hoped for diminution of the risks of war, an advantage enjoyed equally by other countries, she has pledged the whole of her strength to guarantee the most vital, and one of the most dangerous, frontiers in Europe. There has been, perhaps not unnaturally, a growing feeling in the country that in giving national guarantees in support of the general peace structure, Great Britain has assumed an undue and disproportionate burden.

The same characteristics in national outlook, and the slowness and difficulty with which a country adapts a traditional policy to new conditions, are well illustrated by the discussion between Great Britain and America about the Freedom of the Seas. President Wilson had proposed in his Second Point 'Absolute freedom of navigation upon the seas outside territorial waters alike in peace and in war, except as the seas may be closed in whole or in part by international action for the enforcement of international covenants.' The acceptance of this principle was strongly pressed upon Mr. Lloyd George at Paris. But though he ardently desired to establish a firm basis of co-operation with America in general policy, and was himself the most imaginative of British statesmen and the least likely to be bound by obsolete traditions of policy, it was no less strongly, and successfully, resisted by him.

Yet what an incalculable benefit the firm establishment of such a principle in world policy, endorsed by the countries with the principal navies, would have been ! The Achilles' heel of Great Britain is her dependence upon sea-imports of food and supplies. It is to her what her Eastern land frontier is to France, and even more than that, for the submarines of any enemy, and not merely those of a contiguous power, can destroy shipping. And, as against so great a security, could it have been obtained, what had Great Britain to set ? An impairment of her powers of blockade against an enemy on whom she might wish to exercise unilateral pressure not covered by the exception in the Second Point. How likely was it that, having joined the League system, she would be in a position where she would require to exercise such pressure ? And against what countries, if the case arose, could she exercise it effectively under modern conditions, even with no new restrictions on her legal rights ?

But the memory of the blockade against Germany was too vivid, and the knowledge that if the proposed limitations of the Treaty of London had been ratified and observed that blockade could not have been effective. Above all, Great Britain could not yet think of herself as no longer supreme mistress of the seas or as engaging in a war in which she would not be in the position of a blockading power. Neither the restrictions upon her right of independent war, which she had accepted in the Covenant, nor the idea of relying, for her own defence, not solely upon her own Navy but upon that supplemented by international engagements with collective support, had penetrated and transformed instinctive British thought and policy. A collective guarantee of the unrestricted entry of her sea-borne imports might have been the greatest prize she could have hoped to bring from the Conference; and, at a small price, she might have brought it, not by asking but by accepting what was pressed upon her. Yet it was a principal object of her policy, to which other ambitions were subordinated, not to accept but to reject this prize.

The decision at that moment is indeed in retrospect of less practical importance, in view of America's failure to ratify any of the Paris engagements; but it was not determined by any such anticipation; and no subsequent events weaken it as an illustration of the instinctive attitude of Great Britain, not yet changed, towards international engagements against war. She believes in them profoundly, and supports them handsomely, as a means of preventing wars breaking out between others. But she has not yet come to regard them as an integral factor in her own defence. To note this attitude is not to pronounce a verdict upon it; it can be defended as France defends her policy, with its similarities and its differences; it reflects, as hers does, the present inadequate strength of the peace system, which we shall discuss later. But that this is Great Britain's attitude can scarcely be questioned.

§ *America and the Kellogg Pact*

The relative abstention of America is, of course, due to causes which are not difficult to understand. She feels that the principal dangers to peace are likely to originate in Europe, and that it lies with Europe primarily to deal with them. She is separated from them, not, like England, by twenty-one miles, but by three thousand. She is herself impregnable, and able, at a price, to abstain from a European war if she so decides. True, she has much the same export trade and about as many investments abroad as Great Britain; but they are a smaller proportion of her economic life; a policy of isolation and self-sufficiency, though perhaps ultimately impracticable, is not so demonstrably impossible. There were many people in Great Britain before the war, belonging to the so-called Blue Water school, who, with less reason, thought that the country could base her policy on the assumption that she could stay out of a European war if it came. I confess that I was one of them. We were wrong. It is not surprising, however, that many people in the United States of America should hold a similar view. America is beyond question deeply interested in the maintenance of peace, but her actual existence is not involved in the same way as that of European and less self-sufficient countries. This difference in position, combined with certain historic traditions in American policy, doubtless explains the attitude of relative aloofness and the lesser extent to which she has been willing to accept obligations and engagements in order to strengthen the world's system of defence against war.

It is in the light of these considerations that we must examine the significance of America's chief direct contribution to the peace structure, her initiative with France in proposing and carrying through the Pact of Paris, informally known as the Kellogg Pact.

This new Treaty, negotiated and signed in 1928, declared in Article 1 that the high contracting parties (who now comprise all the principal countries including the United States of America and Russia) 'condemn recourse to war for the solution of international controversies and renounce it as an instrument of national policy in their relations one with another'; and in Article 2, that they 'agree that the settlement or solution of all disputes and conflicts of whatever nature or of whatever origin they may be, which may arise among them, shall never be sought except by pacific means.' It is thus more comprehensive than the Covenant of the League, first in including the two great countries, the United States of America and Russia, who are not League members; and second, in making war unlawful even in the case in which it remains lawful under the Covenant. On the other hand, the Kellogg Pact includes no machinery to secure or facilitate its observance; it does not even provide for consultation between the signatories; and no steps have been taken under Article 2 to develop a mechanism or procedure for settling disputes by pacific means, except those which League members have constructed under their own Covenant.

Moreover, the exact meaning of the engagement is far from clear, and was not rendered clearer by the explanatory speeches and reservations (whose relation to the formal Treaty is itself obscure) of some of the principal

countries.   Some of these, made by League members,
implied not only a very restrictive meaning for the
Kellogg Pact, but were so worded as to suggest that the
countries making them placed a very narrow interpretation on their existing engagements under the League.
Instances are to be found in the British reservation as to
certain regions (unnamed) of the world 'the welfare and
integrity of which constitute a special and vital interest
for our peace and safety . . . interference with these regions
cannot be tolerated,' without any recognition of the extent
to which British rights and interests in these regions were
necessarily affected, in certain circumstances, by the provisions of the Covenant ('every region of the habitable
globe is now apparently menaced by British protection'
said one critic at Geneva); and the haste with which not
only America, but Great Britain and France, concurred as
to the right of self-defence remaining intact, without
reference to the right of the League to judge whether
action claiming to be in self-defence could properly be so
termed.

Later statements to the effect that the engagements of
the Covenant remained intact, and that those of the
Kellogg Pact were supplementary, not alternative, did
something to remove this danger to the League itself.
But the real meaning and scope of the Kellogg Pact
remained obscure, and subsequent writing has so far done
little, though it has done something, to clarify the position.   On its most restricted interpretation the Pact might
mean little indeed.   I have heard it argued by a person of
standing and responsibility in America that it is nothing
but a voluntary and simultaneous declaration by certain
countries that they intend to guide their own national
policy by a principle of which each remains the sole and
independent interpreter.   I said, 'Supposing, for example,

that country A, without visible provocation or excuse, invaded country B and declared that she did so because she feared, on grounds not proved, a later attack by B and that therefore she was acting in self-defence, what would America's attitude be ?' I was answered, 'We might, of course, disapprove, as we might have done if there had been no Pact, but as signatories of the Pact we could only note the explanation and should have no right deriving from it to contest the plea; an independent state in 1928 had made a declaration as to a principle by which she intended to guide her policy; at a later date she declared the meaning she herself attached to her own declaration; we had no right to compel the first; we should have no right under the Pact to dispute the second.'

It is obvious that if this were really all that the Pact means it would be worth nothing; indeed less than nothing. For although it is true that the idea of war being renounced as an instrument of national policy may so transform the public thought of the world as to cut away the very roots from which war grows, that is only if it is itself a living and growing idea, both genuine and believed to be genuine. It must never be forgotten, on the other hand, that the only foundation of any possible structure for the maintenance of peace is a belief that countries who sign engagements mean them sincerely. Every time a Treaty is signed which is widely believed not to be regarded by many of its signatories as anything which need seriously affect their policy, much more than the particular Treaty is affected. We have drawn upon and wasted some of the limited capital of public trust in the efficacy of Treaties, without which no common policy, no co-operation, no collective safeguards against war at all can be built. If indeed in later years the Kellogg Pact should seem to the world only a worthless hybrid begotten of idealism out of hypocrisy much more than its own influence would be destroyed; the reputation and future of its older half-brother, the Covenant, would also be involved.

No treaty, or law, falls into desuetude or contempt without damage to much more than itself and its immediate purpose; it undermines the respect for law itself without which no ordered society, national or international, is possible. Let us frankly admit that the world is still uncertain as to whether the Kellogg Pact will or will not fall into this disastrous category. It may grow in its practical influence and in public confidence – and if so it will be a powerful instrument in transforming the world. But if it does not grow it must infallibly shrink – and if it shrinks, it were better that it had never been conceived.

The first vital question is: do the signatories accept the principle of 'no war as an instrument of national policy,' not only as a guide to action which they may initiate, but as the criterion by which they will determine their attitude to the action of other countries ? If A attacks B, will country C, a signatory like the others of the Pact, consider itself free to say, 'It is true that A has acted in a way that I should not have considered it right to act myself, but she must be the guardian of her own conscience; as she is a friend of mine, or my national interest suggests that I should win or retain her friendship, I shall express my sympathy with her, or at least preserve an absolutely impartial attitude ?' Or can we be confident that C will say, 'Whatever my previous relations, and without regard to any specific national interests of my own, I am bound to disapprove of A's action, since it is clear to me that she has contravened the Pact of which we are both members' ?

The next question is, will C regard it as her duty to make her disapproval a really effective influence ? And how far will she go in this direction ? And lastly, will she consult with other signatories faced with the same problem, including those who are prepared or, as League members, required, to exert definite pressure, extending if necessary to economic boycott ? And how far, if at all, will she actively co-operate with them ?

The actual course of events does not yet admit of conclusive inferences on these points. In the dispute between China and Russia in 1929, Mr. Stimson's message clearly implied that he considered that the Pact implied a right and indeed a duty, to adopt a definite attitude based on its cardinal principle towards the action of other countries. The incident remained of some, though not decisive, value as a precedent. More important was the case of China and Japan in Manchuria in the autumn of 1931. The American attitude especially as expressed in the Note of January, confirmed the wider interpretation of the Kellogg Pact. At first it seemed too that there would be real co-operation between America and the League. The issue as regards Manchuria is not yet settled. But it seems unhappily clear that full advantage has not been taken of the opportunity of proving that Kellogg Pact and Covenant can function together as a single instrument.[1] It is still uncertain whether the world's confidence in the effective working of the collective system will, as a net result, be weakened or strengthened; in either case, the consequences will extend to every sphere and every problem of international policy.

Such, in bare summary, is the stage reached after thirteen years of effort to build the new peace structure. The framework is there, but the building is incomplete;

[1] It may yet be retrieved in the subsequent crisis that has arisen in Shanghai.

and the foundations themselves insecure. That the progress made is unsatisfactory is shown by the fact that there was more serious anxiety as to international relations in 1931 than six years before, in 1925, and that this anxiety was grave enough to be a main factor in precipitating the financial crisis. We must now proceed to enquire what can be done to improve the situation.

CHAPTER III

THE WAY TO SECURITY

COVENANT AND KELLOGG PACT

WE have then, in the situation before us, on the one hand a series of separate disputes and occasions of friction; and on the other, a tendency for a grouping of Europe into two opposing alliances. These are the two dangers to peace. What then needs to be done ? What can be done ?

In the first place, of course, it rests with the countries directly concerned, and with the League, to labour continuously to remove or alleviate the particular frictions and disputes; to ease the tension between Germany and France and Poland; between France and Italy, and so on.

The task of fundamental importance, however, is to fortify the 'collective' system itself, to restore confidence that it will function effectively, and to make this confidence a basis of the policy of every country.

Most countries are in varying degree in danger of being attacked by others; all are in danger of suffering loss by the outbreak of war between others. Every country will prepare in some way against these risks. There are only two methods of preparation. One is to build up national armies and armaments, and, so far as they seem insufficient, to supplement them by military alliances; the other is to build up a universal system based on the principle that all abjure war as an instrument of national policy and that all unite to support by their attitude, and action

271

in case of need, the observance of that pledge. The first, since unhappily the forces and weapons of defence are precisely the same as those of offence, creates at every stage more insecurity than security; the second, with every step of advance, is at once a diminution of danger and a defence against it. Just so far as each country feels confident that the universal system will be effective it will make it an integral feature in its own national defence policy; and just in so far as it distrusts that system, it will inevitably turn to armaments and alliances. For this reason it is not enough that the system should in fact be effective when the day of danger arrives. It is essential that there should be confidence beforehand that it will be effective; so that this confidence may affect current politics during the years of peaceful relations, when the scale of armaments and the character of political associations are being determined.

Both these systems will in any event long continue side by side. At the best we shall still have national armaments and more or less overt alliances for common defence. At the worst, the Covenant and the Kellogg Pact will remain as elements in the world's political structure. But everything depends upon which of them, year by year, grows gradually stronger and prevails over the other. If it is the armaments system, Europe will be ranged into two opposing armed camps, the world perhaps into several; armaments will increase up to the limit of the scared taxpayers' capacity and endurance; and a new war destructive of civilisation will in time be inevitable. If it is the collective system, armaments will be reduced by a natural process, the desire for economy having a constantly diminished fear of insecurity to contend against, and alliances will gradually be dissolved under the solvent of the overriding collective obligations, till they disappear or lose their danger.   This is the world's fundamental problem.

The way to its solution is, I believe, to be found, and in the near future to be found only, by strengthening the League and the Kellogg Pact and in co-ordinating them so that in practice they operate as a single instrument.

This task is a double one, partly that of completing the peace system, and partly that of strengthening its foundations; partly, that is, of perfecting the mechanism for dealing with disputes, for securing immediate co-ordination of policy and action when danger arises, for blocking any loophole for legalised war in the net-work of Treaties and Pacts, and partly of ensuring that the existing engagements will be observed and enforced.   In the first part of this task the main need is that it should be made clear that the Kellogg Pact is to be understood in its wider, and not in its more restricted sense.   But it is the second part that is of vital importance.   The real doubt that causes a gnawing anxiety in the world is not whether the present net-work of Treaties covers every possible case, but whether these Treaties will be observed.

Now, in strengthening the peace machinery, and establishing confidence in it, let us say frankly at once, that there is little or nothing more that Europe alone can do.   Every engagement into which European countries may enter is at present undermined by a complete uncertainty as to America's attitude.   We do not know whether America would in fact exercise her influence at a time of crisis to prevent war, and secure a settlement by pacific means.   We do not even know that, for reasons quite independent of the issue itself, she would not interfere with the action taken for this purpose by members of the League.   We do not know that if economic pressure were exercised by League members in accordance

Tʀ

with their engagements against one of their number whom America herself recognised to have resorted to war in breach of both Covenant and Kellogg Pact, America would not protect the interests of her commerce under pre-war rules as to the rights of neutrals and belligerents. And whilst these uncertainties exist it is impossible that European countries should have sufficient confidence in the collective system to modify their national policies.

It is essential that the position of European countries about economic sanctions should be clearly understood. It is easy for those who are themselves in an impregnable position to say that moral influence should be sufficient without economic sanctions. If that is true, the sanctions will never be applied. The chances of moral influence being successful are much greater if the sanctions are in reserve. And if it is not true, the application of these sanctions is incomparably more humane than the war that would otherwise result. It is, of course, true that an economic blockade extended over years causes as much human misery as fighting. But economic pressure of a few days or weeks, which is all that would be necessary if exercised by a united world, causes nothing but some financial loss and inconvenience, whereas even an hour of military action causes the loss of human life. If the collective system has no sanctions at its disposal, it will not be relied upon as an alternative to large national armaments; and it will have much less chance of stopping war in an acute crisis.

Now this, as I have said, is a matter in which the next important step must rest with America. Every engagement between European countries is fatally weakened, and deprived of its effect upon current policy, by the complete uncertainty as to whether it would be – or

whether America's attitude would be such that it could
be – observed.   What then could America do ?

There are obviously certain definite limits set by strong
bodies of American opinion and deep-rooted American
traditions, within which any statesman must frame his
policy and beyond which other countries must not expect America to go.   So far as a foreign observer can
judge what these negative limits are, I should be inclined
to define them as follows.   First it is, I imagine, unlikely
that in a near future, America will be willing to ratify the
Covenant of the League of Nations.   Secondly, it would
be difficult for her, constitutionally or politically, to accept
an engagement which would bind her in a future crisis
to forgo her ultimate right of independent judgment, or
accept the verdict of other countries.   Thirdly, it would
probably be unwise to expect her to commit herself beforehand to taking an active part in enforcing pressure
through blockade operations even against countries which
she herself judged to have inexcusably resorted to war.

Events and ideas are both evolving at such a pace in
the present crisis that it is perhaps rash to suggest that
what has been impossible will continue to be so.   But it
will probably be wise to accept these restrictive limits for
the purpose of considering the most promising line of
evolution, especially since even within them it is possible
to do what is immediately necessary to assure world
peace.

If I were asked to assume these as the limits set by
deep-rooted traditions of American Policy and to say what
American action, on that assumption, would most strengthen the European efforts to re-inforce the 'collective'
principle, I should make the following suggestions.

In the first place American business, expressing itself
through such a representative organisation as the Cham-

bers of Commerce, might remove a reproach which I have often heard made against America, but which is doubtless undeserved. When I have discussed the probable attitude of America if members of the League enforced a blockade against a country which America recognised to have broken the Kellogg Pact, I have often been answered, 'The American Government and people might in such a case wish well to those who were trying to restore peace. But the pressure of a number of exporting interests, which would resent any interference with a part of their trade — and would see an opportunity for securing an extension of it — would probably be irresistible.' American industrialists and merchants, as organised in their Chambers of Commerce, could effectively discourage such pressure by sectional interests. They would render a great public service if they would declare publicly beforehand that they will do so, so that the American Government, with the support of public opinion, may be free to adopt such policy as it considers to be in the wider public interest of the country.

That would, of course, be a purely domestic action. What is needed, however, if the world is to feel that America is really a source of strength, and not of possible weakness, to the structure on which peace depends, is an official definition and declaration of the American attitude endorsed by American public opinion. Would, for example, a declaration substantially to the following effect be possible ?

That the principle of the Kellogg Pact, condemning war as an instrument of national policy is one which will not only determine America's own policy, but will be the criterion with reference to which she will determine her action towards the action of other signatories; that she will not recognise that any country which she herself judges to have resorted to war in breach of the Kellogg Pact has any of a pre-war belligerent's rights; that if America, in the exercise of her own unfettered judgment, considers that action taken by League members under Article 16 is designed solely to stop illegal war by such a country, America will at least not interfere so as to give aid and succour to it; and that in case of actual war or threatened resort to war, she will (while retaining her ultimate right to independent judgment) be ready to consult with the other Kellogg Pact signatories by such methods as may be opportune, but in such a way as not to replace or weaken the machinery of the League for League members.

Several comments on this are perhaps desirable. The exact form and precise procedure are, of course, unimportant if it is in substance America's attitude and if it can be declared. It might take the form of a Presidential declaration which, if in accordance with the predominant public opinion, would become a part of the traditions of American policy, like the Monroe doctrine, or it might be embodied in Resolutions of the Senate and House of Representatives. The part of it relating to consultation would perhaps suitably take the form of an addendum to the Kellogg Pact, signed by all of its signatories, as it doubtless would be if America were willing. The essential thing is that if the real American attitude is such as to strengthen the peace system, it should be known beforehand. Many of us believe that America would, in fact, act in the way suggested above at the actual time of crisis. But in the meantime the policy and armament preparations of different countries anxious about their security will not have been affected by such a prospect. For any Minister of Defence naturally says, 'If America is not now sufficiently sure of what her attitude would be to declare it, how can I, a foreigner, stake my country's security on what I think, or hope, personally, that it will be ?'

It will be observed that nothing in such a declaration would overstep the limits assumed above to be set by deep-rooted traditions of American policy. America would, in all cases, retain her right of sole and independent judgment as to the respective merits of the two countries involved in any hostilities, and as to the essential character and purpose of any action taken by League members in such a crisis; she would only be undertaking to consult with others before making her final decision and so assuring herself that she was deciding with a full knowledge of the facts. She would not be accepting any new restriction upon her own policy or method of dealing with disputes in which her own interests were involved; she would not be committed, in any circumstances, to taking part in a blockade; and she would remain free as at present of the political engagements of the League.

If this were possible, if America were able to declare and pursue such a policy – in effect that of leaving the Wilson Pact intact, and making the Kellogg Pact effective – the political situation would be completely and permanently transformed. The forces in the world supporting the 'collective' system of Covenant and Pact and those drawing them towards the alternative system of increasing national armaments and military alliances are not unequal; the definite addition of America's influence to the first would turn the balance decisively in their favour. Covenant and Pact so linked together by a regular procedure would, in effect, become two solid and mutually supporting pillars in the structure of peace. It would matter little whether or not they were comprised within a single Treaty and united by a formal amalgamation. And the present anxieties and controversies, about the freedom of the seas or the imposition of sanctions, would be solved in the best of all ways; for the collective authority behind the prohibition of war would prevent it from either occurring or being seriously threatened.

Practical experience will be even more convincing

than declarations, however solemn.   It is likely therefore
that the extent to which collaboration is successfully
achieved between the signatories of Covenant and
Kellogg Pact in the present Eastern crisis will determine
the effectiveness of the collective system for long to
come.   It may be established on an unshakeable basis;
or it may be destroyed.

The strengthening of the collective defences against
war is by far the most urgent task.   But that does not, of
course, in itself, give a stable and sufficient foundation
of enduring peace.   It is a dam and a breakwater holding
back the flood while the more permanent foundation is
being laid.   Little by little, behind this immediate protection, a system of world government appropriate to the
needs of the new age must gradually be built.   The exercise
of national sovereign rights in matters affecting the world
as a whole will be restricted or directed by successive
conventions; and the underlying economic causes of war
will thus be gradually eliminated.   But each stage in this
development will be reached by a process of voluntary
agreement, endorsed by a public opinion and clearly demanded by the actual needs of the world.   A new order
so built up will not be liable to the dangers of sudden
and violent national reactions.   It will be broad-based
upon the needs to which it responds, and will be stable
so long as these needs endure.

It is within the power of those now already in adult
life to secure that, for the first time in human history,
man will be free to build his civilisation without either
the crushing burdens of armaments or the shattering
interruption of war.

PART IV

A Programme of Action in Summary

CHAPTER I

FIRST AID MEASURES

THE IMMEDIATE TASK

COLLECTIVE human wisdom will not control the inexorable march of events in the period immediately ahead. Many, perhaps most, of the adjustments that must be made before recovery can come, which might earlier have been made by deliberate policy, with so much less waste and cost, will now come from the pressure of hard facts and the collision of brute forces. Where most debts, private and public, might have retained their value by the aid of selective cancellation or reduction, and by a monetary policy arresting the fall of prices, there will be default. Where the balance of payments might have been maintained by establishing the conditions which would have secured regular and prudent new lending, there must now be a violent change in the course of trade, debtors importing less than they export. Where this adjustment itself might have been made by a new distribution of an undiminished total of world trade, creditors buying more instead of selling less, it is now being made solely by restriction. No debtor country sells more; it only buys less. This process may well continue until the creditor gold-surplus countries can sell no more at all except those few products and articles which can neither be dispensed with nor produced elsewhere. This is not a matter of choice or desire, but an inexorable necessity to the extent to which foreign lending is not restarted and the creditor countries do not buy more themselves.

Doubtless even so we shall touch bottom some time, and the upward turn will come. After wide-spreading bankruptcy and default, hard necessity will drive some debtors to buy a little more abroad and in order to do so to sell their own goods at prices which will enable them to surmount even the highest tariffs and tempt the most reluctant buyer. If there is no rock bottom, there is probably an elastic bottom to our distresses: beyond a certain point the resistance to a further fall will increase. But when the turn comes it is the credit system that should give resiliency; and unhappily the confidence of the lender has already been so shaken, that it is likely to be long before he will again on any considerable scale lend abroad on the credit of a foreign borrower. Not only, then, is the bottom beneath us not rock but elastic, but its elasticity has unhappily lost its upward resiliency. There is also a possible hole through to the abyss. For it may be that before recovery comes there will be revolution and social disintegration. If that comes and spreads we have a world in ruins; with its network of financial obligations in shreds; with the sources of new capital dried up; and with the very basis of law and order, without which none but a primitive society is possible, shattered.

But though much has been irreparably lost and more must be lost, this wasteful and disastrous movement can be first slowed, then arrested, then reversed, long before we reach the nadir of distress to which uncontrolled events will take us if reason and collective wisdom now abdicate. Action will now be less effective and more costly than if it had been taken earlier; but it will still be more potent and less expensive than if we wait. What then can be done ?

There is at least the impelling motive of imminent disaster, and more and more this will henceforth operate, as the natural forces compel their own adjustments month by month, on just those countries which have most power to act. Neither new lending nor movements of gold are now available to disguise or postpone the truth that in goods and services only can payment be made for what is or has been bought.

Let us then gather together the proposals for action made as we have passed the various problems in review, and present them in brief summary.

§ *Reparation and War Debts*

The first collective action has been to deal with the German situation.

Here, as we have seen, the Lausanne Agreement has brought a real solution. It gives a respite of three years, beyond the Hoover Moratorium, provides afterwards for the issue of bonds to a nominal total of 3,000 million marks involving a maximum annual payment of 180 million marks ; and adds certain safeguards designed to secure that the bonds should not be issued under conditions which would have a destructive effect upon German credit. The annual payments only amount to about one-tenth of the payments prescribed in 1929 by the Young Plan and the Hague Agreement. Had a settlement of this kind been possible earlier reparations would never have seriously troubled either the finances of Germany or the exchanges of the world. The Lausanne Agreement requires ratification, and this is associated with the war debts negotiations.   But probably no responsible person thinks that, in any event, Germany will pay, or be seriously pressed to pay, more than the Lausanne Agreement provides.

The negotiations on war debts, already opened by the Notes of December 1932, are the indispensable complement of reparation.   Whether there is any legal or moral connection between the two, there can be no doubt that the financial and economic characteristics and consequences are identical.   It is evident therefore that, after the suspension and reduction of the claims on Germany, an adjustment of war debt is inevitable, whether it comes in the form of agreed concession or collective default.

Earlier, such action might have held up the failing structure of credit and restored confidence which would have prevented the cessation of lending from which the crisis immediately springs.   But in present circumstances, with prices so fallen and falling, and the burden of all debts private and public so increased, new lending would not suffice; nor (except to a limited extent in the form of industrial credits – credits earmarked to the purchase of goods) will new lending soon be possible.

§ *An Increase of Gold Prices*

The next need is therefore that prices should increase, up to say the level of 1929, and then be kept reasonably stable.   This result may be attained in several ways. Three-quarters of the countries of the world are now off gold and on managed currencies.   It is possible that they may remain permanently off and construct a system of their own and build up a mutual trade within that system. But this involves difficulties and dangers.   A managed currency may get out of control; and there may be wide fluctuations of exchange value as between the non-gold countries, wasteful inflation in some of them and a formidable impediment, which may be almost insuperable, to trade with the gold countries. On the other hand, even the risk of this might be a preferable alternative to coming back to a gold system which works no better than at present. And if the countries which have now suspended the gold standard should ultimately decide to abandon it altogether, they could part with such gold as they still have and thus pay for some of the things they have to import and, by adding to the surplus in the gold countries, hasten the time when gold will lose much of its value.

In any case it is common prudence for the countries now off gold to work out a system by which each can maintain substantial stability of prices within its own area; consult together and co-ordinate their policies; and make every possible effort to be prepared to work a concerted managed currency policy which will avoid the dangers that have usually been fatal in the past. These efforts should, however, be regarded not as a goal, but partly as an interim policy, partly as a legitimate means of securing a better bargaining position with the gold countries, partly as a necessary preparation for the adoption of a system which may, after all, be unavoidable. In the meantime, since the advantages of an external metallic standard, if it can be properly secured and worked, and of a single medium for world trade, are so great, these countries should do their utmost to help and encourage the gold countries in the task of enabling the gold standard to work properly – of restoring gold to his throne, not as a tyrant, but as a constitutional monarch. (This, we must never forget, involves much more than monetary action alone.) And the non-gold countries might well wait a substantial period, a year or more, before judging finally whether the prospects of the tyrant behaving well again are sufficiently favourable for them to return to their allegiance, and before making their decision irrevocable.

What then could the gold countries do, especially the two with a large gold surplus ?

They must first perhaps see that their own banking system is so supported as not to threaten large scale default or insolvency and lead to personal hoarding of gold. Subject to this they could first bring back prices towards their 1929 level by creating as much new money as their stocks of gold will bear without endangering the gold parity of their currencies. This policy will be useless unless it is allowed to have its normal effect on the course of trade, increasing internal prices and imports and diminishing exports – an unattractive prospect but perhaps better than the only alternative, which is that the whole adjustment, and not a part only, should be at the expense of their exports. The process would be more successful if it were positively assisted by two further measures, first a direct stimulus to public works at home by Government action, so that as an additional supply of money was forthcoming, a responsive demand would be ready to meet it; and secondly, a reduction of tariffs. If, in these ways, gold prices could be brought back to their 1929 level, every economic and financial problem in the world would be relieved, and their definite solution made more practicable.

The next necessity is that, gold prices having been brought back to the level of 1929, they should thereafter be kept stable. The gold countries might invite the others to a Monetary Conference with the specific purpose of attaining this goal. If agreement on the goal were already reached, the technical methods could be found and their application assured. Since, however, the maintenance of stability is in the nature of a permanent reform, though it might be initiated in 1932, these methods will be summarised in the next chapter.

§ *Foreign Lending*

Let us imagine then that we have a settlement of Reparation and War Debts, an upward movement of gold prices taking us back to the 1929 level, and some assurance that hereafter gold will be kept reasonably stable. The next thing necessary is to restart foreign lending. To the extent that this can be done the violence of the dislocation of the course of trade, and the reduction of creditor countries' exports, will be less. But after the shocks which the investor has already had, and the further shocks that are still awaiting him, this will be extremely difficult. Foreign issuing houses need to consider collectively how they can direct lending better in future; how they can make the loans more secure; how they can convince the private investor that he will be safer. For this purpose they might usefully support the international institutions, the League with its Financial Committee and the Bank of International Settlements, and urge them to give their advice and guidance. Specialised institutions such as the new Agricultural Mortgage Bank and others to deal with certain categories of loans, based on schemes approved by a responsible international authority and equipped to furnish expert advice, may also be valuable.

Gradually, if progress is also being made in other spheres, in political appeasement, in securing an upward movement of gold prices and their subsequent stability, and in reviving economic activity by other means, the investors' confidence will begin to return. But at best it is likely to be a slow process. It may be that (apart from industrial credits) new foreign long-term lending by the private investor, on a considerable scale and in time to relieve the pressure on the balance of trade, will only be possible on the credit, not of the borrowers, but of the Governments of the lending countries. In other words, substantial foreign lending may be impracticable except upon creditor-country Governments' guarantees. If these were forthcoming, the pressure on their export trade could be at once relieved. The loans would need to be carefully directed and controlled. But, on this condition, they could usefully be employed, partly to prevent default on existing debts and to save currencies from further disorganisation, and partly to restart enterprise in debtor countries.

The next important sphere in which action will be urgent is that of commercial policies. We shall start at least with the advantage of having, in one grim sense, almost a 'clean slate.' 'Protection' will have been so complete that very few manufactured articles will be imported by debtor countries or exported by creditor countries. And one obstacle to earlier efforts at reform, inequality, will perhaps have also been removed by the worst of all processes – a levelling up instead of down. At this point, and we are quickly getting near it, the world must decide whether it really wants international trade, with the enrichment of its far-gathered wealth, or an impoverishing self-sufficiency. The way of progress to a freer world trade is suggested in the next, and last, chapter.

§ *Internal Reform*

In the meantime, as we have seen, these measures of monetary, financial and commercial policy, which aim mainly at world consequences, must be accompanied by other action directed primarily to internal reform. In America, for example, the collective action designed to mitigate the danger of many of the Banks being unable to meet their immediate obligations through the 'freezing' of their resources may be developed into less transient measures of reciprocal support. In Great Britain, the task of industrial organisation cannot wait; and it involves the active co-operation of the financial institutions of the country. The basic industries need rationalisation, and they probably require the formation of new corporations which can at once frame the necessary schemes and assist them to establish the basis of new credit with which they can obtain the requisite finance. There is some danger that monetary or financial policy may be regarded as an alternative to the painful process of liquidating basic disequilibria. Until these have been removed there are dangers in stabilisation.

Unless prices increase substantially, the weight of the fixed interest charges will have to be reduced, either by voluntary conversions, or in the last resort by a legislative change in the rate of interest, and the proportion of capital in the form of ordinary shares must be increased. In some cases the only method may be liquidation and the absorption of the concern in a new combination. But in others some substitution of ordinary shares for debentures may be possible by agreement. The Joint Stock Banks now hold a large part of British industry in their mastery, by virtue of the overdraft position, and they have a part to play commensurate with this power. They could initiate and support schemes of re-organisation, and by a collective use of their overdraft power they could enable new reforming bodies to force in reluctant individual concerns whose abstention is fatal to the general plan.

These are, however, only illustrations of national needs to remind us that action designed to affect the general world situation, the real theme of this book, is only a part of what needs to be done. To deal with national require-ments would need as many books as there are countries.

§ *Political Appeasement*

The last, and greatest problem of the world, at once urgent and permanent, is that of establishing the basis of peace and of confidence in good international relations, without which all efforts to revive world finance or trade must always be doomed to failure. And in the immediate future this means ensuring the success of the Disarma-ment Conference, improving relations between France and Germany, and strengthening the peace structure by making it clear that the Covenant of the League and the Pact of Paris will be operative and will be adequately supported. 'Leave the Wilson Pact intact; make the Kellogg Pact effective'; make it clear by declaration and by act – in China for example, where the whole collective system of assurance against war is now being tested – and the world will at last have the foundation on which it can rebuild its civilisation, – and rebuild it securely.

U<small>R</small>

CHAPTER II

A NEW WORLD ORDER

OUR SYSTEM REFORMED AND TRANSFORMED

IT is not easy, in the midst of our daily exigencies, to think not only of the near but of the more distant future; to lift our eyes from the plains to the city on the hills which we would reach. But we must have a goal to guide us through and beyond the tortuous windings of our encumbered path; or we shall follow the lure of many a will-of-the-wisp along by-paths that lead only to some new slough of despond. Mine is no distant or ideal Utopia, beyond either the vision or the reach of the pedestrian. I have taken the system we know, suggesting how it might be strengthened where it is weak, repaired where it has crumbled, and rebuilt where new needs require additions to its fabric. It is our own system, in which we have grown up, that we must reform — and in part transform.

§ *The World's Monetary System*

The keystone of an ordered economic system is a Money that fulfils its function. The world needs a satisfactory medium for the conduct of its trade and the conclusion of its contracts. It is not necessary to abandon different national currencies, pounds, dollars, francs; but if they are to serve the trade of the world they must always be convertible into each other at about the same rates, and must always be able to purchase about the same amount of commodities. In other words, when we have returned to more normal conditions and prices, we want exchange fluctuations to cease, except within narrow margins, and the general level of world prices to be approximately stable. If the principal countries of the world were determined to have such a Money they could secure it. They would need to make a definite and binding agreement as to the goal of policy and as to the functions of Central Banks and of Governments in achieving it. Central Banks, consulting and co-operating through the Bank of International Settlements, could then deal with short-term fluctuations in the general price level. If the situation was getting beyond their control because gold was becoming too scarce or too plentiful – a contingency that would only occur at rare intervals, – Governments would lend their aid. This they could do by securing a simultaneous change in the legal reserve ratios and, in case of necessity, a simultaneous change in the gold content of the currency standards. 'Devaluation' in time of gold scarcity, that is a reduction in the amount of gold to which a currency gives a legal right, would not be open to the ordinary objections if made simultaneously by all principal countries, and so as not to increase prices but to keep them stable; for it would not alter exchange rates or create injustice to creditors.

In this task the Bank of International Settlements, in suitable contact with the League of Nations as a national Central Bank is with the Government of its own country, could play an increasingly useful rôle. A Central Bank is a 'Bankers' Bank.' This could be a 'Central Bankers' Bank.' It could save unnecessary movements of gold, arrange temporary aid where it was needed, and in time exercise the same salutary influence on national Central Banks, as the latter do on the general Banking policy of their own countries. It might even, in time, if given the requisite resources and powers, issue its own notes based on gold; and these notes might be included in national currency reserves or, ultimately, even constitute the legal standard for these currencies.

A managed world currency, without the support, or the cost, of gold, should doubtless be the ultimate ideal. But such a currency needs a degree of international trust which does not now exist, and would best be controlled through an institution which had acquired confidence and a reputation in many years of humbler work. We should aim first therefore at a reformed gold standard, managed by international co-operation. It must maintain a reasonable stability in the general level of world prices, while leaving sufficient elasticity, within the general level, to allow adjustments to changing economic situations. If, however, under the conditions discussed in the preceding chapter, a gold standard cannot be satisfactorily reestablished, and non-metallic managed currencies are therefore necessary, policy must be so concerted that these will, so far as possible, achieve the same end.

A concerted world monetary policy, with an International Bank as an instrument to help in applying it, would be of inestimable value to world trade. But it will be both impracticable and useless unless other policy, in particular commercial policy, is directed to the same end. An international money system or Bank can never function in a nationalistic world.

§ *The Credit System*

The next requirement of world order is a reformed system of credit. Foreign investment must be within a secure framework of world policy; and home investment within a similar framework of national policy; while each is, within this framework, free to adapt itself responsively to the myriad needs of economic enterprise and activities.

In particular, loans to foreign Governments and public authorities need to be made in accordance with definite rules and to be safeguarded by appropriate precautions. Where political factors or the public finances of a small state are concerned, it will usually be desirable that the proposed loan scheme should be examined by a Joint Committee of the League of Nations and the Bank of International Settlements, or some specialised committee or institution established with their approval. The collective influence of the leading financial authorities in each principal financial centre is needed to discipline the lending markets, and to see that the private investor is not easily misled into subscribing to loans floated by irresponsible houses who neglect the required precautions.

At home, similarly, the mechanism for directing the savings of the private investor needs to be improved so as to prevent his money from being wasted. The methods will vary with the different countries, here a new form of home investment bank being established, there an Investment Board limiting itself to the establishment of certain rules within which the existing institutions should operate. Lastly, as an essential counterpart of any reform of the system of credit, the stock exchanges and the banks need to consider how they can diminish the evils of speculation on margins and on borrowed money in a period of boom in share values, by temporary restrictions on borrowing, or limitations on 'buying for the account,' or lower limits on the amount of the transactions.

§ *Commercial Policy*

The next part of the framework within which economic activity develops is that created by commercial policy. In a perfected world order tariffs may still have their place. They may be a means of securing revenue; and of securing to certain countries a greater variety of industrial and social life than would otherwise be possible. They may be kept in reserve as a means of safeguard (preferably on the authorisation of an international authority) to prevent the sudden or temporary 'dumping' which is designed to kill. They will not however be based upon the fallacy that 'difference of cost' should be compensated for by duties, which is destructive of the very foundation of world trade; they will not be 'scientifically' adjusted to the varying needs of differing industries, which in practice means offering the powers of government as a spoil to those who organise themselves most efficiently to corrupt it, and endowing an industry in proportion to the incompetence of those who conduct it. The tariff systems of the world will be the result of international discussion and agreement; they will be stable for long periods, and changeable only after notice and negotiation, and as a rule only to be reduced. Thus alone can industry and trade find a secure foundation for their development. And so only can Government either acquire the time, or maintain the character, required for its public tasks. We have considered how progress towards this goal may be facilitated by regional conventions, requiring a carefully safeguarded extension of the exceptions to the most-favoured-nation principle; and how world conventions might be gradually negotiated.

§ *Economic Organisation*

Meantime, large-scale industrial organisation is changing the free competition which in the past was the protection of the consumer, and therefore needs to be accompanied by new safeguards of the public interest; and, since it has modified the system by which supply used to be automatically adjusted to demand, it requires in return to create a mechanism of deliberately planned direction.

The leaders of industry could in their own associations examine together the future prospects of their industry, in order to estimate demand and eliminate some of the worst risks of dislocation. As one example of a possible means of action, it has been suggested that when it is obvious in any period that excessive production will lead to a crash, a temporary suspension of instalment sales might give just the necessary relief.

It is essential that, if this kind of development is to proceed without injury to the public interest, such private associations should make suitable provision for the representation of the workers, should be increasingly conscious of their responsibilities to the public, and should devote a greater proportion of their attention to such reforms as will result in economies and lower prices which will benefit the consumer. The influence of their own best leaders in this direction can be enforced by informed publicity, by a vigilant public, and by the knowledge that the enforcement of existing laws or the enactment of new ones is in reserve in case of abuse. Meantime, such an organisation within each industry could be accompanied by central industrial associations representing industry as a whole. And such a central industrial organisation could be represented in a National Economic Council in which other institutions similarly formed in other spheres of the national life, finance for example, would find a place side by side with those who represent official action and policy.

National organisation so developing would expand by a natural process into an international sphere. International agreements, cartels and the like, would do for the world what national organisation is doing within each country; and, safeguarded by publicity and the influence of a vigilant and informed public opinion, would bring the benefits of this progress to the consumer. The National Economic Councils would be the basis upon which a World Economic Council could be constituted to fulfil a similar purpose for the world as a whole.

§ *The Task of Government*

And behind all, Government, the ultimate guardian of the public interest, because it alone draws its authority from the public, would fit itself to discharge its responsibilities. Everywhere, at present, Government is proving inadequate for its task. It is doing so because the complexity of the duties which now fall upon it are beyond the limited capacities of human wisdom and human character. The integration of the world's life in every sphere, which results from the improvement in its means of transport and the transmission of news, necessarily increases this complexity; and the machine and methods of Government have not yet adjusted themselves to the new conditions. But above all Government is failing because it has become enmeshed in the task of giving discretionary, partial, preferential privileges to competitive industry, by methods which involve detailed examination and subject it to sectional pressure.

Government can again fit itself for its ultimate guardianship of the public good, which cannot either safely or justly be entrusted to any other institution, in five ways. It can rid itself of the task of giving preferential and changing assistance to sectional interests, and so liberate itself at once from an impossible task and from a fatal source of corruption. It can decentralise, by delegation to local authorities under rules which delimit their responsibility and co-ordinate it with the central policy. It can simplify its duties by resolutely confining its decisions (where it does not assume complete responsibility for an enterprise) to a framework of main principles, within which economic activity must find its own adjustments. It can extend its own mechanism by the establishment of varying kinds of mixed institutions in which private management is diluted by an element of public representation. Lastly, Government can, as we have seen, draw into the service of the public the great private institutions which represent the organised activities of the country (Chambers of Commerce, Banking Institutions, Industrial and Labour Organisations, etc.). Each of these institutions can be left in effect with just so much freedom as its own traditions and conduct show it to deserve. Government itself must watch, and test, and be ready to exercise its residuary powers if, and only if, necessary. It must delegate, but not abdicate, its authority. So the whole organisation can be integrated into what, in the widest sense, is the machine of government itself. And national organisation so developed in each country can be further integrated into an organ of world policy through the great international institutions, the League of Nations and an enlarged and developed International Central Bank.

§ *Peace*

At the basis of any world order must be assured peace. We have seen how political mistrust has been an integral factor in the present crisis and have considered what might immediately be done. But a solid foundation must be established if anything we are to build is to be more than fragmentary and unstable. Human history thus far has been a succession of brief achievements of high civilisation destroyed each in its turn by destructive wars with their attendant train of impoverishment and anarchy.

One policy alone is possible. Two systems are now visibly struggling for the mastery of the world's fate; the collective system of Treaties against war on the one hand – the Covenant, the Locarno Agreements, the Kellogg Pact – and national armaments and military alliances on the other. Under the first every country abjures war as an instrument of national policy and sets its face against any breaker of the world's peace, irrespective of considerations of separate national interest or the ties of previous friendship. Each country turns to the second just so far as it loses confidence in the collective system.

The vital task the world has before it is therefore to strengthen confidence in this system. Europe can in this do little more by herself. The main weakness of the Covenant is not that, in certain cases, war may still be legally permissible under it, but that League members do not know whether they, or each other, would in fact carry out its existing provisions, or be able to do so. And one principal reason for this is that they have no assurance that America would co-operate in restraining an aggressor, or even that she would refrain from interfering with their own efforts to do so. The Kellogg Pact does not give them this assurance, for its terms are ambiguous and it has no machinery, nor even a predetermined procedure, to make it effective.

America could help Europe to make the League effective for its own members, and at the same time make her own Pact a reality, without accepting the political engagements of the Covenant, or forgoing her own liberty of independent judgment on the merits of any future dispute when it arises. If she would undertake to exert her influence to restrain a country which she herself recognised to have broken the Kellogg Pact, to refrain in such a case from impeding the action taken by others to do so, and to consult with other signatories of the Pact, before taking her own decision, in such a way as not to impair the working of the League machinery for its own members, but to supplement it, the whole peace system would at once be strengthened and consolidated. If declarations of this nature were made, and endorsed by American public opinion; and if, as occasion arose, the co-operation between America and League members were seen to be effective; the peace machinery would acquire both the power and the confidence that is needed to make it the determining fact in world policy. Covenant and Kellogg Pact, thus co-ordinated and supporting each other, would become a single instrument without involving the abandonment of either, or any acceptance of substantial new engagements by their respective signatories. It would matter little whether ultimately the two were amalgamated; an effective co-ordination, seen to be adequate in practice, would establish confidence.

Then and then only each country would begin to regard the collective assurance of the Treaties as a principal element in its own national defence. Aided by all the motives for economy, and successive conventions for general and progressive reduction of armaments, each would cut down its military expenditure. And in the same way all military alliances, and all groupings of certain countries *as against others* would fall into desuetude. Even while they remained, the reality would go out of them. The collective system, and its spirit, would prevail. And the psychology, and instinctive habits of thought, needed to establish it securely would gradually develop. When a dispute arose, men would cease to think which of the disputants was a friend and would turn unbiased to the actual issue; and the basis on which alliances are formed would be undermined.

The use of war as an instrument of national policy would become as obsolete in the accepted and instinctive thought of the world as the use of the stake and the torture chamber to extend a particular religion has become among the nations of Western Europe. Then and then only will both actual war be prevented and the prospect of war cease to be the dominant factor in all world policy. Nor is there any other way. The appeasement of existing enmities, or the settlement of present disputes, will not suffice; for others will recur. A growing world needs provision for readjustment. Unilateral and unenforced engagements to refrain from war will not suffice; for they will be broken. The firm establishment of the collective system in the confidence of the world is the only way of assuring peace — until a new world order can eliminate the causes from which wars originate.

Within this framework, itself based upon assured world peace, a framework at once strong and flexible, of a monetary system, of a system of credit, of world commercial policy, of industrial organisation and of world government, man can at last develop fully, and utilise justly, the resources now available to him. Within such a framework of law, custom and institutions, enterprise can still be both free and competitive; with planned direction guiding it so as to prevent its disastrous dislocations; with safeguards of the public interest, so as to prevent the abuses of monopoly and exploitation. The stimulus of competitive enterprise and personal gain, supplementing the traditions of public service, can thus be harnessed to the chariot of the public good. Within a framework so designed and so built, the reciprocal strains of thrusting individual energy can be used to support and strengthen, and not weaken, the whole structure of the world's economic life. Man can then, freed alike from enfeebling impoverishment and harassing anxieties and insecurities, use the resources he now has to give himself both a basis of secure material comfort and adequate leisure. . . . .

And then the real work of civilization can at last begin.

EPILOGUE

BEFORE the vast magnitude of the tasks ahead, man's spirit
has for the moment faltered and his vision contracted.
The public mood is apprehensive where it should be bold,
and defensive where broad and generous policy is most
required. Everywhere men fly to new tariffs and restrictions, to nationalist policies, domestic currencies, paro-
chial purchasing and personal hoarding – like frightened
rabbits each scurrying to his own burrow. Surely it is
for the moment only. Which country of us has not, but
a few years since, shown the resources we now require of
courage, of personal devotion, of industrial and financial
leadership, of public direction, in a need no greater and
in a cause less worthy ? We are, if we could but grapple
with our fate, the most fortunate of the generations of
men. In a single lifetime Science has given us more power
over Nature, and extended further the range of vision of
the exploring mind, than in all recorded history. Now,
and now only, our material resources, technical knowledge and industrial skill, are enough to afford to every
man of the world's teeming population physical comfort,
adequate leisure, and access to everything in our rich
heritage of civilisation that he has the personal quality
to enjoy. We need but the regulative wisdom to control
our specialised activities and the thrusting energy of our
sectional and selfish interests. To face the troubles that
beset us, this apprehensive and defensive world needs
now above all the qualities it seems for the moment to
have abandoned – courage and magnanimity.

INDEX

See also Table of Contents

Advisory Committee under Young Plan, 49, 149

Agricultural Depression, 31–5; Loans, 116–17; Mortgage Bank, 117; Protection and prices, France, 33; Germany, 33

Agriculture, 31

Albania, 65

America, as lender, 99–100

American Banking, 108; Credit System, 94; Policy, 264, 275–9

Anti-trust legislation, 199

Argentine, 31

Armaments and Alliances, 223–40

Assembly of League of Nations, 46

Australia, 31, 47, 97, 101

Austria, 113, 237; aid to, from Bank of England, 43; League reconstruction of, 23, 43, 113

Austro-German Customs Union, 187, 225, 238

Balance of payments, 12, 51–2, 62; gap in, 51–2

Balance of power, 229

Balfour Note, 134–5

Balkans, 237

Bank, Governor of Federal Reserve, 42

Bank Rate, 62

Bank of England, aid to Austria, 43; drain on reserves of, 45; of International Settlements, 76–8, 111, 291–3

Banking, American, 108; system, British, 86–93, 109; French, 95; German, 95–6

Banks and Industry, 96, 109

Banks, Central, 76–9, 216–17; rôle of, 59–60; Deposit, 60, 96, 110

Basle Committee, 44–5, 49, 118

Belgium, 8, 131, 141, 161, 238, 250

Blockade, economic, 274

Bolivia, 104

Brazil, 105

Briand, M., 181, 185, 228, 251

Britain as lender, 96–7

British Broadcasting Corporation, 215

British Foreign Policy, 259–64

Bulgaria, 113, 161, 238

Business cycle, 24, 27–31

'Buy British' campaign, 48

Canada, 31, 47, 80

Capital, long-term, 87–8; working, 87

Capitalist system, 209

Cartels, 196–202; international, 202–7

Central Banks, 76–9, 216–17; rôle of, 59–60

Chamberlain, Sir Austen, 253–4

Charter of Public Loans, 111

China, 47, 55–6, 81, 227, 269

Clearing-house arrangements, 192

Clemenceau, M., 130, 242, 247, 248

Collective system, 120, 158–9, 238–40, 271–9, 298

Colombia, 105

Commercial Policy and Tariffs, 171–95

Commission, Reparation, 131–3

Committee, Advisory, under Young Plan, 49, 149; Basle, 44–5, 49; Dawes, 142–4; Financial, of League of Nations, 48, 111; Macmillan, 52, 59, 86, 92; Transfer, 127, 143; Wiggin, 149

Company promoting, 88
Competitive system, 7–21
Confédération Générale du Travail, 140
Congress, Pan-American, 104
Control, State, 210, 211–18; of large scale organization, 30–1
Council, National Economic, 219–22; Supreme Economic, 22; World Economic, 171, 174, 202–4, 221
Covenant of the League of Nations, 271–9
Credit, 38–9, 292–3
Credit-Anstalt, 42
Credit policy of America, 64–5; System, Part II. Ch. II., 86–121: British, 90; defects in, 90; American, 94; French, 95
Crisis, financial, 42–54; nature of, 51–4; effects of, 49–51
Currencies, managed, 56, 81–4
Customs Union, Austro-German, 187, 225, 238

Dawes Committee, 98, 133, 142–4
Demand and supply, 10–12
Deposit Banks, 60, 96, 110
Depression, World Economic, 22–41; Agricultural, 31–5
Devaluation, 78
Devastated regions, reconstruction of, 128–9, 139
Disarmament, 157–61
Discount rate, 25, 77–8
Dumping, exchange, 48

Economic Blockade, 274; Conference, World, 171, 174, 195, 202–4, 221; Council, Supreme, 22; Councils, 219–21; Depression, 22–41
Exchange dumping, 48–9
England, Bank of, 43, 45, 97, 111
Europe, United States of, 181, 185–92

Factory legislation, 16–17

Federal Reserve, 25; Bank, Governor of, 42; system, 64, 73, 85; policy, 64
Financial Committee, League of Nations, 48, 111; crisis, 42–54; position of Germany, 44
Foreign Lending, 86–110, passim, 110–21, 286–7
France, 157–62, 227–33; as lender, 95, 98; agricultural protection and prices in, 33; industrial production in, 24
Free trade, 171–195
Freedom of the seas, 262–3

Genetics, 33
Genoa, Conference, 76, 137
George, see Lloyd George
German banking system, 95–6
Germany, 101, 233–5; agricultural protection and prices in, 33; financial position in, 44, 49
Glass Steagle Act, 85
Gold, Part II. Ch. I., 55–85; circulation, 65–6; Conference, 84; Delegation, League of Nations, 67; exchange, 66–7; hoarding, 79, 107, 118; maldistribution, 39, 67–9, 73; policy and prices, 283 6; production, 57, 63, 67; standard, 59 seq.; sterilisation of, 39, 64, 68; surplus, 67
Government, task of, 220, 296–7
Governments, loans to, 102–7, 111–16
Grain production, 31–2; surplus, 31–2

Hague Conference, 146–8
Henderson, Mr. Arthur, 147
Hoarding of gold, 79, 107, 118
Hoover-Laval conversations, 49, 149
Hoover moratorium, 44, 148
Hitler, 224, 233
Hungary, 97, 113, 161, 237

Immigration, restriction of, 20
India, 55, 72
Indo-China, 55
Industrial organisation, 30, 196–207; production in, France, 24
Industry and banks, 95–6, 109
Inland bill, 91
Insurance, social, 17; unemployment, 196–7
Internal purchasing power, 82
International cartels, 202–7; Settlements, Bank of, 76–8, 111, 291–3
Invergordon, naval 'mutiny,' 46
Investment, Part I. Ch. IV., *passim*, 42–54; Part II. Ch. II., *passim*, 86–121
Italy, 8, 141, 151, 235–6, 238

Japan, 8, 55, 81, 227, 269
Java, 33
Joint stock banks, 109
Jouhaux, M., 140
Jugo-Slavia, 236

Kellogg Pact, 264–70, 271–9, 298–9

Laissez-faire system, 9–21; achievement and normal working, 10–14; defects and modifications, 16–20; the passing of, 15–21
Lausanne Agreement, 168
Laval, M., 49, 149
League of Nations, 248–50; Assembly, 46; Financial Committee, 48, 111; Gold Conference, 84; Delegation, 67; reconstruction of Austria by, 23, 43, 113
Legislation, anti-trust, 199; factory, 16–17
Lending, foreign, 86–110, *passim*, 110–21, 286–7; Good and Bad, Part II. Ch. II., 86–121
Living, standard of, 23, 24

Lloyd George, 130, 135–7, 242–8, 262
Loans to Governments, 102–7, 111–16; League of Nations, 116; Public, 111–13; Charter of, 111
Locarno, 223, 239, 250–9
Long-term capital, 87–8
Loucheur, M., 140, 148

Macmillan Committee, 52, 59, 86, 92
Maldistribution of gold, 39, 67–9, 73
Managed currencies, 56, 81–4
Manchuria, 227, 269
Mark depreciation, 141
Mechanization of agriculture, 32
Mellon, Mr., 64
Monetary system, 55–85
Moratorium, 167; Hoover, 44, 148
Most-Favoured-Nation Clause, 175–7

National Government in Great Britain, 46, 48
Norman, Montagu, Mr., 42

Open market operations, 70, 73, 87
Organisation, industrial, 30, 196–207
Over-population, 7–9
Overdrafts, 109

Pact, Kellogg, 264–70, 271–9, 298–9; of Paris, 265
Pan-American Congress, 104
Paraguay, 104
Payments, balance of, 12, 51–2, 62; gap in balance of, 51–2
Peace, 298–301
Planning, 30; system, 14
Poincaré, M., 137–8, 142
Poland, 236, 271
Population, 7
Pound, fall of, 45–51
Power, balance of, 229

Prices, fall of, 26, 58–9, 68; wheat, 32–3; fluctuation of wheat, 33; gold, and policy, 283; raw materials, 35
Production, grain, 31–2; in war, 2–3
Protection, agricultural, 33; and prices, agricultural, France, 33; Germany, 33
Public Loans, 111–13

Rationalisation, 196
Raw material prices, 35
Reconstruction Finance Corporation, 73, 85, 94
Reparation, 122–49; and War Debts, 149–57, 282–3; Commission, 131–3
Rhineland, occupation of, 224, 234; evacuation of, 224–5
Ruhr, occupation of, 133, 224
Russia, 4, 31, 47, 134, 162, 236, 237, 269

Scandinavia, 47, 237
Scientific tariff, 183–4
Shanghai, 227
Sherman Laws, 201
Silver, 55, 84
Snowden, Philip (Viscount), 146–7
Social insurance, 17
South America, 46–7
Spain, 47, 237
Speculation, 25, 35–8
Stability of price level, 72
Standard of living, 23, 24
'Standstill' arrangement, 44
State control, 210, 211–18; management, 211–18
Sterilisation of gold, 39, 64, 68
Stimson, Mr., 269
Stock Exchanges, 89

Straits Settlements, 55
Stresemann, 223–4, 252–3
Sugar, 33–4
Supply and Demand, 10–12
Supreme Economic Council, 22
Switzerland, 47

Tariffs, 71, 183–4, 192–5; and commercial policy, Part II. Ch. IV., 171–195
Trade Cycle, see Business cycle
Trade, Free, 171–195
Transfer, 126; Committee, 127, 143

Unemployment, xii., 8
Union, Austro-German Customs, 187, 225, 238
United States of Europe, 181, 185–92

Versailles, Treaty of, 127, 136, 241

Wage level, 69, 70
War Debts, 149–70; and Disarmament, 157–61; and Reparation, 282–3; Settlement, 161–70
War, the, production during, 2–3; recovery after, 3
War-guilt, 234
Wheat, 32; consumption, 32; fluctuation of prices, 33; prices, 33
Wiggin Committee, 149
Wilson, President, 242, 243–8
Working capital, 87
World Economic Conference, 171, 174, 202–4, 221; Financial Crisis, 42–54

Young Plan, 49, 144–8; Advisory Committee under the, 49, 149

Zollverein, 186–91

A Selection of

Opinions of the Press

on

'RECOVERY'

1. THE POLITICAL WORLD: ALL PARTIES

(a) LONDON PRESS

The Times

'Masterly . . . should be read by everybody who wishes to understand the true causes of the world's present distresses, and the only methods by which they can be remedied.

'He has given the general reader a brilliant summary of the various factors, economic and political, which have contributed to the present crisis, with an impartiality of judgment, a breadth of vision and a lucidity of expression which it would be difficult indeed to surpass.

'No account of this stimulating and constructive book would be complete without some reference to the brilliant and vivid character sketches which it contains.'

Daily Telegraph

'Such a book as has been awaited long by the plain citizen.

'The chapters in which the history . . . of the depression is traced have not only a weight of comprehensive knowledge behind them, but are admirably interesting.'

The Morning Post

'Undoubtedly the most fruitful and constructive contribution which has yet appeared . . . marked at every turn by a firm grasp of realities. One of the most valuable parts of the book is the remarkably concise and incisive section devoted to a survey of the European political scene since the war. Not only are the policies of the leading countries analysed with a rare sympathy and understanding, but striking pen portraits are drawn of the principal actors on the stage.'

REVIEWS

The Sunday Times

'Certain men have been behind the scenes in post-war Europe to a quite unexampled degree. And perhaps no one more than Sir Arthur Salter . . . In all that he writes one feels his first hand authority. Facts and men are handled as familiars. . . With the seeing eye and the patiently hearing ear Sir Arthur Salter unites a very rare gift for justice. . . An admirable book.

The Week-end Review

'Its influence may well be spectacular. . . . It puts before the world a programme so practical, so complete and so acceptable in principle to the overwhelming majority that its immediate promise would be difficult to over-rate.'

J. A. Spender in the News-Chronicle

'As a survey of the international field, I know of nothing to compare with Sir Arthur Salter's book.

'To be fair to everybody and to promote understanding is the effort throughout . . .

'He is one of the few experts who are admirable writers.'

A. G. Gardiner in The Star

'Sir Arthur Salter's long awaited book comes in the nick of time. . . . Never was the need more urgent for a large survey of the catastrophe that has befallen civilisation and an instructed and dispassionate blazing of the path out of the wreckage. Nor is anyone more fitted for the task than Sir Arthur Salter . . . he has the ear of the world in a quite exceptional measure.

'His book will be read in every capital by those who influence policy.'

G. P. Gooch in The Contemporary Review

'Sir Arthur Salter's *Recovery* is not only a good book but a good deed. No living Englishman writes with such authority on the supreme problem of our time. . . . It is written so lucidly that any educated reader can understand it, and so brilliantly that our attention is held from beginning to end.'

REVIEWS

The New Statesman

'The most important study of world economic problems since
¿ . . *The Economic Consequences of the Peace.* . . . He knows
from A to Z everything that has happened in international politics
and economics since the League was set up.

'By far the most complete, cogent and sensible programme that
has yet been produced for the reconstruction of world capitalism.
It is far reaching and goes down to fundamentals, and yet everywhere outlines policies which nations as they are might conceivably
be persuaded to accept.'

Professor Harold Laski in the Daily Herald

'It represents in a magnificent way the minimum conditions upon
which our civilisation may hope to survive. It has the analytic
insight of the scientist and the imaginative grasp of the prophet.
Books such as this are written only once or twice in a generation.'

E. F. Wise in The New Leader

'. . . the most significant book on the world's economic problems
that has appeared since the war.

'Salter has an almost unique wealth of experience and knowledge
for the task with which his book deals.'

(*b*) THE PROVINCES AND SCOTLAND

J. A. Hobson in The Manchester Guardian

'No man in this or any other country is better qualified by understanding, temper, and experience to prescribe for the disease, or
tangle of diseases, from which the world is suffering than Sir Arthur
Salter.

'. . . a work which should . . . arrest the mind of all reasonable
men and women, and go far to lift the fatalistic apathy which has
of late beset a world.'

Yorkshire Post

'No individual has had greater experience than Sir Arthur
Salter in the actual work of post-war reconstruction, and I know of
no single book which conveys so lucid a picture in so short a
compass.'

REVIEWS

The Birmingham Post

'He has the gift of lucid and interesting exposition. As a result he is always supremely readable; always easily intelligible . . . and not infrequently genuinely eloquent. . . . Altogether his book is as sane and sound a study of the world's ills as has yet appeared.'

The Western Mail

'This is the book of books on the present world economic situation.'

The Glasgow Herald

'His book may be recommended to all who desire enlightenment on world problems which bear on the daily life of every man and woman. It is easily read and understood, even on the difficult subjects of money and credit, and it never fails to be interesting'

2. THE FINANCIAL WORLD

Hartley Withers in The Spectator

'No one is better qualified than Sir Arthur Salter to diagnose the causes of the world's economic disease and to prescribe remedies, and he has fulfilled this most important task with consummate skill. . .

'He judges world problems with a detached and international mind, nourished by years of intercourse with the statesmen, bankers and business men who have been handling, or bungling, the affairs of the universe.

'Master of an easy and flexible style, he tells a story that can be understood, as he writes it, by all the millions who want or ought to want to know what is the matter.'

The Economist

'Among those best qualified to guide us in reading the lessons of the past ten years, there is no one with higher credentials than Sir Arthur Salter. . . . His judgment on world affairs will . . . carry exceptional weight.'

Truth

'. . . written with great lucidity, with admirable temper, and with the sure touch of a participant in all the great events. . . . The length of a fair-sized novel, only far more interesting.'

REVIEWS

Financial Times

'A valuable contribution to current discussions. . . . Its appearance is particularly appropriate. . . . May it be hoped that it will help to stimulate the nations to remedial action.'

Sir Basil Blackett in The Nineteenth Century

'A fine achievement. . . Will surely be read widely . . . not only in English-speaking countries but in every corner of Europe. . . . Every one of Sir Arthur's suggestions is worthy of the closest attention by the authorities at home and abroad . . .'

Professor J. H. Jones in The Accountant

'I cannot recall any book which was so well-timed and deserved to exercise so much influence upon public opinion in Europe and America. It is impossible, in a review, to do justice to it or to the author.'

Journal of the Institute of Bankers

'The book is very brilliantly written, and fully deserves the wide attention which it has attracted.'

3. AMERICA

Walter Lippmann in The New York Herald Tribune

'The special quality of this book is its perspective and proportion, and it might fairly be said of it, I think, that nothing dealing with the world crisis has yet been written which so nearly represents the consensus of informed opinion throughout the world.

'A few years hence the views he has summarized will, I think, in their general outline seem so obviously true that men will wonder why they were so bitterly repudiated.

'He will find there the considered judgments of an informed, of a patient, of a just and of a courageous mind, and when he lays down the book he will feel that he has been in communication with a vigilant guardian of the human heritage.'

The New York Times

'His experience has given him a rare opportunity for observation. When to this experience are added insight, candour, an engaging style and an unfailing sense of direction through a wilderness of detail, the result is wholly fortunate.'

REVIEWS

The New York Bookman

'In the few months since this book was first published, so many events directly related to its substance have transpired that not only the author's command of his subject but also the book's chances of permanent usefulness have been submitted to a vigorous test. It would be a sufficiently handsome compliment to acknowledge that both author and book have passed this test with flying colours; yet one may justly say even more. Not only do many of the things that have "happened" follow in detail from the premise and logic of Sir Arthur's theories, but also those measures which may at this writing be designated as seemingly curative correspond with astonishing fidelity to the author's prescriptions. As a result, one is left with the choice of deciding whether to put this correspondence down to pure coincidence or—as also cannot fail to occur to the reader—to the enormous influence which the book itself has wielded in international, political, and economic circles since its publication . . . *Recovery* is a masterpiece.'

4. MISCELLANEOUS

Professor George Gordon in The Book Society News

'. . . I should not attempt to reproduce, in this brief but emphatic recommendation, the ordered and luminous reasoning of this deeply considered and admirably constructed book. . . . Once I had begun it was quite impossible to stop.

'His picture of the European scene, his portraits of our international statesmen, and more especially of President Wilson, Briand and of Stresemann, are in the very first class of this difficult and fascinating form of art.

'A book addressed . . . to every educated man and woman in this country. . . . A work of literature. . . . I urge our members by all means to read it.'

Wickham Steed in The Christian World

'In an hour of doubt and darkness it points a way towards hope and sunrise. Best of all it is a work of faith—faith open-eyed and reasonable yet none the less strong and moving. Every public library should possess it, so that many may read. Whoever can should buy it, so as to possess it for himself.'